Ring-tailed cat   *Mallette Dean*

SIERRA NORTH

100 Back-Country Trips in the High Sierra

by Thomas Winnett and Jason Winnett

 WILDERNESS PRESS • BERKELEY

First printing May 1967
Second printing July 1967
Third printing July 1969
SECOND EDITION May 1971
Second printing April 1972
Third printing September 1974
THIRD EDITION January 1976
Second printing February 1978
FOURTH EDITION May 1982
Second Printing July 1983
FIFTH EDITION June 1985
Revised Second Printing May 1987
Third Printing November 1988

Photos by the authors except as noted
Drawings by Lucille Winnett
Design by Thomas Winnett

Library of Congress card number 85-40198
ISBN 0-89997-054-0
Manufactured in the United States

Published by Wilderness Press
2440 Bancroft Way, Berkeley, CA 94704
(415) 843-8080

Write for free catalog

Library of Congress Cataloging in Publication Data

Winnett, Thomas.
    Sierra North.

    Bibliography: p.
    Includes index.
    1. Backpacking—Sierra Nevada Mountains (Calif. and
Nev.)—Guide-books. 2. Hiking—Sierra Nevada Mountains
(Calif. and Nev.)—Guide-books. 3. Sierra Nevada
Mountains (Calif. and Nev.)—Description and travel—
Guidebooks. I. Winnett, Jason. II. Title.
GV199.42.S55W56   1985   917.94'4   85-40198
ISBN 0-89997-054-0

ACKNOWLEDGMENTS

A guidebook like this requires a lot of input, and we have been fortunate enough to meet many gracious and generous Sierra lovers who have helped bring the old trail descriptions up to date and to present the descriptions of the new trips: Jeff Schaffer, Ron Felzer, Margaret and the late Bob Pierce, Ben Schifrin, Ken Fawcett, Joe Grodin, the late J. C. Jenkins, Raleigh Ellisen, Don Parachini, Earl Schnick, John Jencks, Don Deck, Grant Barnes, Harold Furst, Cecelia Hurwich, Norman Jensen, Edwin Rockwell, and Caroline Winnett.

The chapter on "The Care and Enjoyment of the Mountains" was adapted from an article by Michael Loughman.

Hiking in the backcountry entails unavoidable risk that every hiker assumes and must be aware of and respect. The fact that a trail is described in this book is not a representation that it will be safe for you. Trails vary greatly in difficulty and in the degree of conditioning and agility one needs to enjoy them safely. On some hikes routes may have changed or conditions may have deteriorated since the descriptions were written. Also trail conditions can change even from day to day, owing to weather and other factors. A trail that is safe on a dry day or for a highly conditioned, agile, properly equipped hiker may be completely unsafe for someone else or unsafe under adverse weather conditions.

You can minimize your risks on the trail by being knowledgeable, prepared and alert. There is not space in this book for a general treatise on safety in the mountains, but there are a number of good books and public courses on the subject and you should take advantage of them to increase your knowledge. Just as important, you should always be aware of your own limitations and of conditions existing when and where you are hiking. If conditions are dangerous, or if you are not prepared to deal with them safely, choose a different hike! It's better to have wasted a drive than to be the subject of a mountain rescue.

These warnings are not intended to scare you off the trails. Millions of people have safe and enjoyable hikes every year. However, one element of the beauty, freedom and excitement of the wilderness is the presence of risks that do not confront us at home. When you hike you assume those risks. They can be met safely, but only if you exercise your own independent judgment and common sense.

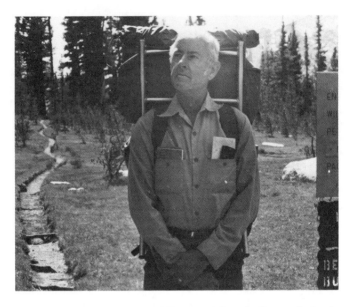

Authors at Buckeye Pass: Thomas (above), Jason (below)

Table of Contents

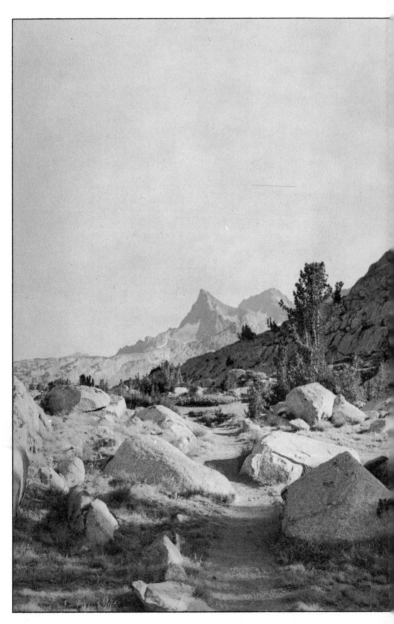

Looking south from Donohue P.

Introduction

This Book's Purpose

The Sierra Nevada is the longest and most extensively trailed mountain range in the United States. With its complex valley-ridge makeup, its lofty eastern escarpment, and its mild weather, it is a backpacker's paradise unequalled in intrinsic beauty and scenic grandeur. Much of the finest scenery and best fishing lie in the back country, accessible only by trail. There has been, therefore, a growing trend toward wilderness trips, and with the trend has come a demand for reliable backcountry trip suggestions. This book is a selective effort to meet that demand.

Galen Clark, Yosemite's beloved "Old Man of the Valley," was once asked how he "got about" the park. Clark scratched his beard, and then replied, "Slowly!" And that is the philosophy the authors have adopted in this book. Hiking descriptions, with the exception of a few "Moderate" ratings and an occasional "Strenuous" trip, are based on a leisurely pace, in order that the hiker can absorb more of the sights, smells and "feel" of the country he has come to see. Pace may not be everything, but Old Man Clark lived to a ripe old age of 96 and it behooves us to follow in his footsteps.

This Book's Terms

Sierra North encompasses the region from the volcanic battlements of Carson Pass to the aspen-lined banks of Mono Creek, where the companion volume, *Sierra South*, takes over. The individual trips were selected on the basis of (1) scenic attraction, (2) wilderness character (remoteness, primitive condition) and (3) recreational potential (fishing, swimming, etc.) After walking the trip, the author decided how long it should take if done at a leisurely pace, how long at a moderate pace, and how long at a strenuous pace. In deciding, he considered not only distance but also elevation change, heat exposure, terrain, availability of water, appropriate campsites and finally, his subjective feeling about the trip. For each trip, then, we suggest how many days you should take to do it at the pace (*Leisurely, Moderate* or *Strenuous*) you prefer. Some trips simply don't lend themselves to a leisurely pace—maybe not even a moderate pace—and some are never strenuous unless you do the whole thing in one day. Such trips have a blank in the number-of-days spot for the corresponding pace at the beginning of the trip.

The last decision about pace was the decision of which pace to use in describing the trip, day by day. Since this book is written for the average backpacker, we chose to describe most trips on either a leisurely or a moderate basis, depending on where the best overnight camping places were along the route.

Subjective considerations also carry over to the evaluation of campsites. Campsites are labeled *poor, fair, good* or *excellent.* The criteria for assigning these labels were amount of use, immediate surroundings, general scenery, presence of vandalization, availability of water, kind of ground cover and recreational potential—angling, side trips, swimming, etc.

Angling, for many, is a prime consideration when planning a trip. The recommendations in this book are based on: (1) on-site samplings and feeding evaluations, (2) word of mouth, (3) *Sierra Trout,* by Dean Cutter, (4) literature of the California Department of Fish and Game, and (5) interviews with commercial packers. When a conflict arose between paper research and trail sampling, the latter was given precedence. Like the campsites, fishing was labeled *poor, fair, good* or *excellent.* It should be noted that these labels refer only to the size, quantity, and general catchability of the fish, not the fishes' inclination to take the hook at any moment. Experienced anglers know that the size of their catch relates not only to quantity, type and general size of the fishery, which are given, but also to water temperature, feed, angling skill, and that indefinable something known as "fisherman's luck." Generally speaking, the old "early and late" adage holds: fishing is better early and late in the day, and early and late in the season.

Deciding when in the year is the best time for a particular trip is a difficult task because of altitude and latitude variations. Low early-season temperatures and mountain shadows often keep some of the higher passes closed until well into August. Early snows have been known to whiten alpine country in late July and August. Some of the trips described here are low-country ones, offered specifically for the itchy hiker who, stiff from a winter's inactivity, is searching for a "warm-up" excursion. These trips are labeled *early season,* a period that extends roughly from late May to early July. *Mid season* is here considered to be from early July to the end of August, and *late season* from then to early October.

Stream crossings vary greatly depending on snow-melt conditions. Often, the same small creek you saw in September will be a raging torrent the next June. We have indicated the problems of fording some creeks as "wet in early season," meaning that in times of high water you will probably have to wade, perhaps in water over your waist, but that the crossing is fairly easy and not dangerous. If a ford is described as "difficult in early season" fording that creek may be difficult because it is hard to walk through deep or fast water, and getting caught in the current would be dangerous. Whether you attempt such a crossing depends on the presence or absence of logs or other bridges and of downstream rapids, your ability and equipment, and your judgment.

Most of the trails described here are well maintained (the exceptions are noted), and are properly signed. If the trail becomes indistinct, look for *blazes* (peeled bark at eye level on trees) or *ducks* (two or more rocks piled one atop the other). Two other significant trail conditions have also been described in the text: (1) degree of openness (type and degree of forest cover, if any, or else "meadow," "brush" or whatever); and (2) underfooting (talus, scree, pumice, sand, "duff"—deep humus ground cover of rotting vegetation—or other material).

Three other terms used in the descriptive text warrant definition. *Packer campsite* is used to indicate a semipermanent camp (usually constructed by packers for the "comfort of their clients") characterized by a nailed-plank table and/or a large, stand-up rock fireplace. *Improved campsite* is a U.S. Forest Service designation for a place where a simple toilet has been installed. A *use trail* is an unmaintained, unofficial trail that is more or less easy to follow because it is well worn by use.

The text contains occasional references to points, peaks and other landmarks. These places will be found on the appropriate topographic maps cited at the beginning of the trip. ("Point 9426" in the text would refer to a point designated simply "9426" on the map itself.)

In recent years the Forest Service and the Park Service have had a policy of letting fires in the backcountry burn so long as they were not a threat to people or structures. One result has been some pretty poor looking scenery on some trips in this book. However, most of the fire-damaged areas have begun to recover soon enough that the authors have chosen not to delete the affected trips from the book.

The Care and Enjoyment of the Mountains

The mountains are in danger, particularly the High Sierra. About a million people camp in the Sierra wilderness each year. Backpacking is something everybody knows about and almost everybody is going to want to try. With California's population edging toward 25 million, the wilderness is threatened with destruction, particularly the High Sierra.

Litter is not the problem! Increasingly, wilderness campsites, even when free of litter, have that "beat out" look of overcrowded roadside campgrounds. The fragile high country sod is being ground down under the pressure of too many feet. Lovely trees and snags are being stripped, scarred, and removed altogether for firewood. Dust, charcoal, blackened stones and dirty fireplaces are accumulating. These conditions are spreading rapidly, and in a few years *every* High Sierra lakeshore and streamside may be severely damaged.

The national park service and the forest service are faced with the necessity for reservation systems, designated campgrounds, restrictions on fire building, increased ranger patrols, and perhaps even rationing of wilderness recreation. Not only the terrain but the wilderness experience is being eroded. Soon conditions may be little different from those we wanted to leave behind at the roadhead.

The solution to the problem depends on each of us. We must change our habits so as to have as little effect on the terrain as possible. We must try to leave no traces of our passing. This was the rule in the wilderness when Indians and trappers traveled through other people's territory. It is still a good rule today. It does take a little trouble. In an earlier day that extra trouble was the price of saving one's scalp or load of beaver pelts. Today it is the price of saving the wilderness. A few basic principles of wilderness preservation—particularly aimed at High Sierra conditions but applicable elsewhere too—are offered below.

Learn to go light. This is largely a matter of acquiring wilderness skills, of learning to be at home in the wilderness rather than in an elaborate camp. The *free spirits* of the mountains are those experts who appear to go anywhere under any conditions with neither encumbrances nor effort but always with complete enjoyment. John Muir, traveling along the crest of the Sierra in the 1870s with little more than his overcoat and pockets full of biscuits, was the archetype.

Modern lightweight equipment and food are a convenience and a joy. The ever-practical Muir would have taken them had they been available in his day. But a lot of the stuff that goes into the mountains is burdensome, harmful to the wilderness, or just plain annoying to other people seeking peace and solitude. Anything that is obtrusive or that can be used to modify the terrain should be left at the roadhead: gigantic tents, gas lanterns, radios, saws, hatchets, firearms (except in the hunting season), etc.

Pick "hard" campsites, sandy places that can stand the use. The fragile sod of meadows, lakeshores and streamsides is rapidly disappearing from the High Sierra. It simply cannot take the wear and tear of campers. Its development depends on very special conditions. Once destroyed, it does not ordinarily grow back.

Be easy with the trees! In the timberline country wood is being burned up faster than it is being produced. The big campfires of the past must give way to small fires or to no fires at all. Wood is a precious resource; use it sparingly. Where it is scarce use a gas stove, not a saw or hatchet. Trees, both live and dead, are part of the scenery. They should never be *cut*. The exquisite golden trunks left standing after lightning strikes should be left completely alone. Sadly, in some popular areas they have already been destroyed for firewood, and you would never know they *were* there.

In established, regularly used campsites a single, small, substantial fireplace should serve for both cooking and warming. If kept scrupulously clean it should last for many years. Unfortunately, fireplaces (and campsites) tend to become increasingly dirty and to multiply. There are now, by actual survey, a hundred times as many fireplaces as are needed in the High Sierra. The countless dirty fireplaces should be eradicated. Many campsites situated at the edge of the water should be entirely restored to nature and not used again. It is a noble service to use and clean up established campsites where they are present, and to restore them to nature where called for.

Elsewhere build a small fireplace, if one is legal, and always eradicate it and restore your campsite to a natural condition before you leave. This is facilitated if you build with restoration in mind: two to four medium-sized stones along the sides of a shallow trench in a sandy place. When camp is broken the stones are returned to their places. The coals are thoroughly burned down and pulverized under a heavy foot until nothing is left but powder. The trench is filled with clean sand. *Fires should never be built against cliffs or large boulders.*

Protect the water from soap and other pollution. In many areas the water is unsafe to drink. This situation can be changed, and hopefully there will always be lakes and streams where the water will be safe and good-tasting.

Giardia is not new to the Sierra but it has recently become a widespread problem. This protozoan (*Giardia lamblia*) can cause acute gastrointestinal distress, as anyone who has had it can tell you. The illness is treatable, but prevention is best. There is giardia in the water in most of the popular areas, and the Park Service and the Forest Service recommend that you treat all water to be sure, as giardia can be anywhere. Among the methods used to treat water (for giardia) are commercial tablets, filters and boiling. It is hard to say which method is the most effective. In popular areas, we use a filter for water that is not boiled for 5 minutes, as in cooking. We have never contracted giardia. Some hikers say they never treat their water and have never contracted giardia. It is likely that most people can ingest some giardia without any problem, and some people are probably immune to giardia. But anyone can be a carrier, whether they have symptoms not. It takes 2-3 weeks for symptoms to appear after exposure.

Scatter organic garbage in dry, out-of-the-way places. It disappears most quickly when dry and exposed to the air. Talus slopes and dry brush are the best hiding places. Garbage should never be burned in the fireplace. Orange peels are an exception. They seem to be destructible only in a hot fire.

Thoroughly cold and pulverized charcoal may be broadcast away from camp in a fireproof site. Charcoal is part of the natural scene.

Pack cans and foil back to the roadhead. Smelly or oily cans and foil can be cleaned easily in a hot fire but please do remove them. The accumulation of garbage, cans, and charcoal around fireplaces is the principal reason campsites are abandoned and new, redundant fireplaces and campsites are created.

Latrines. By and large, the giardia in Sierran waters comes from improper disposal of human wastes. Keeping giardia and other infectious organisms out of the water supply requires proper burial, 6-8 inches deep, at least 50 yards away from lakes, streams, dry watercourses and campsites. Be sure to completely bury or burn your toilet paper.

Maps and Profiles

Today's Sierra traveler is confronted by a bewildering array of maps, and it doesn't take much experience to learn that no single map fulfills all needs. There are base maps (U.S. Forest Service), shaded relief maps (National Park Service), artistically drawn representational maps (California Department of Fish and Game), aerial-photograph maps, geologic maps, three-dimensional relief maps, soil-vegetation maps, etc. Each map has different information to impart, and the outdoorsman contemplating a backcountry trip is wise to utilize several of these maps in his planning.

For trip-planning purposes, the reader will find a plan map in the back of this book. Trails and trailheads used in the trip descriptions are shown on this map in red, the access roads in black, water in blue, and the topographic map grid in orange.

The profile of each trip in this book gives a quick picture of the ups and downs. All profiles are drawn with the same *ratio* of horizontal miles to feet of elevation except 44 and 87. The vertical scale in all is exaggerated.

On the trail most backpackers prefer to use a topographic (*topo*) map, because it affords a good deal of accurate information about terrain and forest cover. Topo maps come in a variety of sizes and scales, but the best, because it covers the whole Sierra in one useful scale, is the U.S. Geological Survey's 15' Topographic Quadrangle series. The 15' series scale is approximately 1" = 1 mile; the contour interval (elevation difference between contour lines) is 80 feet in the Sierra; and the area covered by each map is about 14 × 17 miles. They show most of the maintained trails (exceptions are noted in the text of this book), the elevations, the relief, the watercourses, the forest cover and the works of man. Learning to read these maps takes a little practice, but the savings in shoe leather and frayed tempers make it a worthy undertaking. For the reader's convenience, the appropriate 15' topo maps for each trip are cited in the text.

By far the best topo maps—for the quadrangles for which they are available—are the 15' quadrangle maps published by Wilderness Press. These maps are based on the USGS versions, but were completely updated in the late 1970s and early

1980s after thorough fieldwork. Trails are much easier to see on these maps because they are shown as solid black lines. And each map has an index grid and an index for locating all the features on it. In the area of *Sierra North,* Wilderness Press 15′ maps are available for these quadrangles: Hetch Hetchy, Tuolumne Meadows, Yosemite, Merced Peak and Devils Postpile. In addition, Wilderness Press has published an updated topographic map of Yosemite National Park and Vicinity. This map alone shows more than half of the trails described in *Sierra North.* In the tabular matter at the start of each trip in the book, the topo maps needed for the trip are listed. If the map's name is in **boldface,** that quadrangle is available in the Wilderness Press series, and it is the best one available.

Another useful map series is the ½″ = 1 mile series published by the U.S. Forest Service. Being base maps, they lack contour lines, but they are revised with some frequency, and they show newer roads and trails. They also show water, man-made structures and some elevations.

HOW TO ACQUIRE YOUR MAPS

USGS 15′ *Topo* maps:

U.S. Geological Survey,
Federal Center, Denver, CO 80225
$2.75 each
State index map is free

California
15′ *Topo* maps:

The Map Center
2440 Bancroft Way
Berkeley, CA 94704

USFS base maps:

U.S. Forest Service,
630 Sansome St.,
San Francisco, CA 94111
An index map is free.
Individual forest maps can be
purchased at ranger stations.

Topo maps plus free state index maps can be obtained *in person* from USGS offices located at:

7638 Federal Building
300 North Los Angeles Street
Los Angeles, CA

504 Custom House
555 Battery Street
San Francisco, CA

345 Middlefield Road
Menlo Park, CA

Wilderness Permits and Quotas

The wilderness traveler will need a permit from the Forest Service (for federally designated wilderness areas) or from the National Park Service (for national-park backcountry and wilderness). You may obtain a permit from the Park Service or Forest Service ranger station or office that administers the area. In Yosemite permits are available on a first-come-first-served basis not more than 24 hours before your departure into the backcountry. In Tuolumne Meadows you can get your permit from a booth in the parking lot near the west end of the Tuolumne Lodge spur road. The Park Service realizes that many Yosemite hikers are weekend visitors, so from late June through Labor Day weekend they keep the booth open on Friday nights and open it early (sometimes 6 a.m.) on Saturday mornings. In Yosemite, you can also get a permit in person at the Big Oak Flat entrance station on Highway 120, in Yosemite Valley and at Wawona.

Rules for obtaining a permit for a national-forest area have been in flux, so we suggest that you write the supervisor of the national forest you plan to visit, to find out the procedure in force at the time of your trip, using the addresses below. In addition, permits for Yosemite may be obtained by mail *between Feb. 1 and May 31* by writing: Wilderness Permits, Box 577, Yosemite National Park, CA 95389. After May 31 you must appear in person. Groups of 15 or more are requested to make mail reservations for any trip between Memorial Day and October 1.

Emigrant Wilderness
Stanislaus National Forest
19777 Greenley Rd.
Sonora, CA 95370

Hoover Wilderness
(for eastside entry)
Toiyabe National Forest
Bridgeport, CA 93517

Hoover Wilderness
(for southside entry)
Inyo National Forest
P.O. Box 10
Lee Vining, CA 93541

Ansel Adams Wilderness
(for westside entry)
Sierra National Forest
North Fork, CA 93643

Ansel Adams Wilderness
(for eastide entry)
Inyo National Forest
P.O. Box 148
Mammoth Lakes, CA 93546

John Muir Wilderness
(for westide entry)
Sierra National Forest
P.O. Box 300
Shaver Lake, CA 93664

John Muir Wilderness
(for eastside entry)
Inyo National Forest
873 N. Main
Bishop, CA 93514

Ansel Adams Wilderness
(for southside entry)
Sierra National Forest
P.O. Box 300
Shaver Lake, CA 93664

Mokelumne Wilderness
El Dorado National Forest
   Visitor Center
3070 Camino Heights Dr.
Camino, CA 95709

Carson-Iceberg Wilderness
(for westside entry)
Calaveras Ranger District
P.O. Box 500
Hathaway Pines, CA 95232

Carson-Iceberg Wilderness
(for eastside entry)
1536 S. Carson St.
Carson City, NV 89701

If your trip extends through more than one national-forest wilderness, or through more than one national forest, or through both a national forest and a national park, obtain your permit from the forest or park where your trip starts.

A wilderness permit is issued for a single trip during a specified period of time. A separate permit is necessary for each trip.

The wilderness permit also serves as a campfire permit while you visit the wilderness area. A campfire permit is required for campfires outside of wilderness areas.

Capacities have been established for high-use areas in the region covered by this book, including all the backcountry of Yosemite. If the capacity of the area where you want to go has been filled, you must select another overnight destination. A number of other rules exist for backcountry use, many of which are simply codifications of the principles in the chapter "The Care and Enjoyment of the Mountains." One rule that is all too often broken is that you must camp at least 100 feet from lakes and stream—where terrain permits. In a few places, such as Barney Lake and Peeler Lake, that distance is increased to 200 feet. Copies of all these special regulations are available from the government agencies that issue wilderness permits.

When writing for a permit, please state 1) where and when you will enter and leave the wilderness, 2) your entire route, and where you will stop each night, 3) how many people in your party (the limit is 25—15 in the Hoover Wilderness), 4) how many head of stock you are taking, if any, and 5) your mode of travel: hiking, skiing or riding horses.

Land of Fire and Ice

Called the "land of fire and ice" by one awestruck pioneer emigrant, this large slice of the northern Sierra encompasses the area stretching south from U.S. 50 to the North Boundary of Yosemite National Park. The pioneers who first trod this wilderness recognized the black basaltic crests of this region for their fiery origins, and in stories of arduous crossings over snow- and ice-capped summits, they expressed a profound appreciation for the evolutionary contrasts. Today's geologists tell us that lava once covered that area from around Sonora Pass west to Knights Ferry to a depth of 1500 feet. Millions of years passed before the juggernaut forces of time, glacial ice and water cut through this thick layer, and today more than half of this region consists of re-exposed white-and-gray granite, the hallmark rock of the Sierra. The traveler passing through the backcountry cannot help but notice the sharp delineation between the older batholithic granites and the volcanic overlays.

Historically, this region offers much to intrigue the visitor—particularly if this visitor is on foot (either on two or four). Many of the trips described here trace old emigrant trails, and it is easy for backpackers, afoot like the emigrants, to identify with these pioneers. Preceding the emigrants were the footloose pathfinders. Explorers like John Fremont, Joseph Walker and Jedediah Smith first looked upon these mountains, and Fremont and Walker made crossings that cut across some of the routes described here. Before the white man, however, the Indian established hunting trails that made a network over the foothills on both sides of the Sierra crest. The Maidu and the Miwok occupied and hunted the west side of the crest, and the Washoe and Piute coexisted on the east. It is of interest to the mountaineer to know that most of these Indian trails are located on top of the ridges, and not, as is the white man's custom, along the muddy, snowy canyon bottoms.

After the Indians and the explorers came the emigrants. The Bartleson-Bidwell party of 1841 was the first overland emigrant group to cross the Sierra, and its route, tentatively identified, showed the way—later changed in places—for those who followed. This route still bears blazes cut in trees by westward-bound emigrants. There is, for example, a blazed tree near Emigrant Lake in Emigrant Basin which still shows the epitaph of a traveler who died there in October 1853. Still another emigrant route followed Fremont's old route up the West Carson River to Caples (formerly Twin) Lake, and thence descended the west slope past yet another Emigrant Lake.

These routes were the predecessors of roads—first toll roads, and finally public highways. Today, with the devastating intrusion of roads into these wild spots, Californians have come to a reluctant recognition of the necessity of preserving wilderness integrity. To this end they have established, through federal auspices, wilderness areas that are supposed to preserve a wild area in its intrinsic primitive state. The Mokelumne Wilderness was established in 1964, and in 1974 the Emigrant Basin Primitive Area was enlarged and renamed the Emigrant Wilderness. There is also a plan for a Carson-Iceberg Wilderness that would encompass the area between the Ebbets Pass highway and the Sonora Pass highway. Unfortunately, in the Emigrant Wilderness it was decided to exclude the mining claims and their access road, which cuts across the Sierra crest at Emigrant Pass. And in the planning stages of the Carson-Iceberg Wilderness it is proposed that the present Clark Fork road be left to intrude like a dagger into the heart of the wilderness area. Administrative decisions of this caliber offer slim hope that future decisions will be made to extend the protective mantle of a wilderness area designation to other deserving areas such as that scenic east-side region in the West Walker River drainage. Here the present policy remains one of wilderness attrition by "recreation roads" (a gross contradiction) and unless prompt action is taken, it too will become another dusty traffic jam suitable only for trail bikes and tent cities.

The backcountry hiker who knows the beauty of unspoiled wilderness comes to know the threat implicit in the unrestrained use of machines. With an objectivity born of an appreciation of fundamentals, and an individual wholeness that results from relying on his own resources, he recognizes the automobile as a cultural blight that is responsible for the destruction of thousands of acres of Sierra wilderness. Only recently have Forest Service officials begun to realize the burgeoning threat of trail bikes and snowmobiles, and this dawning awareness has prompted an administrative proclamation that has closed many of the trails on the Eldorado and

Stanislaus National Forests to jeeps and trail bikes. One hopes similar restrictions will be placed upon the equally disastrous presence of snowmobiles in the backcountry.

The Emigrant Basin area has long been a fisherman's mecca, and for good reason. Hundreds of lakes and miles of streams offer excellent angling for brook, rainbow, brown and golden trout. Some of the better fishing in the area may be found at Wire Lakes, Cow Meadow Lake, the North Fork of Cherry Creek, and the upper reaches of Falls Creek (Jack Main Canyon). California fishing licenses are required.

The Trailheads

Horse Canyon Trailhead. Go 0.8 mile north on State Highway 88 north from Silver Lake to Oyster Creek Roadside Rest, where there is plenty of parking, and walk 100 yards farther up the highway to the signed trailhead. There is room for a very few cars right by the trailhead.

Plasse's Resort. Go east on State Highway 88 to the last downhill stretch before arriving at the shore of Silver Lake and turn right on a road signed PLASSE ROAD. At the bottom of the hill, turn right and drive past the resort's main buildings to an informal parking area where there are many signs of use by horses and horse trailers. East across the stream here is your trailhead.

Echo Summit. Go ⅓ mile south from Echo Summit (on U.S. 50) to the end of a graded summer-home-tract road.

Carson Pass. Go 0.9 mile west of Carson Pass on State Highway 88 to a small parking area with a sign OLD MEISS TRAILHEAD.

Upper Wolf Creek Meadows. About 2½ miles south on State Highway 4 from State Highway 89, turn left and go southeast up Wolf Creek Road 3⅓ miles to a fork left, where you could descend northeast to the north end of Wolf Creek Meadows. Continue straight ahead—south—1½ miles beyond the fork to road's end, from which a short, rocky road veers northeast to signed *Wolf Creek Meadows Undeveloped Camping Area.* The Wolf Creek Trail heads south up a creekside jeep road.

Wolf Creek Meadows. Follow Wolf Creek Road 3⅓ miles to a fork left and descend northeast on it to the north end of Wolf Creek Meadows. In ⅔ mile from the fork, the road reaches a spur road heading southeast. This spur climbs ¼ mile to two adjacent trailheads, but it is best to park on a small flat, on your right, about midway along this spur road, before the road curves left. The two trailheads serve the High Trail and the

East Carson River Trail.

Ebbetts Pass. This is the highest point on State Highway 4. The Pacific Crest Trail crosses State Highway 4 only 0.1 mile northeast of the pass, and in another 0.3 mile a short spur road veers right up to a PCT parking lot. A short spur trail up to the PCT leaves from the lot's south end.

Heiser Lake Trailhead. From the east end of Lake Alpine go 6 miles northeast up State Highway 4 to the west end of Mosquito Lake, beside which is the signed trailhead.

Bull Run Lake Trailhead. From the east end of Lake Alpine go 4 miles northeast up State Highway 4 to a spur road branching right signed *Stanislaus Mdw, Bull Run Trail*. Follow this road ½ mile to its end.

Lake Alpine. At the east end of Lake Alpine on State Highway 4 turn right ⅓ mile to the Silver Valley Overnight Campground. Just within the campground, at a *Speed Limit 10* sign, is the trailhead for the Highland Creek Trail.

Rodriguez Flat. From the State Highway 4/89 junction with U.S. 395, go 5½ miles south on U.S. 395 to Coleville, then another 2¼ miles to a road west, signed both *Lost Cannon Creek Road* and *Mill Canyon Road*. Alternatively, from the State Highway 108/U.S. 395 junction, drive 13 miles north to Walker, then another 2½ miles to Lost Cannon Creek Road. This dirt road west quickly becomes the Golden Gate Road. Go up it 6¼ miles; following *Little Antelope Pack Station* signs. From the mountain crest junction at broad, open Rodriguez Flat, drive ½ mile south to road's end at signed Trail 1020.

Kennedy Meadow. Go 1 mile up an oiled road from State Highway 108, 29 miles east of the Pinecrest **Y**. You can let passengers out at the resort, and park there for a fee or drive ½ mile back to a public parking area.

Crabtree Camp. From the traffic light in downtown Sonora, go 25½ miles northeast on State Route 108 to tiny Cold Springs, and 1.2 miles beyond turn right on signed Crabtree Road. Follow this paved road 6.8 miles to a junction just before a pack station. Go straight ahead onto dirt road and drive 2.65 miles to a junction. Go right here for 0.7 mile to the trailhead parking lot beside Bell Creek.

Gianelli Cabin. Proceed as above to the last-named junction. Turn left and go 4 miles to road's end.

Sonora Pass West. About 0.85 mile west of Sonora Pass on State Highway 108, turn north to park on a closed-off dirt road.

Sonora Pass. This is the highest point of State Highway 108, 67 miles northeast of Sonora and 15 miles west of the U.S. 395 junction.

Silver Lake to Scout Carson Lake

1

TRIP

From Silver Lake to Scout Carson Lake (round trip). Topo map *Silver Lake*. Best mid season; 11 miles (17.8 km).

Grade	Trail/layover days	Total recom- mended days
Leisurely	2/1	3
Moderate	2/0	2
Strenuous	....	....

HILITES

The mountains around Silver Lake are a startling amalgam of light-gray granite and dark-brown lava, the granite being gently rounded, but the lava arrayed in tiers of jagged cliffs. This trip follows a boundary between the two types of terrain, ascending gently southward under the soaring lava cliffs of Thunder Peak and Thimble Peak to a lovely, small lake near timberline.

DESCRIPTION

1st Hiking Day (**Silver Lake** to **Scout Carson Lake,** 5.5 miles—8.9 km): From the aspen grove at the trailhead just north of Oyster Creek Roadside Rest, the duff-colored trail ascends gently, sometimes moderately, through a red-fir forest in which some wind-toppled firs across the trail require small detours. In early season, open patches in the forest are carpeted with lupine, and showy red columbines grow here and there. Eroded blocks of lava beside the trail have taken on grotesque and fascinating shapes which your imagination can identify as what it will. Even more compelling are the dark lava cliffs on the northern skyline, the crenelated battlements of a 3-mile-long igneous castle. About 2 miles up from the trailhead an unsigned trail comes in on the right beside a large boulder; this is one route up from the Boy Scout Camp below. A more-used path from the camp, the trail shown on the topo map, meets our route ½ mile farther up, on an open hillside, and 70 yards beyond this junction is the first water you will cross in midsummer, flowing very slightly but fit to drink. From this cooling pause, we break out onto an open slope dotted with red fir and great numbers of yellow-flowered mule ears, mixed with bits of blue lupine. Then the blazed trail re-enters red-fir forest, and just how brittle the wood of this conifer species is, is shown by the tremendous amount of broken wood littering the forest floor—seemingly enough for a thousand campfires.

Leaving the forest, our rocky trail climbs across an open hillside dotted with many large granite boulders, a large assortment of wildflowers and a few lodgepole pines, red firs and Sierra junipers. As we come into earshot of a plunging stream, we turn steeply uphill and in 100 yards reach and jump-ford this creek. The walk up the far bank is enhanced by the gurgling sounds and by the brilliant chutes and cascades of this unnamed stream, which drains the bowl between Thunder Peak (not named on the topo map) and Thimble Peak. About 300 yards later the trail veers away from the stream to make an unrelenting steep ascent, then levels off just before it tops out on a granite ridge. Here again the hillside is very open, and we now have excellent views of Silver Lake and mountains surrounding it. Then a short, strolling descent brings the hiker to an all-year stream with flanking flower gardens, a good place to stop for lunch. The many mountain birds around here will eat any crumbs you leave.

Beyond the stream our trail contours along an open hillside where the flower display in season is among the best for miles around. Using one of the guides listed in the Recommended Reading chapter, the budding botanist will recognize woolly sunflower, Indian paintbrush, sulfur flower, scarlet gilia, pennyroyal, mule ears, corn lily and sagebrush, among others. Soon our route passes the signed-but-hard-to-find trail to Kirkwood Meadow and Caples Lake, and ½ mile farther, at a ford of an unnamed stream, meets the signed lateral trail to Scout Carson Lake. From this junction an unmaintained trail leads south for a good ¼ mile to this small, grass-and-heather-fringed lake with good campsites.

2nd Hiking Day: Retrace your steps, 5.5 miles (8.9 km).

Silver Lake to Summit City Canyon

2

TRIP From Silver Lake to Summit City Canyon (round trip). Topo map *Silver Lake*. Best mid season; 20 miles (32.2 km).

Grade	Trail/layover days	Total recommended days
Leisurely	4/1	5
Moderate	3/0	3
Strenuous	2/0	2

HILITES The first leg of this trip is a long traverse of very flowery open hillsides with fine views of the Silver Lake basin and its surrounding battlements. Then the trail enters a new stream valley and winds down through solitude-filled Horse Canyon to a variety of streamside campsites along beautiful Summit City Creek.

DESCRIPTION (Leisurely trip)

1st Hiking Day: Follow Trip 1 to **Scout Carson Lake**, 5.5 miles (8.9 km).

2nd Hiking Day (**Scout Carson Lake** to **Summit City Canyon**, 4.5 miles—7.2 km): First we retrace the long ¼ mile of use trail to the Horse Canyon Trail and turn right (east) on it. Our sometimes muddy trail ascends moderately through a thinning tree cover almost to timberline, passing through upland meadows rife with flower color in early season. Approaching Squaw Ridge, we cross a set of little-used jeep tracks and in 100 yards arrive at an unnamed pass which is the border of the Mokelumne Wilderness, a region of 50,450 acres where only foot travel is permitted and trails are generally kept up to a standard sufficient for walkers but not horses or mules.

The descent into steep Horse Canyon proceeds on a great number of switchbacks that zigzag down among tall, elegant silver pine trees past plentiful patches of daisies, groundsel, phlox, brodiaea, paintbrush and whorled penstemon, among other blossoms. At a natural overlook spot less than a mile down, the far-gazing hiker can see deep into Summit City Canyon and the Mokelumne River Canyon. Farther south, standing above the south canyon rim, are some peaks beyond Kennedy Meadow, including Cooper Peak, Granite Dome and Three Chimneys. Shortly after, our descending trail passes a trail that leads back to Squaw Ridge. After a few more switchbacks, the trail grade abates to moderate, and then almost to level, as it winds through a delightful meadowy area with lots of grass growing underneath a moderate cover of lodgepole pines, and flower swaths flanking bubbling little streams. This would be a fine camping area for lovers of seculsion. It was not always so secluded. Horse Canyon was part of the route of one emigrant trail, and eye bolts can still be found in some trees, where they were used to rope the wagons up or down.

After a mile of this meadowy forest, our trail crosses the Horse Canyon stream to its east side and leaves the main draw of the canyon, passing east over a ridge. Then the trail plunges down a rocky way where it is disguised as a rock-filled watercourse, and one had best watch one's footing. A brief stop will allow the careful descender to lift his eyes to enjoy the surrounding greenery and flowers, and to look down to the bottom of Summit City Canyon, far below. Soon the steepness decreases, and the rocky chute gives way to gentle switchbacks that lead ½ mile down to the Tahoe-Yosemite Trail beside Summit City Creek. Fair-to-good campsites lie near the junction. Fishing is fair-to-good for rainbow (to 10″) in Summit City Creek.

3rd and 4th Hiking Days: Retrace your steps, 10 miles (16.1 km).

Silver Lake to the Mokelumne River   **3**

TRIP   From Silver Lake to the Mokelumne River (round trip; part cross country). Topo map *Silver Lake.* Best mid season; 29 miles (46.6 km).

Grade	Trail/layover days	Total recommended days
Leisurely	6/2	8
Moderate	5/1	6
Strenuous	4/0	4

HILITES   The largest wilderness river in the northern Sierra is the goal of this trip. Virgin forests here shade the cool, green river, brown trout often rise to the fly, and except at trail crossings solitude is plentiful.

DESCRIPTION (Leisurely trip)

1st and 2nd Hiking Days: Follow Trip 2 to **Summit City Canyon**, 10 miles (16.1 km).

3rd Hiking Day (**Summit City Canyon** to the **Mokelumne River**, 4.5 miles—7.2 km): Some readers have complained that previous editions didn't mention the rattlesnakes in Summit City Canyon and along the Mokelumne River. Now they are mentioned. But we have yet to see one there.

Several hundred yards below the Horse Canyon Trail junction, our route, following the Tahoe-Yosemite Trail, easily crosses the Horse Canyon stream and then winds down Summit City Creek to cross Telephone Gulch. The main canyon narrows, but not so much as to force our path right next to the creek, and we follow a sandy duff tread across flats dotted with many lodgepole pines and aspens. The commonest

flower here, as it has been since before we reached the floor of
Summit City Canyon is the pink-cupped sidalcea. The second
commonest has been squaw root, also called yampa, with
hundreds of little white flowers making up flattish
flowerheads. An overgrown sign points to *Grouse Creek,* and
finally the regular trail ends just beyond a charming if now
illegal campsite.

From here to the Mokelumne River, the essentially
cross-country route is variously marked, and sometimes more
clear, sometimes less, but at worst you will be delayed in your
passage; you can't get lost. You should cross Summit City
Creek about 200 yards downstream from the illegal campsite,
at a point where deep, narrow channels in the bedrock can
contain all the stream flow except in early season, and
immediately scramble up the east slope before veering south
to parallel the stream. You will go behind a knoll about 30 feet
high with a small Jeffrey pine on it, and then proceed parallel
to the creek but separated from it by a series of rocky
prominences. From time to time ducks give some guidance, as
do a few remaining orange plastic ribbons tied by trail
surveyors when the Forest Service intended to construct a
trail here.

About ½ mile from the main stream crossing, we dip down
beside a very small stream and parallel it for ½ mile, then
cross it and contour high on a red-fir-shaded hillside, looking
down on a green, aspen-dotted flat where Summit City Creek
meanders south. After a little bushwhacking through willow
thickets, we descend on open granite to an almost flat area
near the stream, then on a fallen log cross a tributary that
runs till late summer. After penetrating more brush, we again
descend on open granite, this time to a large, sandy-bottomed
pool below a spectacular cataract on Summit City Creek. This
pool makes a fine lunch spot.

From the pool we pick up the ducked route again and make
two half-loops away from the creek and back to it. In some
places there are competing ducks, but they all lead in the
correct general direction. About ¼ mile from the pool we get a
good look down into the river canyon, and see that it is not too
far below us now. After the second half-loop returns to the
creek momentarily, our route veers east, tops a small ridge,
and descends steeply south for ¼ mile to a crossing of Summit
City Creek. A fallen tree here still with its bark, which does
not quite reach the north bank, would help one across the
creek during high water. About 100 yards beyond the crossing,
a faint trail forks left and we follow it 300 yards to an unsigned

junction in a sandy flat. Turning right here, we reach, in 300 more yards, a sign indicating *Cedar Camp Trail*. A few yards farther is the beautiful, clear Mokelumne River.

If you miss these faint trails, you can of course just follow Summit City Creek down to its confluence with the river. There are good campsites near the confluence. Fishing in the river for brown and rainbow trout (to 14″), is good—better if you go upstream, because that's tough walking.

4th, 5th and 6th Hiking Days: Retrace your steps, 14.5 miles (23.3 km).

Mokelumne River near Summit City Creek

4   Silver Lake to Long Lake

TRIP   From Silver Lake to Long Lake (round trip). Topo map *Silver Lake*. Best mid season, 13 miles—21 km (maximum).

Grade	Trail/layover days	Total recommended days
Leisurely	2/0	2
Moderate	....	....
Strenuous	....	....

HILITES   This easy weekend trip is even shorter for those with mountainworthy cars, and the very swimmable lake which is the destination makes a fine base from which to explore the gentle plateau north of the Mokelumne River Canyon.

DESCRIPTION (Leisurely trip)

If your car has good clearance you can probably drive past Allen's ranch to a parking area just beyond a runoff stream not long before Squaw Ridge (see the description below). You find the start of your dirt road at the top of the hill on State Highway 88 southwest of Silver Lake, and just east of Tragedy Spring, beginning among some summer homes. The parking area is 5 miles in from the highway. About 1¾ miles up this dirt road a signed fork to the right leads past Mud Lake and then back to the main dirt road before you reach Allen's ranch, and cars with only medium clearance can probably reach the parking area by taking this detour. Using either road will save you 2½ miles of walking each way.

1st Hiking Day (**Silver Lake** to **Long Lake,** 6.5 miles—10.5 km.): Near the informal parking area at Plasse's Resort, a dirt road fords a small unnamed stream and heads south past Stockton Municipal Camp on the right. Our wide, dusty trail leaves the road as we continue southbound in a moderate forest of small lodgepole pines east of the creek. Soon the trail begins to rise gradually, and then more steeply, under a welcome forest canopy of red fir and lodgepole pine. It passes several long, grassy meadows flanking the unnamed stream, fine spots for a breather stop or an early lunch. In 1½ miles our route passes a junction with a trail to Hidden Lake and then reaches the steep south wall of the basin we have been ascending. Here the path proceeds by way of long switchbacks up a mountain-hemlock-shaded volcanic slope. Views from the ridgetop include Silver Lake and Hidden Lake in the northern foreground, the Crystal Range and the Jacks Peak-Dicks Peak range farther north in Desolation Wilderness, and in the south, the meadow that we will walk through south of Allen's ranch, and the top of buff-brown Mokelumne Peak.

About 75 yards downhill from this saddle we meet a dirt road. (The northbound hiker could identify the place to leave the dirt road by noting that beyond Allen's ranch a two-track rough road veers right from the main dirt road at a pile of several hundred tan volcanic rocks.) Our route eastward on the dusty dirt road descends gently past the entrance to Allen's ranch and crosses the headwaters of Bear River—at this point not even a trickle in late summer. Shortly beyond, we ford running water in the lee of hundreds of brilliant yellow mimulus flowers and reach a sort of parking area for 4WD vehicles. Just beyond, we veer right on a trail as the jeep road ascends leftward, and traverse gently up in the shade of pine and hemlock to Squaw Ridge.

The junction on the ridge is in the middle of a forest of signs, identifying the Squaw Ridge Trail going northeast and southwest, the site of Plasse's Trading Post of Gold Rush days, and our Cedar Camp Trail, numbered 17E27. Here also we enter the 105,000-acre Mokelumne Wilderness. About 130 yards down our trail from this sign, a jeep road continues toward Pardoe Lake. In another 110 yards, at the bottom of the hill and across the road from a blazed lodgepole tree, is Horsethief Springs, where amid more yellow mimulus a pipe delivers the best drinking water on this entire trip, a fine place for lunch. Continuing on the two-track road, our route soon arrives at the former border of the Mokelumne Wilderness, which was enlarged in 1984 by Congressional action from 50,000 acres to 105,000 acres, to be held forever in trust for those who prefer their outdoors unmechanized.

In the wilderness our route for the next mile is almost level, slightly down, past several large meadows awash in corn lilies, groundsel and lupine in midseason. After a short descent on open hillside, the trail leads down through cool forest with a very green understory. Then it levels again in a moderate forest cover of pine and fir and passes the trail to Black Rock Lake. The next descent, over open granite slabs that look south to the plateau around our destination and to

Mokelumne Peak, passes a signed trail to Cole Creek Lakes. The sign is nailed to a lodgepole pine near its base, and easily missed. These lakes are a fine alternative campsite for this trip. The largest lake is ½ mile south on the lateral trail, and swimming and fishing for rainbow and brook trout are excellent.

Continuing on the Cedar Camp Trail, we wind among boulders shaded by silver and lodgepole pine and descend rockily to cross the dwindling outlet of a small lakelet which is the southernmost of the Cole Creek Lakes. A use trail up its east side leads to the main lake, mentioned above.

Now in red-fir forest, our path switchbacks down for a mile of decreasing gradient, recrossing the dwindling outlet, to the signed turnoff to Long Lake. Here we turn east and wind levelly beside snowmelt ponds for a short ½ mile to the west end of warm, reedy, tree-bound Long Lake. There is no stream, but the lake water is drinkable. In late season Halazone would be an extra precaution. Fishing for brook trout (to 14″) is fair, with a midsummer slowdown, and swimming from the granite slabs at the east end is first-rate. At night, you may be entertained by the excited calls of convening coyotes. On my first visit here, before I knew any were around, I let out a yip-yip, and was astounded that two real ones answered.

2nd Hiking Day: Retrace your steps, 6.5 miles (10.5 km).

Brook trout from Long Lake

Silver Lake to Camp Irene

5

TRIP   From Silver Lake to Camp Irene (round trip). Topo map *Silver Lake*. Best mid season; 25 miles (40.4 km).

Grade	Trail/layover days	Total recommended days
Leisurely	5/1	6
Moderate	4/0	4
Strenuous	3/0	3

HILITES   The hiker taking this trip will stop overnight at two highly contrasting places. Long Lake is at 8000 feet elevation, in the cool belt, and the green water is still, with no visible inflow or outflow after early season. In contrast, the Mokelumne River is a good-sized, clear-flowing river at an elevation of only 5000 feet, where middays can be very hot.

DESCRIPTION (Moderate trip)

1st Hiking Day: Follow Trip 4 to **Long Lake**, 6.5 miles (10.5 km).

2nd Hiking day (**Long Lake** to **Camp Irene**, 6 miles—9.7 km):   After retracing the short lateral trail to Long Lake, this day's route turns left (south) on the Cedar Camp Trail and rises gradually through a dense forest of fir and pine. Many rivulets lace this slope into midseason, and their courses are fertile growing grounds for lavender shooting stars and other meadow flowers. As the grade levels off, the trail swings eastward and soon arrives at green, sloping Munson Meadow, where in late season you will find the first flowing water since Horsethief Springs. For northbound hikers, it is the first water since the beginning of the long, unshaded climb up the manzanita-lined sandy trail from the "oasis" in the Mokelumne River canyon.

From Munson Meadow the trail wanders southeast over a forested plateau for a mile before it starts to descend in earnest into the river canyon. At first, the trail is rocky and dusty, shaded by a sparse forest cover of red firs. Then it steepens and becomes completely exposed to the sun as it leads down a series of long switchback legs on very sandy underfooting. Views across the canyon are quite expansive, and time passes quickly—for the descending traveler. Coming back is a very different story.

Nearly 2 miles from the start of the switchbacks, the trail, still steep, enters much more hospitable territory where all-year water allows alders, willows, aspens and a great panoply of wildflowers to flourish. About 100 yards below the first of these wet "oasis" areas is a flat spot where one could camp if he were up-bound and exhausted. The trail continues to descend, moderately to steeply, but it is well shaded much of the time, and it often crosses unmapped streams that flow all year. At these streams the thirsty hiker can pleasure his mouth with the sweet pure water, and pleasure his eyes with the multicolors of orange tiger lily, pink columbine, yellow groundsel and white milfoil flowers, and the rich green of bracken ferns. After about four stream crossings—depending on the season—it is a steep 200-yard descent on a rocky-dusty trail to the junction of the unmapped trail up the river canyon and the trail down to Camp Irene.

Turning right here, our route descends to a stream not shown on the map and follows it down to the river, passing a 1974 burn shortly before reaching Camp Irene. This camping area has a sandy beach, fine granite slabs, lovely pools—and a lot of campers, since it is a popular overnight stop along the Tahoe-Yosemite Trail. Those who need solitude will find it up or down the river. Fishing in the Mokelumne is good for brown and rainbow trout (to 14").

3rd and 4th Hiking Days: Retrace your steps, 12.5 miles (20.9 km).

Silver Lake to the Mokelumne River 6

TRIP From Silver Lake to the Mokelumne River via Summit City Canyon, return via Munson Meadow and Long Lake (shuttle trip). Topo map *Silver Lake*. Best mid season; 28.2 miles (45.4 km).

Grade	Trail/layover days	Total Recom- mended days
Leisurely	6/2	8
Moderate	5/1	6
Strenuous	4/0	4

HILITES This tour visits examples of all the landscapes of the Carson Pass region—volcanic peaks, rounded granite domes, deep-cut river canyons and lake-dotted plateaus. Anyone in good condition who has the basic skills for hiking cross country will enjoy this long shuttle trip.

DESCRIPTION (Moderate trip)

1st, 2nd and 3rd Hiking Days: Follow Trip 3 to the **Mokelumne River**, 14.5 miles (23.3 km).

4th Hiking Day (**Mokelumne River** to **Long Lake**, 7.2 miles—11.6 km): (This trail description as far as the junction with the trail to Camp Irene is quite detailed because the multiplicity of trails and paths in the region west of Summit City Creek makes route finding a problem.) From the *Cedar Camp Trail* sign, retrace your steps 300 yards to the unsigned junction in a sandy flat and turn left. A bare hundred yards south of this junction, very noticeable ducks lead up a granite slab, more or less straight ahead. Don't follow them. Instead, veer right, and when you top the crest of granite a few feet above you, you will (if it's still there) see a duck which will lead you onto the little-used trail on which you came here from the Tahoe-Yosemite Trail. If you do accidentally follow the proscribed ducked route, you will soon find yourself going down beside the river. Eventually you will have to leave the riverside and climb some cliffs above a gorge, perhaps using rope to haul your pack once or twice. Finally you will arrive at Camp Irene, and from there you can take the Tahoe-Yosemite Trail north 1 mile to its junction with the Munson Meadow Trail, a junction described in later paragraphs.

Back at the Tahoe-Yosemite Trail where we left it yesterday, we turn left, top a small ridge, cross a tributary stream, and descend into a dense forest of second-growth ponderosa pine and incense-cedar with a few delicate ferns on the level forest floor. Then, emerging from this forest, we see that we are close under granite cliffs on the right (north). From here a gentle downgrade takes us past a 5-foot-thick ponderosa, burned through at the base, into a fine forest of first-growth sugar pines, their great cones strewn about the forest floor. After crossing a stream that flows in early season, our route soon leaves the forest and climbs more than 100 feet on rocky-dusty underfooting, leveling off under a sparse-to-moderate cover of Jeffrey pines, incense-cedars and black oaks. In ⅛ mile after the climb, the eastbound hiker would notice a fork veering right, but he should keep left. From this junction our path makes a steep, sandy ascent for several hundred yards, then drops slightly across exposed granite outcroppings. Just after it swings right, there is another unofficial junction that might beguile an eastbound hiker: he should keep right at this junction. Then one arrives at the signed junction of the trails to Camp Irene (left) and Munson Meadow (right). From here, retrace the steps of most of the 2nd hiking day, Trip 5, to Long Lake. The ascent you will make out of the Mokelumne River canyon is very stiff indeed, and the earlier you start this hiking day, the better.

5th Hiking Day: Reverse the 1st hiking day of Trip 4, 6.5 miles (10.5 km).

Carson Pass to Showers Lake   7

TRIP   From Carson Pass to Showers Lake (round trip). Topo map *Silver Lake.* Best mid season, 10.2 miles (16.4 km).

Grade	Trail/layover days	Total recom- mended days
Leisurely	2/1	3
Moderate	2/0	2
Strenuous	....	....

HILITES   Showers Lake is one of the best camping places between U.S. 50 and State Highway 88, with numerous campsites and good angling for brook trout. En route, the trail through the upper Truckee Valley offers panoramic views of immense volcanic formations and promises potential close-up glimpses of many birds and mammals.

DESCRIPTION

1st Hiking Day (**Carson Pass** to **Showers Lake,** 5.1 miles—8.2 km): From a large parking area (8350′) ¼ mile west of Carson Pass our dusty route climbs steadily northward on an old jeep road now closed to motor vehicles. The slope is moderately forested with red fir, lodgepole pine and clumps of aspen. Leaving the tree cover behind, we climb steeply up a slope covered by sagebrush and mule ears. In the warm sun of this open slope the sage odor adds spice to the thin, clear air. After ascending 400 feet in ½ mile, the trail reaches a saddle on the divide between Truckee River drainage and American River drainage. From this saddle views southward of Round Top Peak and its snow-draped satellites are excellent. In the north, we see Mt. Tallac, Dicks Peak and Jacks Peak, all west of Tahoe. Here we begin a descent down the long, green, tree-dotted valley of the upper Truckee. Nearby on the east, Red Lake Peak is topped by slablike volcanic outcroppings resembling a stegosaur's back plates. Little runoff streams that spring from porous volcanic rocks trickle their water onto flower gardens of iris, yarrow milfoil, Mariposa lily, sulfur flower, lupine and paintbrush. Descending moderately to steadily from the summit, we cross three runoff streams (dry in late season), then a westward-flowing tributary, and finally the infant Truckee River—all via easy fords.

Just past another easy ford are the buildings of a cow camp, and near them the Round Lake Trail (not shown on the topo map) branches right. The meadows here are full of little gray Belding squirrels, commonly called picket-pins, and often a Swainson hawk soars overhead, hoping to surprise one of them. Continuing the level walk from the Round Lake junction, we pass an unsigned trail to Meiss Lake, visible as a meadow-fringed blue sheet in the northeast. Then one last time we ford the river, on boulders, and a few feet beyond the ford an old jeep road forks right toward Meiss Lake, as our route bears left. (From this point on our route is not shown on the topo map.) We pass a trail to Schneider Camp (not shown on the topo map and unsigned but marked by a blazed **S** on the lodgepole), and ascend out of Dixon Canyon on a gentle grade. From the crest of this little ascent, the trail dips past a shallow, weedy pond and continues on the old two-track jeep road. After crossing two runoff streams (dry in late season), we begin a steady-to-steep ascent of ¼ mile, first up a wash filled with smoothed, round rocks, and then on a rocky-dusty trail, under moderate-to-dense forest cover of red fir, hemlock, silver pine and lodgepole pine. Sixty yards after the jeep tracks emerge from this forest onto a meadowy slope lush with lupine and mule ears, a trail veers slightly left and uphill from the tracks, and we take the trail. (The old jeep road also goes to Showers Lake.) This trail section traverses a bountifully flowered, meadowy slope to a forested saddle overlooking Showers Lake, from where it descends to the fair-to-good campsites on the west and east sides of the lake (8650'). Fishing is good for eastern brook (to 12"). From a base camp here, one may easily walk cross country to Four Lakes, where fishing and swimming are often good in mid-to-late season.

2nd Hiking Day: Retrace your steps, 4.3 miles (6.9 km).

Carson Pass to Echo Summit 8

TRIP From Carson Pass to Echo Summit (shuttle trip). Topo maps *Silver Lake,* ***Fallen Leaf Lake.*** Best mid season; 12.6 miles (20.3 km).

Grade	Trail/layover days	Total recom- mended days
Leisurely	2/1	3
Moderate	2/0	2
Strenuous	....	....

HILITES This trip offers one of the easiest ways in the whole northern Sierra to get away from the crowd, and it is an excellent choice for a two-party shuttle. With a minimum of effort, the hiker can traverse some high, scenic, little-used country, where the wildlife is as plentiful as the people are scarce.

DESCRIPTION

1st Hiking Day: Follow Trip 7 to **Showers Lake,** 5.1 miles (8.2 km).

2nd Hiking Day (**Showers Lake** to **Echo Summit,** 7.5 miles— 12.1 km). Heading northwest from the southwest shore of Showers Lake, we soon find the trail, and then ascend gently for several hundred yards through mixed conifers. Coming out onto open slopes, we ford a year-round stream fed by the snow cornice that drapes the ridge of Little Round Top above. Where we cross this stream, its banks are lined with thousands of blossoms of the showy yellow flower *Arnica chamissionis.* In fact, this whole open bowl is laced with runoff streams and lavishly planted with colorful bushes and flowers: blue elderberry, green gentian, swamp whiteheads, mountain bluebell, aster, wallflower, penstemon, spiraea, cinquefoil, corn lily and columbine. As we walk around this bowl on the boundary between volcanic rocks above and granite below, we have good views of Stevens Peak and Red Lake Peak, both built up of layers of richly colored volcanic flows.

Finally, the trail ascends out of the bowl and enters a sparse cover of lodgepole and silver pine. At the crest of this ascent, the pine gives way to hemlock as we pass a cattle drift fence (close the gate) and level off through open high country. Reaching a willowy meadow, one may lose the trail momentarily, but it is easy to find if one continues straight across the meadow. A short distance beyond is a junction with a signed trial to Schneider Cow Camp, which leads west. One third of a mile beyond this junction our route crosses, at right angles, an unsigned but well-grooved trail which is used by local stockmen, and then continues its almost level, winding course northward under a sparse-to-moderate mixed forest cover.

We then pass a collapsed stock fence and make a short, steep descent down a hemlock-covered hillside to a meadowy slope where marsh marigolds, their white and yellow petals set off by their rich green leaves, bloom in the wetness of melting snows until late in the season. Our sandy footpath soon passes a trail that winds down Sayles Canyon, and then we continue north to a summit from where views of the Crystal Range, including Pyramid Peak, are good. From here it is a gentle descent under hemlock, silver and lodgepole pine to Bryan Meadow. Here one may camp except in late season, when the stream is dry. A collapsed log cabin in the meadow sprawls near the confluence of routes leading to Showers Lake, U.S. 50 and Benwood Meadow.

Heading for Benwood Meadow, we ascend a gently rising sandy trail through meadowy, open stands of lodgepole pine, with some sagebrush. The alert hiker here may spot a red-shafted flicker on one of its characteristic undulating flights between trees. At the top of this sandy climb the trail levels off and becomes indistinct, but the route is well marked by blazes. A short, steep descent then brings us to a willow-filled bowl where an unnamed stream rises. We cross the young stream and on the far slope veer right, on a trail that soon switchbacks steeply down a red-fir-covered slope. At the foot of the slope is another willowy meadow, and shortly beyond that another steep downslope, also shaded by red fir, where following the route may require attention to the occasional ducks. The trail then levels out in a large meadow that was once a lake, skirting the west side of it.

The trail from this meadow to Benwood Meadow is sometimes indistinct, but there are sufficient blazes and ducks. At Benwood Meadow the flora is quite noteworthy: along the wet meadow margin the flower-spotter is kept busy by the plenitude of aster, corn lily, snow plant, alpine lily, monkey flower, penstemon, false Solomon's seal, squawroot, pennyroyal, groundsel, columbine, larkspur and mountain bluebell, to say nothing of the ferns, grasses and sedges.

Past Benwood Meadow, our nearly level trail meets a junction with a new segment of trail that goes left to Echo Summit. Then it dips to cross the outlet of a lily-filled pond, and ascends gently up a rather exposed slope, where a few mixed conifers partially shade a ground cover of huckleberry oak, pinemat manzanita and Sierra chinquapin. Finally, the rocky-dusty trail ends at a graded road (7520') that serves a small tract of summer homes ⅓ mile south of Echo Summit.

Showers Lake

9   Mosquito Lake to Bull Run Lake

TRIP   From Mosquito Lake to Heiser Lake, Bull Run
Lake, return to Stanislaus Meadow (shuttle trip).
Topo maps *Markleeville, Dardanelles Cone* (this
new trail is not shown on either map). Best mid
season; 8 miles (12.8 km).

Grade	Trail/layover days	Total recom- mended days
Leisurely	3/0	3
Moderate	2/0	2
Strenuous	....	....

HILITES Two of the better, scenic, trout-stocked lakes of the
Lake Alpine area are visited on this easy hike.
Dayhikers and fishermen may wish to hike only to
Heiser Lake via the Heiser Lake Trail or only to
larger Bull Run Lake via the Bull Run Trail,
thereby avoiding the short 2½-mile shuttle.

DESCRIPTION (Leisurely trip)

1st Hiking Day (**Mosquito Lake** to **Heiser Lake**, 2 miles—3.2 km):
At the west end of Mosquito Lake in a picnic ground, look for a
faint trail that follows old blazes southeast, directly up a
forested slope. In about 30 yards, the trail becomes obvious,
leading up granitic bedrock that has a veneer of volcanic
rocks. The steep trail quickly levels off, then makes a short,
moderate descent and winds south close to a pond that is
erroneously labeled "Heiser Lake" on the *Markleeville* topo
map. The true Heiser Lake is seen on the *Dardanelles Cone*
topo as the lake one mile north-northeast of Bull Run Lake.

Leaving the pond's environs, we climb steeply through a
thinning forest of silver and lodgepole pine and mountain
hemlock, and surmount a granitic ridge at its low point. On
fresh-looking, glacially scoured rock we descend from the

ridge and follow a winding route that takes the path of least resistance down slabs. After leveling off in deep forest, we climb ⅓ mile to a junction on a little flat. Tomorrow we'll head southwest from here down a creekside trail, but since our immediate goal is Heiser Lake, we turn east, hike a short ¼ mile uphill, then switchback and climb south over a low granitic ridge that hides the shallow lake. Dotted with several small islands of granitic rock, this conifer-fringed lake presents the fisherman with a picturesque distraction while he contemplates a meal of fresh brook trout. Campsites lie on the north and south shores under a pleasant canopy of red fir, lodgepole pine, silver pine and mountain hemlock.

2nd Hiking Day (**Heiser Lake** to **Bull Run Lake**, 2.5 miles—4 km): First, retrace your steps ½ mile to yesterday's trail junction. From here our route, usually well blazed and ducked, takes us southwest to the brink of a rocky slope, and then down the slope via very steep switchbacks. We then stay fairly close to Heiser Lake's outlet creek, paralleling it west across a flat basin shaded by mountain hemlocks. Approaching the basin's west edge, we cross four closely spaced branches of a tributary that joins the outlet creek just south of the trail. After a brief climb west, our trail turns south and leads to a signed junction with the Bull Run Trail.

From the junction, this route almost immediately fords Heiser Lake's outlet creek, a ford that could require a little doing in early season when it is a small torrent of white water. After following an almost level granitic bench for ⅓ mile, this route angles south and crosses the first of many creeklets. Our winding route goes from slab to granitic slab as it climbs and gyrates up toward the lake. Were it not for a superabundance of blazes and ducks, some hikers would get off route. This climb is broken into distinct ascents, the first one trending southeast up and around a secondary ridge, the second one trending southwest past a trailside pond before it approaches Bull Run Lake's outlet creek and ascends near it to the lake's bedrock dam.

Although not large by Sierra standards, this popular lake can accommodate dozens of campers, particularly on the spacious flats beneath large red firs. Swimming in the lake is good in early August, and fishing is often good for brook trout.

3rd Hiking Day (**Bull Run Lake** to **Stanislaus Meadow**, 3.5 miles—5.6 km): After backtracking to the trail junction just west of Heiser Lake's outlet, our route stays on the Bull Run Trail as it winds, steeply at times, 350 vertical feet down rock slabs covered with lodgepole and silver pine, red fir and mountain juniper, well above the outlet creek from both lakes before it eases off in a shady flat. A short forest traverse brings us to a crossing of this creek, which in early season can entail a cold, wide, knee-deep ford. Beyond the ford we follow the creek a shady, long ⅓ mile to a refording of two branches of it, which will give early-season hikers another challenge. The trail from the ford maintains a westbound course for 100 yards to an even wider ford, the headwaters of North Fork Stanislaus River. As usual, look for logs across the stream, which may make fording drier and perhaps much quicker.

Immediately beyond the North Fork we cross a seasonally dry wash before turning north and roughly paralleling the North Fork upstream. A wide path leads up this moderate grade, and, near its top, we may be greeted by a chorus of cowbells, which incessantly ring as their wearers munch away in Stanislaus Meadow. A fence keeps the cattle in the meadow and us in the forest while an easy ½ mile hike along its west side brings us to the Bull Run Lake trailhead.

Bull Run Lake   *Jeff Schaffer*

Wolf Creek Meadows to Soda Springs **10**

TRIP   From Wolf Creek Meadows to Soda Springs Guard
Station via High Trail, return via East Carson
River Trail (semiloop trip). Topo map *Topaz Lake*.
Best mid season; 20.5 miles (33 km).

Grade	Trail/layover days	Total recommended days
Leisurely	3/1	4
Moderate	2/0	2
Strenuous	....	....

HILITES   One can acquire a good feeling for eastside Sierra
flora and geology on this trip, ideally suited for
weekend backpackers. Because the landscape is
viewed from a crest route going and a canyon route
returning, the hiker sees it from two very different
perspectives.

DESCRIPTION (Moderate trip)

1st Hiking Day (**Wolf Creek Meadows** to **Soda Springs Guard
Station,** 9.5 miles—15.3 km): At the edge of a volcanic slope
covered with sagebrush, mule ears and bitterbrush, the High
Trail climbs upward into an open forest of Jeffrey pine and
white fir. With the brief views of Wolf Creek Meadows behind
us, we now enjoy the shade that the forest provides on this
steep climb. Beyond a large split boulder and its surrounding
mountain mahogany bushes, the High Trail parallels the
ridge up to a level crest, then climbs steeply to a small, grassy
flat. Just beyond this flat, we start an uphill traverse across a
grassy, gentle slope that contains a curious combination of
water-loving, white-barked aspens almost next to drought-
resistant, mangy-barked junipers. Jeffrey pines, white firs,
willows, mule ears and sagebrush complete the cast of
principal plants. Here, taking a break, one can easily fall
asleep to the soothing sounds of rustling aspen leaves.

Up these shady slopes we climb, and about ½ mile beyond
the meadow, the steep trail eases up and then levels off as it

comes to an open slope. Here the trail provides a momentary view of the Vaquero Camp buildings in the east, down in Silver King Valley, and more enduring views of the granitic Freel Peak area, in the northwest, beyond whose summits lies Lake Tahoe. Along our short, open traverse we find a good exposure of a type of blocky volcanic rock that is common to this "land of fire and ice." It is called an *autobrecciated* ("self-broken") lava flow. From the middle Miocene epoch through the late Pliocene epoch (roughly from 18 to 5 million years ago), thick andesitic lava flows poured from summits that probably resembled today's Oregon Cascades, and they covered an area of the Sierra Nevada that extended from Sonora Pass north to Lassen Park and from east of the present Sierra crest westward to beneath the Central Valley. When the thick lava flows cooled as they flowed along their downward paths, they became less and less able to move, particularly along their rapidly cooling edges, and eventually these edges solidified. But then the pressure of the still-flowing internal material fractured the edges, creating the broken-up texture we see here.

At the base of an autobrecciated flow decorated with vine maples, we enter a shady white-fir forest and encounter a refreshing, flowery, mossy, spring-fed creeklet. Beyond it our trail climbs moderately eastward, then descends slightly to a low knoll covered with ragged mountain mahogany. Leaving the knoll, we pass through a forest of pines and firs, and descend steeply south into two seasonal, parallel creeklets that drain Snowslide Canyon. Volcanic rocks give way to granitic ones as we leave this broad, brushy canyon, descend through a shady forest, round a jagged, granitic ridge, and then reach another seasonal creek.

One-fourth mile beyond this creek, our trail tops out at a bedrock saddle on a ridge above the East Carson canyon. From it, short switchbacks lead steeply down a brushy slope covered with huckleberry oak and manzanita; then our trail diagonals southwest down to a gentle slope on which we cross an unsigned east-west trail. Soon we reach a bubbling creek, and cross it only 90 yards before arriving at the East Fork Carson River. If you don't like river fords, you can camp along or near the riverbank, and later backtrack $^1/_5$ mile to the east-west trail and follow it east ¼ mile to another river ford. (Those who ford the East Carson southbound on this trip will reford it here.) Before mid-July, the river is usually waist-deep, about 50°F at most, and swift, but by Labor Day it has dropped to knee depth. A rope helps in an early-season traverse across the river's bouldery bottom, but it is unnecessary for the experienced backpacker, since there are no dangerous rapids downstream.

For those who fish this river, a likely catch is the mountain whitefish, which looks like a cross between a trout and a sucker. A small mouth on the lower part of its head is the sucker characteristic, but the presence of an adipose fin on the lower back identifies it as a close relative of trout and salmon. Like these fish, it is good to eat. This river also contains the Tahoe sucker, whose protractile mouth, on the bottom of its head, is ideally suited for scavenging the river bottom. Although bony, it is tasty.

Across the river, the High Trail ends in 80 yards at a signed junction with the East Carson River Trail—an old jeep road closed to motor vehicles. On this gravelly road we parallel the river ⅓ mile upstream to the north edge of a sagebrush flat. Here the river angles west, but our tracks head south through dense sagebrush. Reaching a dry wash debouching from a small, very bouldery gorge, we climb up it to a low bedrock saddle. From the saddle we make a short descent past a small, steep cliff, on the right, then reach a larger, longer, steeper one, on the left. This cliff we parallel southeast, then continue to three close-spaced Jeffrey pines in a sagebrush flat. From between the west and south pines, the main route goes 200 yards southwest to a ford of the East Carson, then south along jeep tracks through a shady forest to a refording of the East Carson one mile later. This refording takes place at the

Bagley Valley (autobrecciated rock in foreground) *Schaffer*

"bottom" (south) curve of a large meander, whose west half
dries up late in the summer, when the lower river shoots
directly east 150 yards to the ford (see the accompanying map).
Eventually, the meander will disappear as the river estab-
lishes a more efficient, more direct course. About 250 yards

south of this ford, in a field of granitic boulders left by a glacier, an indistinct trail heads east-southeast through the grass another 250 yards to Poison Creek, just beyond whose east bank is a path that leads south 300 yards to the Soda Springs Guard Station.

Most hikers, when they arrive at the three Jeffrey pines, will prefer not to ford and reford the East Carson, even though these two fords are considerably easier than the High Trail ford. For them there is a dry route to the Soda Springs Guard Station. After leaving between the south and east pines, follow a path south-southeast for 100 yards. If you're on the right path—there are many cow paths—it will bend south and soon reach a granitic cliff that plunges down to the East Carson only ¼ mile due south of the three pines. Once around the bouldery base of this small cliff, you have an easy, open walk southward that parallels the East Carson. About ¾ mile beyond, the river bends west and you follow it on a faint trail through sagebrush to the northeast corner of the large meander mentioned in the alternate route. From this corner a set of jeep tracks leads southeast ⅕ mile across a flat to a signed junction with the Poison Flat Trail, just within forest cover. Trip 13 heads north along this trail, and trips 15 and 16 head south along it to this junction. We turn south, up-canyon, and follow the jeep tracks, which quickly reduce to a path in the 100 yards it takes to reach the first of as many as half a dozen distributaries of Poison Creek. Between two of them, the alternate route—a footpath from the west-northwest—ends at our broad path. A little beyond we meet the fenced-in compound around Soda Springs Guard Station. You can camp by multibranched Poison Creek, or a small creek ⅓ mile along the trail west of the guard station provides another possibility.

2nd Hiking Day (**Soda Springs Guard Station** to **Wolf Creek Meadows,** 11 miles—17.7 km): First, retrace your steps 2¾ miles to the signed High Trail junction. This day's route continues on a jeep road going northeast from the junction, then quickly curves right as it rounds an open flat. In 0.4 mile from the High Trail junction, we arrive at an East Carson ford which is almost as difficult as the High Trail ford. Our next segment of jeep road starts northeast up a flat and crosses it, then is almost cut in two by a river's meander that has eroded deeply into the flat. Beyond the meander, a traverse across an equally long flat ends at the East Carson one mile below the High Trail junction.

Here, look for two large Jeffrey pines just north of you, between which a barbed-wire gate marks the start of a trail.

From the gate this trail stays on the west side of the East Carson, paralleling the river at first, but gradually veering away from it. We cross two long, but not high, moraines— those bouldery, sandy ridges left by a glacier before it retreated back up the East Carson canyon and into extinction. Beyond the second moraine is a seasonal creeklet which we cross only 70 yards west of the East Carson. The trail now parallels the river to a junction with some jeep tracks.

We follow these north almost ½ mile up to a low ridgecrest of a rocky moraine that marks the northernmost extent of a former glacier in Silver King Valley. Atop this moraine is a barbed-wire fence across the jeep tracks. Motor vehicles are allowed on the north side of the gate, and to avoid them our route goes through an impressive gorge of the East Carson. This challenging route leaves the jeep tracks atop the moraine, follows the fence west about 300 yards to a gate, descends to the entrance of the gorge, and follows the river's west side 2½ miles. The difficulty of this gorge route varies, the hardest part occurring in the scenic first half. When the water is low—after Labor Day—you can walk along the river's edge, but in early season you'll have to climb above it many times. Nevertheless, a rope is not necessary. At first, you'll pass by impressive, deeply cut cliffs of autobrecciated lava flows. Farther down, you're likely to see columnar flows in addition. Campsites in this isolated gorge are plentiful, but unfortunately the best ones are on the opposite bank. Midway down the gorge campsites are replaced by talus slopes whose boulders came down from the loose, pinkish-brown cliffs above. This route ends at the official trail, which fords the East Carson at Gray's Crossing, directly west of a low gap.

From the crossing, the East Carson River Trail heads west, then climbs steeply up to gentler slopes above the river. Soon we reach a gate, pass through it, and gradually curve westward into Railroad Canyon. Up this canyon we hike, seemingly too long to be on the right route, and then we cross its creeklet. From here, the last permanent source of fresh water, our trail climbs north out of the canyon, circles along the edge of a flat-topped autobrecciated lava flow, then traverses ⅓ mile northwest to the south tip of shallow Wolf Creek Lake (not the larger, better known Wolf Creek Lake at the east base of Sonora Peak).

From the lake's southeast corner, our trail climbs west up to the base of steep volcanic slopes, then ascends to the ridge above the trailhead, along which runs a fence. On the other side of its gate, we meet the end of a jeep road, and on it walk west a short distance to a saddle, recognizing that the large, scattered granitic boulders resting on the volcanic bedrock are "erratics"—boulders carried here by a large glacier that once flowed north down Wolf Creek canyon. From the saddle we can look up-canyon and imagine how impressive this canyon would have appeared about 6,000 years ago, when a river of ice, hundreds of feet thick, slowly flowed past this spot, quite likely reaching, and occasionally damming, the East Fork Carson River. After a moment's reflection on this subject, we leave the saddle and descend 100 steep yards to our trailhead, which is beside the trailhead of the High Trail.

East Fork Carson River   *Jeff Schaffer*

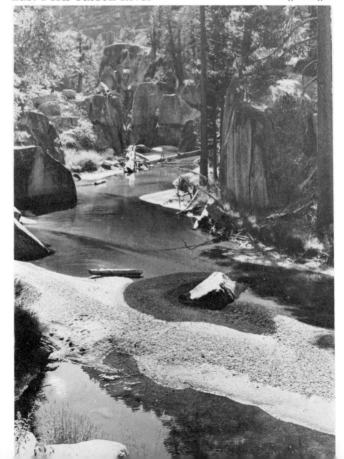

11 Wolf Creek Meadows to Wolf Creek

TRIP   From Wolf Creek Meadows to Wolf Creek via Soda
            Springs Guard Station, Murray Canyon and Wolf
            Creek canyon (shuttle trip). Topo maps *Topaz
            Lake, Sonora Pass*. Best mid or late season; 24
            miles (38.6 km).

Grade	Trail/layover days	Total recommended days
Leisurely	3/0	3
Moderate	2/0	2
Strenuous	....	....

HILITES   Like trip 2, this trip starts as a scenic crest route,
            then it proceeds through parts of three glaciated
            canyons. Plenty of creekside campsites await
            anglers who would like to try their skill at trout
            fishing.

DESCRIPTION (Moderate trip)

1st Hiking Day (**Wolf Creek Meadows** to **Murray Canyon Trail
junction,** 12 miles—19.3 km): First, follow trip 10 to Soda
Springs Guard Station, 9.5 miles (15.3 km). Leaving the shady
campground at the guard station, we hike west on a jeep trail
and after ⅓ mile cross a spring-fed creeklet. Just beyond this
creeklet is a well-used campsite under lodgepole pines, only 20
yards downslope. Immediately below it is a trail coming from
the larger meander mentioned in Trip 10 (see the map in Trip
10). Westward, this trail parallels our jeep trail, dying out in a
grassy meadow. Our easy route through sagebrush reaches
this meadow in ½ mile and the jeep tracks, like the trail, die
out in it. They quickly reappear at the northwest end of the
meadow and lead us 200 yards northwest to a wide ford of the
East Carson.

Continuing northwest we arrive at an unsigned junction.
From here our route goes 1½ miles over a trail that is often a

multilane cowpath. The trail tends to stay away from the river as it ascends gently through Jeffrey-pine forest. After the canyon heads south, the trail emerges on the edge of a large, cow-infested meadow, on the northwest side of which is a signed junction about 50 yards beyond Murray Canyon creek. Several fair campsites can be found near the cottonwoods along the creek. This creek, and the river provide fair-to-good fishing for rainbow and paiute-rainbow hybrid (to 10″).

2nd Hiking Day (**Murray Canyon Trail junction** to **Upper Wolf Creek Meadows**, 12 miles—19.3 km): At the signed trail junction, we leave the gentle gradient of the East Fork Carson River Trail and climb, steeply at times, up 15 switchback legs that lead high on a brushy, open-forested slope and then into Murray Canyon. Like virtually every tributary canyon of the East Carson above Soda Springs, this one usually had a glacier in it when there was one in the main canyon. Being much smaller, however, the Murray Canyon glacier was unable to keep pace with the tremendous excavating power of the East Carson glacier, which in this area was sometimes more than 800 feet thick. As a result, the East Carson glacier cut down faster, leaving Murray Canyon as a hanging valley—which we have just entered at the top of the switchbacks.

From the top of these switchbacks we go another 200 yards to the verdant banks of clear Murray Canyon creek. After 100 steep yards, the trail resumes a moderate grade and takes us past the first of many flower-lined creeklets. One-third mile up from the creek crossing, we pass through the gate of a cattle fence, then continue up the flowery path. At a trail junction where Murray Canyon splits in two, our trail, the main one, bends right and climbs steeply west up the canyon.

About ¼ mile above the junction is a permanent creek, lined with willows and alders; then in another ¼ mile the trail crosses a second creek. Beyond it the route steepens, on a few short switchbacks up a granitic slope. Talus that has fallen from volcanic formations above has buried much of the granitic bedrock, and it becomes very widespread as the grade eases and the trail enters a small gully flowered with mule ears. Beyond this gully, we climb steadily north ½ mile to a crest saddle, where, a few yards northwest of the actual crest, is a junction with a fairly new trail. Trip 15, which has coincided with this hiking day up to this saddle, departs south along this crest path.

As we switchback northwest down rather open volcanic slopes, ahead is a flat-topped ridge composed of several thick, horizontal lava flows, below which lies a huge talus slope. This

rocky slope was built up after the last glacier retreated
up-canyon when water, freezing and expanding in the flows'
cracks, pried off countless blocks.

At the bottom of the descent into deep, long Wolf Creek
Canyon, we encounter a cattle fence, pass through its gate,
and follow the trail as it widens to a jeep road. Joining this
short stretch is a jeep spur from the south and, merged
together, they head 100 yards northwest to a signed junction,
near a conspicuous snow-depth marker, with the Asa Lake
Trail. Our route, a jeep road for the remainder of this hike,
starts north and quickly reaches a ford—usually a wet one—of
Wolf Creek. Across the creek, we amble along an easy path ⅓
mile to a meadow and a signed junction.

Continuing northeast on the jeep road around the fenced
meadow, we descend to a creeklet and then parallel Wolf
Creek at a short distance, staying above the small gorge it has
cut through volcanic rock. Small, tempting pools can be seen
in the creek, particularly just before a gate on a low, descending ridge. Beyond the ridge gate, our route descends very
steeply to a crossing of Bull Canyon creek, a wet ford except in
late season. At this alder-lined crossing, granitic bedrock once
again is and it becomes more abundant down-canyon.

Strolling down-canyon to Dixon Creek, we approach and
veer away from Wolf Creek several times. A long, wide, rocky
stream bed has formed behind a constriction in the canyon
created by a prominent granitic ridge on the east side and by
Dixon Creek's alluvial fan on the west. Since the *Topaz Lake*
topo was made, Dixon Creek has shifted its course to a more
northern position down across this fan. For most of the
summer Dixon Creek runs too high to ford without getting wet
feet. Once across it, though, you'll keep your feet dry the rest of
the way. The jeep road first parallels the creek, then veers
northwest away from it, skirts a grove of aspens and
cottonwoods, and curves east around a well-weathered granitic knob. From here it is an easy 1 mile stroll to the trailhead,
the Wolf Creek Meadows Undeveloped Camping Area.

Wolf Creek Meadows to Sonora Pass 12

TRIP   From Wolf Creek Meadows to Sonora Pass via
Soda Springs, White Canyon and Wolf Creek Lake
(shuttle trip). Topo maps *Topaz Lake, Sonora Pass*.
Best mid season; 30 miles (48.5 km).

Grade	Trail/layover days	Total recom- mended days
Leisurely	5/1	6
Moderate	4/0	4
Strenuous	3/0	3

HILITES   One of the longest and deepest canyons east of the
Sierra crest, the East Fork Carson River canyon at
times contained glaciers up to 19 miles long. Our
trip heads south up this spectacular canyon, stops
at scenic Wolf Creek Lake, then passes through a
sculptured volcanic "badland" on the south slope
of Sonora Peak. This peak—the highest summit
between State Highway 108 and Mt. Shasta—is
easily climbed in a short side trip.

DESCRIPTION (Strenuous trip)

1st Hiking Day: Follow Trip 11 to **Murray Canyon Trail junction**,
12 miles (19.3 km).

2nd Hiking Day **Murray Canyon Trail junction** to **Wolf Creek
Lake,** 13 miles—20.9 km): Next to granitic bedrock just south
of the Murray Canyon Trail junction is a fair campsite. At this
campsite Murray Canyon creek blocks our path in early and
mid season. During these seasons you may have to wade
several yards downstream before you can resume your brief

walk along the west side of this creek. In about 200 yards, Murray Canyon creek bends east and joins the meadering East Fork Carson River. Immediately south of the creek's bend, we join the main path from our starting point. This path, obvious to northbound hikers, makes four fords of Murray Canyon creek and, due to willows and grass, is difficult for southbound hikers to locate. Staying along the East Carson canyon's meadowy west edge, we now hike about ½ mile south to a usually flowing creek, cross a very low ridge, and make a very steep but short ascent, 200 yards to a junction. Here, a ¼-mile-long alternate route leads east to Carson Falls before turning south and rejoining the main route. Since both routes are equally strenuous, the more scenic Carson Falls Trail is certainly recommended. Midway along this short trail you'll descend briefly to almost level granitic slabs near the lip of the river's gorge. Take your pack off here and then *cautiously* explore the falls and pools of the gorge. Over a period of thousands of years large potholes have been drilled into the bedrock as strong currents have swirled large boulders round and round. When the river's water is low, some potholes make brisk, invigorating swimming holes. If you climb to the top of an almost isolated granitic mass just downstream, you can get the best view of the main falls.

After the Carson Falls Trail rejoins the main trail, we walk through a flat that is being "logged out" by beavers. Entering an aspen grove at the edge of this flat, we curve southeast along a granitic base just above the sometimes swampy flat, and soon reach a ford of the East Carson. If you don't find any dry logs, cross at a wide, shallow place just downstream. A short ½-mile farther, where the river—trapped in a small gorge—turns abruptly west, we leave its company and hike up-canyon to a junction with the Golden Canyon Trail. From the junction our route curves southeast and quickly becomes a steep, brushy climb 400 vertical feet to the top of a granitic mass that has withstood repeated efforts of past glaciers to eradicate it. Leaving its southeast end, our route rollercoasters for ½ mile and touches upon a river meander just before it starts a fairly long climb.

This winding climb crosses a few creek beds before going south up the gully of a north-flowing seasonal creek. Beyond the top of the gully, junipers together with Jeffrey, lodgepole and silver pines are momentarily left behind as we descend into a shady red-fir forest, home of the red squirrel, or chickaree. Our path levels off at a year-round creek and beyond it we parallel the East Carson—usually at a small distance—for 3 miles upstream. The shady path crosses many creeklets as it progresses gently to moderately up-canyon, and along the way one has glimpses of the high cliffs along the canyon's east side.

At the south end of the cliffs, a descending ridge forces our route across the East Carson, which can be a slippery and wet ford in early and mid season. On the west bank, we hike south and in about 150 yards arrive at a junction with the Pacific Crest Trail. One mile from the PCT junction we cross the path of a recent avalanche which built up so much force on its descent of the west slope that it swept across the snow-covered East Carson River and knocked down trees on the east slope.

Beyond a second avalanche path we enter a forest of mature lodgepole pines and in it see more evidence of glaciation. Here, erratics—boulders transported by a glacier—were left behind as the glacier melted back some 12,000 years ago. The glacier that left these erratics was perhaps only 2½ miles long, a midget compared with the massive giant that flowed 19 miles down-canyon perhaps 60,000 years ago. The granitic bedrock over which the more recent one flowed is polished smooth and remains little changed from the day the glacier left it.

A ⅔-mile walk leads to a crossing of a permanent stream, tricky in early season. Then the trail's gradient increases noticeably. Unfortunately, when we sight the windswept saddle we're puffing up to, there is still ⅔ mile of climbing—now up a steep gradient—ahead. Whitebark pines and even late-season snow patches become evident as we make the final push. Finally struggling up to the 10,240-foot-high saddle, we take a well earned rest to pause and admire the view down the glaciated, **U**-shaped canyon of the East Fork Carson River.

From the saddle, the Pacific Crest Trail leads southwest along Sonora Peak's northeast slopes, but this day's hike ends by descending ⅓ mile south to campsites at the west edge of the grassy, frog-inhabited meadow that contains shallow Wolf Creek Lake. A post marks the start of the ducked path down to the lake. In 200 yards along it you'll see the lake, and can take one of several ducked routes down a moderately steep slope to it. At 10,090 feet, the lake is usually pretty cold for swimming, and fishing would yield only frogs. The lake's serene setting however, renews one's spirit, and while relaxing, you may be fortunate enough to see a large marsh hawk glide across the meadow.

3rd Hiking Day (**Wolf Creek Lake** to **Sonora Pass**, 5 miles—8.1 km): After retracing the steps back to the saddle, we follow the Pacific Crest Trail south. Winding among fractured granitic blocks, we reach a steep, conspicuous ramp up which a new trail segment has been built. The ramp, unfortunately, is narrow, leaving the trail pitifully small latitude to switchback up it, and snow can obscure parts of this climb well into August. Emerging from it, we encounter two creeklets on a slope covered with wind-cropped willows. View-seekers wishing to climb Sonora Peak can leave the trail here for a stiff but technically easy 1000-foot climb up to its lofty, dark summit.

Granitic bedrock gives way to volcanic rocks and talus as we now traverse south along the east slopes of Sonora Peak. Along this easy stretch one can see how the whitebark pines have been reduced to shrub height by winter's freezing winds. To the east, the effects of glaciation are evident in Wolf Creek canyon, but they are negligible in the distant Sweetwater Mountains. At times, you may see camouflaged U.S. Marines from the nearby Mountain Warfare Training Center. In the field from May through October, these troops participate in war games in an area that includes the Sonora Peak environs, Wolf Creek canyon and Silver Meadows canyon. From the saddle southeast of Sonora Peak, the high peaks on the Yosemite border are seen on the distant southeast horizon.

Our trail, now well graded, winds in and out of bleak gullies before coming to the tops of a conspicuous group of volcanic pinnacles that sit right on the Alpine-Mono county line. A 30-yard scramble south to one of their summits permits a sweeping panorama, north-to-east-to-south, of the Pacific Crest Trail and the slopes it traverses, and it also provides a panorama of the Sierra peak summits in the south.

More gullies lie ahead as we descend west. In ½ mile we reach a ridge and double back eastward. Then, hiking south near the crest, we again cross many gullies, so typical of this eroded volcanic landscape. Several of them have good water all year. The sunny slopes between are coated with sagebrush, mule ears, creambush, and a scattering of lodgepole and whitebark pines. Overhead, Clark nutcrackers flap and caw, and red-tailed hawks wheel and soar. Finally, we descend gently to signed Sonora Pass and a small parking area. (Northbound hikers can park 100 yards west of the pass and walk 70 yards up a closed jeep road to intercept the trail.)

Wolf Creek Meadows to Poison Lake **13**

TRIP   From Wolf Creek Meadows to Poison Lake via Soda Springs and Poison Flat, return via East Fork Carson River (semiloop trip). Topo maps *Topaz Lake, Sonora Pass*. Best mid season; 36.5 miles (58.8 km).

Grade	Trail/layover days	Total recommended days
Leisurely	5/1	6
Moderate	4/0	4
Strenuous	2/0	2

HILITES   Good fishing and swimming await hikers who backpack into Poison Lake. Along the way, they'll obtain numerous panoramas of large, glaciated canyons and visit several carbonate and soda springs.

DESCRIPTION (Moderate trip)

1st Hiking Day: Follow Trip 10 to **Soda Springs Guard Station**, 9.5 miles (15.3 km).

2nd Hiking Day (**Soda Springs Guard Station** to **Poison Lake**, 8 miles—12.9 km): From the campground at Soda Springs Guard Station, we head north on the trail we hiked in on. In ¼ mile we arrive at a signed junction with the Poison Flat Trail. This trail we follow north as it hugs the east edge of Dumonts Meadows and then begins to climb above the canyon floor. As we climb higher, we pass a large, white terrace built up by carbonate molecules that precipitated out of spring water. Behind us, the west wall of the East Carson canyon becomes ever more impressive as we climb moderately to steeply up to a ridge just north of Poison Flat creek. From the ridge, we head east up toward a small exfoliating dome that at first resembles those of Yosemite, but closer up is seen to be volcanic. Our trail's gradient eases off as it passes the dome and comes to a signed spur trail to Soda Cone, about 100 yards away on the south bank of Poison Flat creek.

The conifer-lined meadow that we follow beyond the Soda Cone Trail junction is often inhabited by cattle, which give Poison Flat creek a disagreeable taste and odor. The hike through the meadow is an easy one up to a low, shady divide. Then, under the canopy of the forest's edge, we parallel the south side of the meadow eastward, cross an aspen-lined gully, and come to a barbed-wire gate, then another. Immediately beyond, we reach the signed Poison Lake Trail. Travelers who are hiking this trip at a very leisurely pace may want to descend 100 yards on the Silver King Trail to a junction with the Driveway Trail, near Silver King Creek. From this junction to a crossing 300 yards upstream you can find many good, shady, creekside campsites beneath lodgepole pines. Along this creekside route Trip 14 descends before turning east up the Driveway Trail.

Our trail up to Poison Lake starts steeply, then eases as it climbs up to a ridgecrest. It stays on or near the ridge for about a mile, where shade is provided by an open forest of Jeffrey pines and red firs. Where the ridge ends at the base of a steep slope, we climb steeply southwest to a minor ridge that provides a major, sweeping view of rounded hills in the north, granitic cliffs in the east, Silver King canyon in the south, and the ragged Sierra crest in the southwest. From the ridge our trail continues to climb through thick brush, which at times includes shiny-leaved, aromatic tobacco brush. Soon, short, very steep switchbacks lead up into the forest's shade once again, and the gradient becomes pleasant.

Another climb leads to a small, rocky flat, dense with sagebrush and bitterbrush, from whose south end we can look up-canyon into Lower Fish Valley, Upper Fish Valley and Fourmile Canyon. From the flat our trail makes an undulating traverse west toward a small canyon and nearly reaches it at its top. Here the trail turns northwest and goes past several meadows before leveling off on a broad ridge above Poison Lake. A short, steep descent down this ridge leads to the lake's willow-clad south shore. Good campsites lie under lodgepoles and hemlocks on its northwest shore and fishing is good for brook trout.

3rd Hiking Day: Retrace your steps to **Soda Springs Guard Station**, 8 miles (12.9 km).

4th Hiking Day: Follow the 2nd hiking day of Trip 10, 11 miles (17.7 km).

Rodriguez Flat to Lower Fish Valley 14

TRIP   From Rodriguez Flat to Upper Fish Valley via Corral and Coyote valleys, return via Lower Fish and Long valleys (semiloop trip). Topo maps *Topaz Lake, Sonora Pass*. Best mid or late season; 14 miles (22.6 km).

Grade	Trail/layover days	Total recommended days
Leisurely	2/1	2
Moderate	....	....
Strenuous	....	....

HILITES   A fine weekend selection, this two-day trip visits five subalpine valleys. The country traversed contains some of the largest Sierra junipers to be found anywhere. In addition, over half a dozen side trips can be made from the Silver King Trail.

DESCRIPTION

1st Hiking Day (**Rodriguez Flat** to **Lower Fish Valley**, 7.5 miles—12.1 km): Our trail, the Snodgrass Canyon-Fish Valley Trail, makes a moderate climb southwest and shortly passes two trails from the Little Antelope Pack Station. A forest cover of white fir, silver pine and lodgepole pine persists for the next ⅓ mile of steep ascent, then yields to sagebrush as the old, metamorphosed sediments of Rodriguez Flat give way to much younger volcanic rocks. The view here is quite spectacular, and on a clear day you can see desert ranges northeast well beyond broad, open Rodriguez Flat.

The short, open ascent soon curves around the base of a volcanic hill and gives us new views—of Slinkard Valley below in the north, and the Sierra crest in the northwest. A traverse across broad, gentle, sagebrush-covered slopes leads to a signed junction, at which the Driveway Trail—our returning route—forks right (southwest). Our trail, the smaller of the two, soon passes through a fence gate and descends moderately past sagebrush and bitterbrush to the well-used grazing lands of spacious Corral Valley. On the valley floor, we cross two branches of Corral Valley Creek. The north branch, which drains the area most used by cattle, tends to be muddy, but the south branch, which drains more-forested slopes, looks and is drinkable. In it you'll see piute trout, which, like those in Coyote Valley and upper Silver King Creek, are an endangered and protected species. Please, no fishing here!

Beyond Corral Valley Creek, our southbound trail goes into the forest, curves west, parallels the valley a short distance, and then climbs an ever-increasing slope up to a dry saddle. From here the descent into Coyote Valley is a steep one, but it is made easy by the cushioning effect of the deep gravel. Near the bottom of a gully, the trail crosses a seasonal creek and goes but a short distance southeast before coming to an enormous, two-trunked juniper. With a diameter of 12 feet and a girth of 36, this specimen just might be the largest juniper in the Sierra. Beyond it, our trail winds south down toward Coyote Valley, reaching its sagebrush-covered floor beside a large, five-foot-diameter lodgepole (the key landmark to look for if you're hiking this trail in the opposite direction).

On the valley floor we walk a level ¼ mile to an easy ford of Coyote Valley Creek. Beyond the ford, the trail veers away from the creek and gradually climbs south. Near the crest above Upper Fish Valley, the forest becomes more dense and the aspens more dominant. At the crest's broad saddle a fence greets us, and from its gate we descend, usually past grazing cattle, steeply down to Upper Fish Valley. On the valley floor, a signed trail junction lies near a tall, orange snow-depth marker. Our trip proceeds north about 300 yards beyond the junction to a meeting of three fences, each with its own gate. Go through the north gate and follow the path that parallels the west side of the north-northeast-heading fence. Our trail soon starts to curve northwest, climbs over a low moraine left by a retreating glacier, and then comes to within hearing range of unseen Llewellyn Falls, just southwest of us. Let your ears direct you to this significant 20-foot-high cascade.

Llewellyn Falls creates a barrier trout cannot get over. As a giant glacier slowly retreated up Silver King Canyon, perhaps 50,000 years ago, cutthroat trout followed its path. They were able to swim into Upper Fish Valley and higher valleys before Silver King Creek eroded away bedrock to form the falls. Once isolated. they evolved into a subspecies known as the piute cutthroat trout (*Salmo clarki seleniris*), or simply piute trout. These trout became endangered not through overfishing but rather through the introduction of Lahontan cutthroats and rainbows, which then bred with the piutes to form hybrids. Once this miscegenation was discovered, Fish and Game workers removed purebreds and in 1964 treated Silver King Creek with rotenone to kill the hybrids. After the purebreds were reintroduced above the falls, their numbers grew from about 150 in the late 1960s to about 600 in the early 1970s. By 1975 the population had changed very little more, and it appears to be stable. Fishing, nevertheless, is strictly prohibited, for the piute trout could be easily fished out of existence.

From Llewellyn Falls gorge, our trail descends briefly northeast into Lower Fish Valley. The trail approaches Silver King Creek several times before reaching the north end of this overgrazed grassland, where you can cross the creek (wet in early season) and camp among the trees wherever people and cattle have not made too much of a mess. Fishing along Silver King Creek is good-to-excellent for rainbow, paiute and rainbow-paiute hybrid (to 9").

2nd Hiking Day (**Lower Fish Valley** to **Rodriguez Flat**, 6.5 miles—10.5 km): Continuing downstream, we walk northwest toward a low ridge that hides the forested, little-visited valley of Tamarack Creek. Our path leaves Lower Fish Valley, turns northeast and climbs a low granitic saddle before entering the south end of Long Valley. To avoid springs and boggy meadows, take the trail that circles around the valley's east side. Part way down the flat valley, the trails join and then approach Silver King Creek. This creek meanders lazily through the glacial sediments that long ago buried its canyon's bedrock floor, and our trail approaches several of these meanders before leaving the valley's north end.

Following Silver King Creek, our trail passes its confluence with Tamarack Creek. After ½ mile of easy, shaded descent along the creek, we ford it about where granite outcrops force the trail to the north bank (wet in early season). About 200 yards downstream we meet the Driveway Trail near a large gate.

Our route then descends to cross Silver King Creek just below its confluence with Corral Valley Creek (wet in early season). Climbing steeply, we ascend a brush-covered slope where the thin soil supports only a few scattered junipers for shade. Soon the grade eases to moderate and then gentle, and after 2½ miles we reach a junction with the Snodgrass Canyon-

Fish Valley Trail, from where we retrace the first part of the previous hiking day. Before hiking the last mile along this familiar trail back to the trailhead, stop and look at the over-sized cairn just before this junction. Built seven feet high by careful hands, this cairn stands as a monument to the loneliness of the Basque shepherds who once tended flocks in this area. Called *arri mutillak,* or "stone boys," monuments like this were built by lonely shepherds for lack of any other way to pass the time. Today, hikers *seek* to be alone and *look* for places of solitude in this east Sierra landscape.

an arri mutillak   *Jeff Schaffer*

Rodriguez Flat to Ebbetts Pass 15

TRIP   From Rodriguez Flat to Ebbetts Pass via Corral
          Valley, Coyote Valley, Silver King Creek, Soda
          Springs Guard Station, Murray Canyon, Asa Lake
          and Nobel Lake (shuttle trip). Topo maps *Topaz
          Lake, Sonora Pass, Dardanelles Cone,
          Markleeville*. Best mid season; 34 miles (54.8 km).

Grade	Trail/layover days	Total recom- mended days
Leisurely	5/1	6
Moderate	4/0	4
Strenuous	3/0	3

HILITES   Ridges and canyons east of the Sierra crest wait to
          be explored along this scenic route. You'll en-
          counter mammoth junipers, a rare trout, soda and
          carbonate springs, diverse scenery and good
          fishing. The last 11 miles are along the famous,
          ridge-hugging Pacific Crest Trail.

DESCRIPTION (Moderate trip)

1st Hiking Day: Follow Trip 14 to **Lower Fish Valley**, 7.5 miles
(12.1 km).

2nd Hiking Day (**Lower Fish Valley** to **Murray Canyon Trail
junction**. 9.5 miles—15.3 km): Follow the 2nd hiking day, Trip
14, to the Driveway Trail junction and walk 100 yards up the
Silver King Trail to the Poison Lake Trail junction. From it,
reverse the steps of the first half of the 2nd hiking day, Trip 13,
to Soda Springs Guard Station, and then follow the 1st hiking
day, Trip 11, to the Murray Canyon Trail junction.

3rd Hiking Day (**Murray Canyon Trail junction** to **Asa Lake**, 10
miles—16.1 km): Follow the first part of the 2nd hiking day,
Trip 11, up Murray Canyon to the crest junction. Our trail

starts southeast from the crest, crosses a pebbly flat, and then returns to the crest to follow it a short distance. Through the thinning forest we see Highland Peak and other volcanic summits to the northwest, and in the southwest are the volcanic cliffs of Arnot Peak. Our trail soon leaves the crest and contours ½ mile south across a brushy slope to a saddle just north of a low knoll. We cross the saddle, descend southeast, and gradually curve southwest through lodgepole forest over toward a grassy meadow south of the knoll. At the east end of this meadow our trail disappears, but you'll find it again at the west end. From here, you can look down across a large, open bowl. Our route, very vague, starts southwest down into the bowl, contours south just below the forest's edge, and then climbs southeast toward a saddle on the southwest side of a very prominent summit of highly broken volcanic rock. Just before the saddle, you'll reach a new segment of the Pacific Crest Trail.

Choosing the Pacific Crest Trail at the junction, we descend northwest along the west side of the bowl. As the bowl gives way to steeper slopes, the PCT circles west around a ridge, descends southwest and momentarily enters and then leaves a small but deep side canyon before reaching the slightly cloudy east fork of Wolf Creek, flowing down a wide, rocky wash. The cloudy color is due to fine volcanic sediments suspended in the water. In your drinking cup, these harmless sediments will settle out quite fast. A ⅓-mile traverse west past caves and fingers of a cliff of deeply eroded volcanic deposits gets us to the wide, silty middle fork of Wolf Creek.

Leaving this stream, we curve west briefly, then climb steadily northwest up to several branches of the west fork of Wolf Creek. The Pacific Crest Trail climbs north up a slope just beyond the main, east-flowing branch, switchbacks west, and climbs more steeply through a thinning forest. Rather than traversing west to a forested saddle, our trail continues to climb northwest above its east end—a route designed to avoid cattle-grazing lands on the other side. On reaching the west slopes of summit 8960+, we diagonal northwest down them, then curve north down to a small, flat saddle that lies at the base of the summit's northwest ridge. Here, it is important that you not continue north and cross the saddle. Rather, head west down a small gully, then parallel a low ridge, staying on its southwest side. A large cow meadow will quickly appear below you, and you'll almost touch it just before reaching a small gorge. The meadow's creek joyfully cascades down the resistant, volcanic end of the gorge, then flows out into Lower

Gardner Meadow. The Pacific Crest Trail descends to a jeep road at the east end of this meadow, and on this road Trip 14 parallels the creek westward. At this junction, situated on a broad, low ridge known as Wolf Creek Pass, the road curves north immediately into a grassy, boggy meadow.

From the jeep road, the Pacific Crest Trail climbs northwest up a low ridge crest, then curves north above the boggy meadow. The trail crosses the old Asa Creek Trail, then in ¼ mile arrives at a small pond just southeast of unseen Asa Lake. A minute's walk upstream off trail from the pond leads to the lake's east shore, where it is apparent why this small lake stays full and clear even in late summer: refreshing springs gush from the volcanic rocks above its east shore, and with the aid of a canal, their water is continually channeled into the lake. Under shady red firs above its northeast shore are some good campsites, and brook trout await the skillfull—or lucky—angler.

4th Hiking Day (**Asa Lake** to **Ebbetts Pass**, 7 miles—11.3 km): Get back on the Pacific Crest Trail by walking about 150 yards up-slope from Asa Lake's northeast corner. Once on the trail, follow it moderately to steeply up around a ridge, then through a small cove shaded by red firs. On the climb out of the cove, the forest of hemlocks and pines gives way to sagebrush as the trail traverses northwest toward a saddle. Tryon Peak looms ahead, and in the southwest, the large popular Highland Lakes stand out clearly in their broad, glaciated canyon. At the often windy saddle we encounter whitebark pines, which, better than any other conifer in this area, thrive in the harsh winter climate of this high elevation (9300').

We cross a crest-line fence, then follow a descending path that diagonals through tight clusters of whitebark pines and mountain hemlocks before crossing the willow-lined head-waters of Nobel Creek to intersect the faint Nobel Canyon Trail. Beyond this intersection the Pacific Crest Trail skirts above the east edge of a meadow and descends gradually southwest. Then our route curves north to a low saddle above the southwest corner of Nobel Lake. Staying high above the lake, the route curves northwest across a low ridge. The trail here is vague over the next hundred yards. It quickly dies out, but can be found again on the east side of the small gully immediately below. From the gully, the trail curves east to Nobel Lake's outlet creek, crossing it about 200 yards below the lake. Now the obvious trail heads north and soon switchbacks down a bizarre landscape of eroded, broken-up, *autobrecciated* lava flows (see Trip 10) that support only a few hardy junipers. We recross Nobel Lake's creek, head west briefly to a ridge of glacial sediments, and follow it north ¼ mile to a fork. Here, just east of the ridge crest, the Nobel Canyon Trail leaves the PCT.

The PCT rounds the ridge, descends to the bouldery main arm of Nobel Creek, and begins a traverse northwest. After ⅓ mile it starts climbing in earnest and momentarily leaves volcanic rock behind as it approaches granitic knobs atop a northeast-trending ridge. Our trail climbs north to the ridge's crest, curves around one knob back to the crest again, and then starts southeast around a second knob. At its south side we cross the crest for good and commence a winding traverse west along the base of some impressive, deeply eroded, volcanic cliffs. Northeast across Nobel Canyon is Silver Peak (10,774'), site of hectic mining activity beginning in 1863.

A brief climb north leads to the top of another northeast-trending ridge, this one just east of State Highway 4. Then a ¼-mile descent southwest from it brings the hiker to a junction, from which the PCT winds ⅓ mile southwest to a crossing of State Highway 4 only 200 yards north of Ebbetts Pass. From the junction, our route leads north and descends a spur trail ¼ mile to the Pacific Crest Trail parking lot.

Nobel Canyon from above Nobel Lake   *Jeff Schaffer*

Rodriguez Flat to Lake Alpine

16

TRIP From Rodriguez Flat to Lake Alpine via Corral, Coyote and Fish valleys, Soda Springs Guard Station, White Canyon, Highland Lakes, Hiram Meadow and Rock Lake (shuttle trip). Topo maps *Topaz Lake, Sonora Pass, Dardanelles Cone* (*Markleeville* optional for Asa Lake). Best mid or late season; 49 miles (78.9 km).

Grade	Trail/layover days	Total recommended days
Leisurely	8/2	10
Moderate	6/1	7
Strenuous	4/0	4

HILITES This exciting route traverses several major Sierra ridges along its westward course. As you progress west, the vegetation changes dramatically, sagebrush and juniper giving way to dense forests of pine and fir. Sections of two famous trails are hiked along this route: first, the 2600-mile-long Pacific Crest Trail, then later, the 180-mile-long Tahoe-Yosemite Trail.

DESCRIPTION (Moderate trip)

1st, 2nd and 3rd Hiking Days: Follow Trip 15 to **Asa Lake**, 27 miles (43.5 km).

4th Hiking Day (**Asa Lake** to **Hiram Meadow,** 9 miles—14.5 km):   From Asa Lake, retrace your steps ½ mile south down the Pacific Crest Trail to the jeep road at Wolf Creek Pass. This road we take ½ mile west, following a creek through spacious, cow-inhabited Lower Gardner Meadow. Leaving the creek, we traverse southwest across undulating country for another ½ mile to a north-flowing creek. In 150 yards we reach a signed fork, turn northwest, and wind ¼ mile up to a gap, 100 yards

beyond which our road is joined by a faint trail from Upper
Gardner Meadow. In another 80 yards, this trail resumes its
course, veering left. We follow it northwest ¼ mile up to a low
crest, on which we cross a north-leading jeep road. From this
junction the hiker will follow the trail about 200 yards to a
reunion with the road 70 yards before a creek crossing.
Draining lower Highland Lake, this creek can be a wet ford in
early season. A trailhead parking lot is seen just above the
west bank, and from it our road curves west 100 yards to the
Highland Lake Road.

Wide, level Highland Lake Road contours around the west
shore of lower Highland Lake, popular with fishermen for its
population of brook trout. Beyond the lake, our road climbs
gradually to Highland Lakes Campground, just north of the
upper lake, which is divided into two camps. Backpackers will
usually find quieter sites in the camp at the end of a short,
eastbound spur road.

At the far end of upper Highland Lake the road ends and the
well-signed Highland Creek Trail to Lake Alpine begins with
a steep descent along the lake's outlet creek, then bends more
westward away from it. Beyond a small knoll on the left, we
descend west ½ mile down a steep, winding trail, passing a
small gorge before we reach upper Highland Lake's outlet
creek. In early season large boulders just downstream will
make the crossing a dry one. Heading south, we pass through
two small meadows, each with an abundant garden of corn
lilies, then in ¼ mile approach a creek that drains what the
map calls "Poison Canyon." (Poison Canyon is incorrectly
called "Champion Canyon" on the topo map. All the canyon
labels on the topo map from "Poison Canyon" to "Slaughter
Canyon" should be moved one canyon to the southwest; the
canyon labeled "Poison" on the map is actually unnamed.)

We follow the creek ¼ mile downstream, cross it near its
union with Highland Creek, and in another ¼ mile come to a
good campsite, under large cottonwoods, on the east bank of
Highland Creek. At times, logs placed by hikers make this
wide-creek crossing a dry one, but if you are here before
mid-July, you can expect to wade. Then we round the base of a
granitic ridge, enter a lodgepole flat, traverse the west side of a
damp meadow, and return to forest cover as the trail and the
nearby creek both bend south. In this part of the canyon,
Highland Creek has several shallow pools that are ideal for a
quick bath.

Our trail soon reaches a second ford of Highland Creek—just as wide and a little deeper than the first. Once across, we veer away from the creek on a minor climb, then descend to the stream that drains Champion Canyon ("Hiram Canyon" on the topo map). Its ford is an easy one, and on a moderately descending trail we head down to the sunny flats of Hiram Meadow. Only 80 yards south of Highland Creek's union with Weiser Creek is a third usually wet ford of the former.

Late-season hikers will note that this ford is a wet ford long after most Sierra snow has melted. This is because Highland Creek canyon and its tributary canyons have abundant volcanic sediments that act as a reservoir to hold water well into September. Good campsites lie across the ford on the west bank.

5th Hiking Day (**Hiram Meadow** to **Rock Lake,** 8.5 miles—13.7 km): About 100 yards west of the Highland Creek ford is a junction with the Weiser Trail. At the start of the deer-hunting season on the last weekend of September, hunters will descend this trail on motorcycles, bringing noise and pollution with them. Plan accordingly. From the junction we hike west across wide, flat Hiram Meadow, re-enter lodgepole cover, and quickly arrive at a cabin. Our path turns southwest, soon reaches willow-lined Highland Creek, and then crosses some low knolls of highly fractured, fine-grained igneous rock. One mile southwest of Hiram Meadow the Highland Creek Trail briefly climbs away from the creek just before it turns south and cascades down a sizable gorge. Our trail parallels the watercourse at a distance as we descend steeply to a junction with the Woods Gulch Trail. This trail east—part of the Tahoe-Yosemite Trail—crosses Highland Creek in 60 yards, just north of its union with the creek from Jenkins Canyon ("Slaughter Canyon" on the topo). Westward, the next 13-mile stretch of the Tahoe-Yosemite Trail coincides with the Highland Creek Trail.

Leaving the junction, our route turns west and in a few minutes brings us beside some small, lovely Highland Creek pools. We follow the creek only momentarily, then gradually veer away and climb up a brushy, granitic slope to an open forest of Jeffrey pines. In it, we descend quickly to a shady flat from which our trail descends moderately to the canyon bottom, where we cross a usually trickling creek that originates in a small, shallow lake northwest of Hiram Meadow. Traversing around the east shore of this lake is the Bull Run Creek Trail, which we meet only ¼ mile west of the trickling creek. Although motor vehicles are allowed on this

trail, few successfully make it up or down due to its excessively
steep, very sandy nature. In 100 yards we cross refreshing Bull
Run Creek, shaded by cottonwoods and white firs.

Reaching Gabbot Meadow we hike briefly alongside
Highland Creek, then leave it and parallel the northwest side
of a southwest-running fence. In ½ mile is a gate, and in
another ¼ mile a second gate. From this second gate the level
trail follows the fence line 300 yards, then turns abruptly
up-slope. During the summer of 1975 the Highland Creek
Trail was rebuilt and/or relocated from this point west to the
saddle above Lake Alpine. The trail climbs steeply northwest,
but then turns southwest and almost levels off, giving one a
chance to catch one's breath on the traverse through a shady
forest of white fir and Jeffrey pine. Emerging from the forest,
we begin to climb steeply again, this time up brushy slopes to a
small gap in the granitic bedrock. Almost immediately, we
pass through a second gap, then start a short traverse
southwest, from which we can admire the dark, volcanic
formations called the Dardanelles. This monumental ridge,
composed of lava hundreds of feet thick, is only a small
remnant of a long lava flow that originated near Bridgeport,
California, about nine million years ago. From that source it
flowed about *100 miles* down-canyon, stopping at the western
edge of the Sierra foothills. In the ensuing millions of years,
the walls of the canyon it flowed down were eroded away while
the canyon bottom it buried was preserved beneath the flow.
Two million years of glacial attacks further eroded the
Dardanelles landscape until the granitic floor of Highland
Creek lay a good 1000 feet below the base of the Dardanelles.
We can expect future glaciers to excavate Highland Creek's
canyon even more. Visible up-canyon are Iceberg, Airola and
Hiram peaks—all with volcanic summits but none of them
related to the Dardanelles flow.

Crossing the crest, which stands 550 feet above Highland
Creek, we hike southwest just west of the crest. That the last
Highland Creek glacier was *at least* as thick as the crest is
high is obvious from the fresh polish it gave the granitic
bedrock here. The glacier was, in fact, about 1300 feet thick.
At a point where one could head south cross-country 1 mile
down to Highland Creek, our trail turns northwest and climbs
to a glaciated saddle. Then, midway along the mile-long
rollercoaster path to Wilderness Creek, we cross one of its
tributaries. The ford of Wilderness Creek is difficult in early
season, but the stream disappears in late season. Beyond this
creek our trail passes the Sand Flat Trail, climbs north to a

gravelly, barren flat, and then briefly parallels Wilderness Creek. Continuing a moderate-to-easy climb north, we reach the east end of Rock Lake in ¾ mile. Grassy and unappealing at this end, Rock Lake provides good swimming and fishing (brook trout) near its southwest end. Along its south shore are several forested campsites.

6th Hiking Day (**Rock Lake** to **Lake Alpine,** 4.5 miles—7.2 km): From the lake's east end, our route starts northwest along the old Highland Lake Trail, and then, just out of sight of the lake, turns northeast and follows a new tread ¼ mile up a granitic ridge. Then, from the slightly higher main ridge, we curve north, cross a small, dry wash, and descend to a flat ¼ mile east of the North Fork Stanislaus River. From it, a short climb north and then a steep descent bring us to the river (difficult ford in early season).

Beyond this ford we climb steeply northwest to cross a ridge, and then wind ½ mile down glacier-polished slabs to a large, forested flat with a trail junction. From here the old trail goes 1¼ miles west past the south shore of Duck Lake to a cabin-side junction with a jeep road. Through July and part of August the mosquitoes along this swampy route are almost unbearable. Turning right on the new trail, we immediately cross a creek, and wind west along the north edge of this forested flat. When the trail reaches a point about 200 yards north of Duck Lake, it abruptly turns north and climbs up a ridge. After 300 yards it turns abruptly west and then climbs more moderately ⅓ mile west up to a switchback in the jeep road that ascends northward from the Duck Lake basin. On this closed road we climb west briefly up to a saddle, pass through a gate, follow the crest southwest, and then descend ½ mile to the trailhead at the east end of Lake Alpine's Silver Valley Campground.

17 Sonora Pass to Clark Fork

TRIP   From West Sonora Pass Trailhead to Clark Fork
             Meadow (round trip, part cross country). Topo map
             Sonora Pass. Best mid season; 7 miles (11.2 km).

Grade	Trail/layover days	Total recommended days
Leisurely	2/0	2
Moderate	....	....
Strenuous	....	....

HILITES Clark Fork Meadow is secluded by the steep sides
             of the deep bowl which protects it, and here—only
             two airline miles from a state highway—one can
             get away from it all even on a short weekend. On
             the way, the views from the pass are among the
             most sweeping in the entire Sierra.

DESCRIPTION

1st Hiking Day (**Sonora Pass Trailhead** to **Clark Fork Meadow,** 3.5
miles—5.6 km.): The trailhead is located at the foot of a
barred road which leads north from Highway 108 about 0.85
mile west of Sonora Pass. From a parking area (9760′) we
walk up the jeep road toward timberline, through sparse
lodgepole and whitebark pine understoried by considerable
sagebrush. The pinkish soil here slowly and steadily gives off
its stored winter water, and these slopes are dotted with a
pleasant variety of high-elevation wildflowers throughout the
season. Beyond a small runoff stream that flows all summer,
the road becomes trail, and after a short level section we veer
eastward and ascend steadily. A breather stop here allows us
to look south and see the great peaks of the Emigrant Basin
and northern Yosemite. Below us is the threadlike highway
curving up to Sonora Pass, and beyond the pass we see unnamed Peak 11245. West of this imposing if nameless height,
the long chocolate-brown west ridge of Leavitt Peak shows its

snowy north slope, and even a few tiny glaciers.

The crest of this little climb (10440′) is called St. Marys Pass. Here we obtain a view far to the north—on clear days, as far as the peaks west of Lake Tahoe. Looking north and south, we realize we are standing right on the boundary between the rugged High Sierra of Yosemite and beyond, and the lower, less rugged northern Sierra. Immediately below us to the north, the bowl that contains Clark Fork Meadow is so deep that we cannot see the bottom of it.

From the pass we turn southwest and follow a sporadically ducked route near the top of a granite ridge for about one mile, dipping slightly to cross several runoff streams not shown on the topo map. In midseason these seemingly bare slopes boast a profusion of blue flax, lavender phlox and yellow woolly sunflower. Once past the billowy granite outcroppings that line most of the route for the first mile from St. Marys Pass, we veer north and start down the valley of a little stream not shown on the topo map. We follow the ridge that lies east of the upper basin of this stream until, at about timberline, we drop down next to the stream and parallel it, on its east side, into thick hemlock forest, where we may find occasional ducks. This route passes close under the west face of the cliffs that are ½ mile southeast of the meadow.

At the bottom of the steep ascent we ford the infant Clark Fork on a log, turn west, and soon ford a tributary on boulders. Half a mile of level walking under a moderate forest cover of silver, lodgepole and whitebark pine and some hemlock brings us to the good campsite at the northwest edge of the meadow (8875′) beside a clear stream. Fishing in the Clark Fork is good for eastern brook (to 9″).

2nd Hiking Day: Retrace your steps, 3.5 miles (5.6 km).

South from St. Marys Pass

18   Sonora Pass to Iceberg Meadow

TRIP   From West Sonora Pass Trailhead to Iceberg
             Meadow (shuttle trip, part cross country). Topo
             map *Sonora Pass*. Best mid season; 11.5 miles
             (18.5 km).

	Trail/layover *days*	*Total recom-* *mended days*
Grade		
Leisurely	2/1	3
Moderate	2/0	2
Strenuous	....	....

HILITES   Few trips are downhill most of the way, but this
             one ascends only 800 feet and then descends 4000
             feet. The descent follows the canyon of Clark Fork
             Stanislaus River from its wellsprings above
             timberline through meadows and down granite
             gorges to a thickly forested, gently flowing section
             of the river.

DESCRIPTION

1st Hiking Day: Follow Trip 17 to **Clark Fork Meadow,** 3.5 miles
(5.6 km).

2nd Hiking Day (**Clark Fork Meadow** to **Iceberg Meadow,** 8
miles—12.9 km): From the campsite, we walk to the foot of the
meadow and cross the Clark Fork on boulders. On the west
side, a few yards downstream, we encounter ducks, and this
ducked route soon becomes a trail—although none is shown on
the topo map. The trail passes a stock-drift fence (close the
gate) and makes a short, steep descent under a moderate forest
cover of hemlock, silver pine and lodgepole. At the foot of the

descent we enter red-fir forest, and this superb conifer is frequent for the rest of the hiking day. A short mile from Clark Fork Meadow is a boulder ford to the east side of the stream, and several fair-to-good campsites lie just beyond it. After the ford, the sandy trail veers away from the stream and descends gently to moderately, fording a small runoff stream every half mile or so.

After paralleling and then fording a larger tributary, the trail enters a sloping meadow considerably marred by the hooves of grazing cattle. The route across the slope is indistinct, but we find the trail again in granite sand under red firs near the Clark Fork. After crossing another tree-shaded meadow with fair campsites, we begin a steep, switchbacking descent on a rocky dusty trail down to an almost level valley, where the Clark Fork swings west. At the foot of the descent, the trail crosses Boulder Creek and meets a trail up the creek. From this junction the route descends along a shaded sand-and-duff trail, close to the alder-lined Clark Fork, now big enough to call a river. Numerous good campsites line this shaded canyon, with its dense forest cover of white fir, alder and Jeffrey pine. Nearing Iceberg Meadow the trail makes a short, steady-to-steep descent and then parallels the river on pleasant, sandy underfooting to the roadend (6460′).

Clark Fork Meadow

19   Kennedy Meadow to Summit Creek

TRIP From Kennedy Meadow to Summit Creek (round
trip). Topo maps *Sonora Pass, Tower Peak*. Best
early-to-mid season; 13.6 miles (21.8 km).

Grade	Trail/layover days	Total recommended days
Leisurely	2/0	2
Moderate	....	....
Strenuous	....	....

HILITES A part of this route follows the historic Emigrant
Trail used by the pioneers in crossing the Sierra
from the area around Bridgeport to Columbia and
points west. Relief Peak was a major landmark for
these early travelers, and the terminus of this trip,
lies in this unusual formation's shadow. The
scenery along the way is an absorbing study in
glacial and volcanic terrain.

DESCRIPTION

1st Hiking Day (**Kennedy Meadow** to **Summit Creek**, 6.8
miles—10.9 km): The trailhead (6400′) is located alongside
Middle Fork Stanislaus River at Kennedy Meadow resort.
Amid a dense forest cover of Jeffrey pine, incense-cedar, sugar
pine, juniper and white fir, the trail crosses a small ridge to
Kennedy Meadow itself and skirts the east side of the meadow,
offering sweeping views of the lush grasslands. Beyond the
meadow, the trail crosses the river via a bridge and
immediately veers west onto a new trail section. This trail
section ascends gently past the foot of a small granite dome
and then switchbacks up a steeper grade between this dome
and its larger neighbor. Under a sparse-to-moderate forest
cover of mixed conifers, the route ascends steadily up a little
canyon to a saddle, where it turns eastward to descend a
sandy, multi-tracked slope to Summit Creek. After paralleling the creek for a few steps, the trail crosses it on a bridge and

meets the old, abandoned trail a few yards south of the Kennedy Lake Trail junction, near the PG&E dam-maintenance station.

Our route then contours high above the east side of Relief Reservoir. The trail section paralleling the shore offers excellent views to the south and west before it descends to the timbered shallow at the Grouse Creek ford. From Grouse Creek the trail ascends steadily over a series of rocky switchbacks, and then veers southeast to pass the Lower Relief Valley Trail after one mile. Then our trail begins a steady-to-steep uphill climb as it leaves the shaded riparian zone and enters the brush-covered volcanic rubble above Summit Creek. Along the rock-strewn trail one can compare varieties of penstemon flowers in various hues. This steady ascent is relieved when the trail drops into the little pocket encompassing Saucer Meadow. The gravesite indicated on the topo and Forest Service maps was that of a passing immigrant, but all that remains of this last resting place of a would-be immigrant is a small, vandalized sign on a tree.

The section of trail beyond this point was part of a major trans-Sierra route, used during the middle of the 19th century—the Emigrant Trail. With the many-hued volcanic rock of Relief Peak on the left, and white, glaciated granite on the right, the trail climbs along Summit Creek to several fair campsites. Fishing along the creek is poor.

2nd Hiking Day: Retrace your steps, 6.8 miles (10.9 km).

South of Grouse Creek

20 Kennedy Meadow to Emigrant Meadow

TRIP   From Kennedy Meadow to Emigrant Meadow
            Lake via Brown Bear Pass (round trip). Topo maps
            Sonora Pass, Tower Peak. Best mid or late season;
            25.2 miles (40.4 km).

Grade	Trail/layover days	Total recommended days
Leisurely	4/0	4
Moderate	3/0	3
Strenuous	2/0	2

HILITES   A good portion of this trail follows the historic
            Emigrant Trail, and travelers today have an
            excellent opportunity to identify with these hardy
            pioneers. Scenically, this route splits the terrain
            into two distinctly different parts: To the north,
            the basaltic and pumice slopes vividly disclose the
            vulcan overlay that gives the country its colorful
            reds and blacks. To the south, mirrorlike stretches
            of glacially polished granite add contrast and
            interest.

DESCRIPTION (Leisurely trip)

1st Hiking Day: Follow Trip 19 to **Summit Creek**, 6.8 miles (10.9
km).

2nd Hiking Day (**Summit Creek** to **Emigrant Meadow Lake**, 5.8
miles—9.3 km): Our level trail continues up-canyon on
red-fir-dotted slopes for a mile, then makes a rocky 400-foot
ascent to a little saddle which is the portal of the camping area
called Sheep Camp, a very overused area. Winding above
Summit Creek beyond Sheep Camp, the trail soon leaves
timber cover, and crosses a pumice slope above Lunch
Meadow. This large meadow is subalpine, dotted with sparse

stands of lodgepole and mountain hemlock. At the east end of Lunch Meadow our route passes the trail to Emigrant Lake. North of our trail, red and black volcanic columns thrust up from the otherwise smooth, red, pumice slopes, and punctuate the skyline with their tortured shapes. Directly to the east the traveler can discern the shallow saddle that is Brown Bear Pass. The trail to the pass is a gradual but steady ascent offering colorfully contrasting views of Granite Dome and Relief Peak to the west. It is easy to see why the emigrants who used this same route relied upon the distinctive outline of Relief Peak as a landmark. At the summit of Brown Bear Pass (9700'), the grassy expanses of historic Emigrant Meadow present themselves, and the serenity of this pioneer waystop is enhanced by the placid blue waters of Emigrant Meadow Lake.

As the trail descends from Brown Bear Pass on a long traverse, the visitor cannot help being impressed by the gigantic scale of this grassy, granite-walled basin. It seems a fitting stage for the enactment of the "great move westward," and it doesn't take a great deal of imagination to hear boisterous shouts, the creaking of wagons, the barking of dogs, and the tired, hungry lowing of trail-weary stock. This great meadow saw the frenzied summertime travel of thousands of pioneers headed for the western slope, but of their passing all that remains is an echo in the wind. Fair campsites may be found along the west side of Emigrant Meadow Lake (9400'). Fishing for rainbow (8-13") is good, with a midseason slowdown.

3rd and 4th Hiking Days: Retrace your steps, 12.6 miles (20.2 km).

Author at Brown Bear Pass   *Jason Winnett*

21   Kennedy Meadow to Emigrant Lake

TRIP   From Kennedy Meadow to Emigrant Lake (round trip). Topo maps *Sonora Pass, Tower Peak*. Best mid-to-late season; 26.8 miles (43 km).

Grade	Trail/layover days	Total recommended days
Leisurely	4/1	5
Moderate	3/1	4
Strenuous	3/0	3

HILITES   A long-time favorite of anglers, Emigrant Lake is often used as a base camp for short fishing trips to the surrounding lakes. This route to Emigrant Lake allows the traveler to take in the geological variety of the country. Alpine meadows surrounding isolated melt-off tarns compete for attention with vast slopes of red pumice and fields of polished granite.

DESCRIPTION (Leisurely trip)

1st Hiking Day: Follow Trip 19 to **Summit Creek,** 6.8 miles (10.9 km).

2nd Hiking Day (**Summit Creek** to **Emigrant Lake**, 6.6 miles—10.6 km): First follow Trip 20 to the trail junction at the east end of Lunch Meadow. Here our route branches right (south), fords Summit Creek, and ascends through a sparse mountain-hemlock cover to a long, low saddle. Views along this segment of trail present a wide range of colors. The superimposed vulcanism of Relief Peak and the ridge to the east are a potpourri of pastel shades of reds, blacks, yellows and ochres. Black Hawk Mountain to the west is granite in varying shades of dun, gray, and buff-brown.

The long saddle through which our trail winds is a series of granite fields that are delightfully broken by tiny, wildflower-filled meadows. Many of these meadows are further enhanced by one or two small melt-off tarns. The long, shallow valley on the other side of the saddle contains a tributary of North Fork Cherry Creek, and from it there are excellent views across the Cherry Creek watershed south to Michie and Haystack peaks. The trail descends on the east side of this tributary for ½ mile and then fords to the west side. This ford is the correct place from which to head east cross country to reach Mosquito Lake, which has pink-fleshed rainbow trout. Continuing down the east bank, we ford a little tributary and then recross the main stream to the west side. From here our trail descends to the large meadow at the inlet to large (230-acre) Emigrant Lake (8800'). There are several good-to-excellent campsites at the inlet, on the north side, and at the outlet. This popular lake is glacial in character, with a sparse forest cover, and fishing for rainbow (8-18') is good (excellent in early and late season).

3rd and 4th Hiking Days: Retrace your steps, 13.4 miles (21.6 km).

near Lunch Meadow

22 Kennedy Meadow to Emigrant Lake

TRIP   From Kennedy Meadow to Emigrant Lake via
                Middle Emigrant and Emigrant Meadow lakes
                (semi-loop trip). Topo maps *Sonora Pass; Tower
                Peak*. Best mid or late season; 30.4 miles (48.9 km).

	Trail/layover days	Total recom- mended days
Grade		
Leisurely	5/2	7
Moderate	4/2	6
Strenuous	3/2	5

HILITES   Like the previous trip this route tours a part of the
                historic Emigrant Trail and visits large Emigrant
                Lake. In addition, linking Emigrant Lake with
                Emigrant Meadow Lake, this route makes a good
                fisherman's loop and takes in more scenic variety.

DESCRIPTION (Leisurely trip)

1st and 2nd Hiking Days: Follow Trip 21 to **Emigrant Lake**, 13.4
miles (21.6 km).

3rd Hiking Day (**Emigrant Lake** to **Emigrant Meadow Lake**, 4.4
miles—7.1 km): Beginning at the trail junction above the
inlet to Emigrant Lake, this route crosses a log bridge over
North Fork Cherry Creek and ascends a moderately forested
slope to Blackbird Lake (9000′) and a junction with a trail to
Middle Emigrant Lake, where we turn left and follow part of
the 5th hiking day, Trip 23.

4th and 5th Hiking Days: Reverse the steps of the 2nd and 1st
hiking days, Trip 20, 12.6 miles (20.2 km).

Kennedy Meadow to Cow Meadow Lake 23

TRIP From Kennedy Meadow to Cow Meadow Lake via Emigrant Lake and Buck Lakes (loop trip). Topo maps *Sonora Pass, Tower Peak*. Best mid or late season; 45 miles (72.5 km).

Grade	Trail/layover days	Total recom-mended days
Leisurely	7/2	9
Moderate	5/2	7
Strenuous	4/2	6

HILITES This is a fine choice for a midseason fishing trip, as it circles the lake-dotted Cherry Creek watershed. A day's walking from one or another base camp will permit the fisherman to sample almost 100 lakes. The route also tours some of the finest scenery in the Emigrant Wilderness, which should provide adequate incentive for the nonfisherman as well.

DESCRIPTION (Leisurely trip)

1st and 2nd Hiking Days: Follow Trip 21 to **Emigrant Lake**, 13.4 miles (21.5 km).

3rd Hiking Day (**Emigrant Lake** to **Cow Meadow Lake**, 6 miles—9.7 km): From the trail junction at the inlet to Emigrant Lake, our route traverses the long, timbered north side of the lake, and passes a junction with a poorly maintained trail to Cow Meadow Lake via North Fork Cherry Creek. It then crosses a low, forest-covered saddle and descends to ford Buck Meadow Creek. After crossing the long meadow at the north end of upper Buck Lake, the trail circles the west side of upper Buck Lake, passing a trail to Deer Lake, crosses the isthmus separating the two lakes, and follows the east side of lower Buck Lake, often being back in the trees away from the lakeside. Upper Buck Lake is a good-sized

(50-acre) glacial lake with numerous good campsites around the shore. Fishing for rainbow (to 18′) is good. Lower Buck Lake is somewhat deeper and rockier, though about the same size, and fishing is usually about the same as at the upper lake. About ¼ mile beyond the south end of Lower Buck Lake, the trail passes the Wood Lake lateral, and amid a nice forest cover of lodgepole descends steeply (600′) to the Emigrant Lake Trail junction and lovely Cow Meadow Lake (7840′). There are excellent campsites along the north edge of the lake. This 55-acre lake is connected by lagoons with overhanging banks. A DF&G dam at the south end keeps the water level fairly constant, and fishing for rainbow and some brook is excellent (8-18′). Angling on the stream above the lake is good.

4th Hiking Day (**Cow Meadow Lake** to **Maxwell Lake**, 7.5 miles—12.1 km): From the east side of Cow Meadow Lake, the trail ascends 560 feet via a frequently blasted, usually cobbled trail to the bench containing rocky, deep Lertora Lake (8400′), passing a trail to the west and Huckleberry Lake before arriving at Lertora. This 25-acre lake offers only fair angling for brook and rainbow (7-13″). From the west end of Lertora Lake this route veers east along the south side of the lake, and descends over a very rough trail to the northeast end of large (200-acre) Huckleberry Lake (8000′). This subalpine lake provides good fishing for brook and rainbow (8-18″), and East Fork Cherry Creek above the lake often provides excellent angling. From the meadows at the northeast end of Huckleberry, the trail heads upstream and soon fords East Fork Cherry Creek as it ascends the canyon. Views of the unusual granite island known as Sachse Monument dominate the northern skyline as the trail passes a tungsten mine. At this point the trail joins the mining road, and then it refords the stream before passing the Twin Lakes Trail lateral. At the south end of Horse Meadow our trail branches northwest up a timbered slope to Maxwell Lake (8700′). Maxwell Lake (46 acres), an emerald-green gem with a tufty meadow fringe, affords excellent angling for brook trout (8-14″). The polished granite of Sachse Monument towers over the south side of this charming lake, and the choice campsites on the north side of the lake have an uninterrupted view of both the lake and the peak.

5th Hiking Day (**Maxwell Lake** to **Emigrant Meadow Lake**, 5.5 miles—8.9 km): From Maxwell Lake the trail climbs by a series of switchbacks through a moderate forest cover of lodgepole pine and then winds through a long, rock-lined meadow past several beautiful lakelets to Blackbird Lake and a junction with a trail to Emigrant Meadow Lake. Here our route branches right (north) past several small tarns that are usually dry by late season. The trail soon becomes faint, since this lateral is unmaintained, and one must keep a sharp eye out for ducks and blazes. This footpath ascends along the south side of the wandering North Fork Cherry Creek for about 1½ miles, and then fords the creek. From the ford onward, the trail is rutted into meadowy turf, but has become overgrown due to lack of maintenance. The trail becomes a little steeper just south of Middle Emigrant Lake, and then levels out at the wet meadows at the foot of the lake. Anglers who wish to try their luck on this fair-sized, granitic lake will find the fishing fair-to-good for rainbow (7-10″). The trail rounds the west side of the lake, fords the inlet stream, and crosses a low, rocky ridge to the Emigrant Meadow Lake basin (9400′). This huge meadow was the traditional stopping place for emigrant trains on the first leg of their Sierra crossing. This hiking day terminates at the open and exposed fair campsites on the west side of the lake. Fishing in Emigrant Meadow Lake is good for rainbow (8-13″).

6th and 7th Hiking Days: Reverse the steps of the 2nd and 1st hiking days of Trip 20, 12.6 miles (20.3 km).

Maxwell Lake

24 **Kennedy Meadow to Hetch Hetchy**

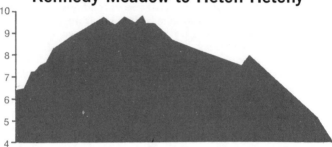

TRIP   From Kennedy Meadow to O'Shaughnessy Dam (Hetch Hetchy Reservoir) via Brown Bear Pass and Jack Main Canyon (shuttle trip). Topo maps *Sonora Pass, Tower Peak, Pinecrest, Lake Eleanor.* Best mid or late season; 44 miles (70.9 km).

Grade	Trail/layover days	Total recommended days
Leisurely	7/2	9
Moderate	5/1	6
Strenuous	4/0	4

HILITES   This is a trip of contrasts. The route begins by bisecting the volcanic and glacial terrain north of Bond Pass. This terrain is, as one writer aptly described it, "a land born of fire and ice." As beautiful as the terrain is northwest of Bond Pass, the primitive, unspoiled beauty of Jack Main Canyon has to be the high point of this trip. Glacial, subalpine meadows like those around Emigrant Meadow Lake impress the visitor, but it remains for the lower grasslands of Grace Meadow, with its meandering Falls Creek, to claim the heart. This is an excellent trip for the intermediate as well as the seasoned wilderness traveler.

DESCRIPTION (Leisurely trip)

1st and 2nd Hiking Days: Follow Trip 20 to **Emigrant Meadow Lake**, 12.6 miles (20.3 km).

3rd Hiking Day (**Emigrant Meadow Lake** to **Dorothy Lake,** 5 miles—8.1 km): From Emigrant Meadow the route climbs over a rocky ridge to Grizzly Meadow (9700′) and two unnamed lakes. Fishing here is fair-to-good for rainbow (to

10″). This area is subject to the Forest Service's Multiple-Use land program; hence the traveler may encounter summer-grazing steers. Further evidences of this program mar the serenity of this wilderness just beyond the lakes, where the trail encounters a mining road. Our route follows this road as it descends to the Summit Meadow "trail" junction, a distance of about 2 miles. From here our route follows another mining road across the northern fringe of the meadow, and then ascends by a series of switchbacks to the gentle saddle called Bond Pass (9700′). Amidst a clump of red fir marking the summit, the trail leaves the dirt road and crosses into Yosemite National Park. There are excellent views, east from the summit, of Saurian Crest and Tower Peak.

The descent on the east side winds through dense lodgepole and fir to a junction of the trail to Dorothy Lake (9440′). After turning north on it, a ½-mile gentle ascent brings the traveler to the scattered campsites on the west shore. Anglers should ready their tackle for the good-to-excellent fishing for brook and rainbow (8-15″). Dorothy Lake, with its pleasant meadow fringes and bunched stands of lodgepole, makes an excellent base camp from which to explore the surrounding lakes and terrain. Of particular interest is the "rock glacier" beneath nearby Forsyth Peak. A discovery side trip to the lake just south of Dorothy Lake provides excellent views of this geologic wonder. Like their ice counterparts, rock glaciers are moving masses.

4th Hiking Day (**Dorothy Lake** to **Grace Meadow,** 3.2 miles—5.2 km): First, retrace your steps ½ mile to the first junction, then continue down-canyon. Jack Main Canyon begins at Dorothy Lake, and from the start it is a great hiker's route. A whole spectrum of wildlife may be found along this trail, and the abundance of the wildlife is testimony to the effectiveness of the National Park system. In the meadowed fringes of Dorothy Lake, the piping of the Belding ground squirrel ushers the traveler past the marmot-inhabited opposite slopes. If one is on the trail early enough, deer still out grazing will keep him entranced with their graceful movements. Ample signs of the black bears that roam this section of the park will be found along the trail—particularly during gooseberry season. Scenically, this short stretch of trail is an idyllic series of tiny meadows alongside murmuring Falls Creek. To the east, somber Forsyth Peak and abruptly divided Keyes Peak (juxtaposed black gabbro and white granite) cap the canyon walls. The trail gradually descends through a dense forest cover to the north end of long, rolling Grace Meadow (8620′). In contrast to the wide-open, windy stretch of Emigrant

Meadow, Grace Meadow has a soft, intimate feel that makes it a favorite base camp. Anglers should be ready for excellent brook and rainbow (to 13″) along Falls Creek.

*5th Hiking Day (***Grace Meadow** to **Paradise Valley,** 8 miles—12.9 km): From Grace Meadow our trail heads south through more meadows and lodgepole-pine stands on an almost level descent. During breaks in the trees you can get a good view back up-canyon at the straight, glaciated valley, while ahead is rounded Chittenden Peak. As we come abreast of Chittenden Peak, the grade steepens and becomes a bit rocky. We pass the trail to Tilden Lake and wind gently down slabs, sometimes near now-dashing Falls Creek. Where we climb onto a sandy flat, we meet a junction where we leave the Pacific Crest Trail. Continuing down-canyon, we rejoin the languid creek opposite lovely Wilmer Lake, which is separated from the creek by a natural levee. Just below the lake, the canyon narrows and the grade steepens. Along this stretch the trail parallels the creek, which is a series of rapids, falls and pools in smooth granite. Where the canyon bends south, we descend to a lodgepole-pine-and-meadow-covered valley that was a lake in the recent geologic past. The glacial lakes in this canyon will all eventually fill with sediment or another glacier, whichever comes first.

The next section of Falls Creek is very tranquil, winding through willowy marshes from pool to pool. The trail, sometimes near the creek, sometimes climbing over bedrock ridges, leads through ferns and aspens at the base of the steep north canyon wall. After leaving the creek for ⅓ mile, we arrive at a small lake which is bordered by an aspen grove on the north and a cliff on the south. At the west end of this brook-trout-filled lake is a good campsite, strategically located near both this lovely lake and Falls Creek, which is several hundred feet to the south.

*6th Hiking Day (***Paradise Valley** to **Beehive,** 8 miles—12.9 km): A short distance west of the lake our trail meets a signed trail to Tilden Canyon by a large pool. Continuing west we pass some "improved" campsites and cross a large, overgrazed meadow. Beyond this seasonally wet meadow our trail climbs over sun-baked slabs and descends to join the creek again by a large pool where it begins yet another slow-moving stretch. Along this section the trail goes between the creek and a nearby lake on a narrow, aspen-covered levee. Leaving the creek again, we pass another, smaller lake and skirt the marshy north shore of a larger one. For the next two miles our trail winds down glacially modified Jack Main Canyon, sometimes on slabs, sometimes through trees and sometimes near Falls

Creek. From where the creek turns south to cascade down into the valley containing Lake Vernon, we climb a rocky stairway up a gully and onto the timbered flanks of Moraine Ridge. After a 500-foot ascent we leave forest cover and arrive at the summit of aptly named Moraine Ridge. From the summit we can look back at much of northern Yosemite. Most of what you see was covered with ice at various times during the Pleistocene Epoch. We see the glacial aftermath of rounded ridges, polished domes and scoured valleys.

Following the crest of Moraine Ridge, we descend along a very wide, dusty trail through an open forest of Jeffrey pine and white fir. After we cross a burned section, we pass the trail to Lake Vernon, and the grade eases. Back in denser forest now, we cross a very low saddle where we can find lodgepole pine, Jeffrey pine, aspen, incense-cedar and black oak—species rarely found together. A little farther on we make a short, steep descent, and then a gentle descent through a wet area to the forest-bound meadow at Beehive (6500'). The water supply here is a small spring west of the junction with the trail to Laurel Lake. As this lovely meadow is popular with people, there are usually bears around.

7th Hiking Day (**Beehive** to **O'Shaughnessy Dam,** 7.2 miles— 11.6 km): Leaving Beehive, we descend gently through a burned area past a second trail to Laurel Lake. Fire is an important part of the ecology of this forest. You will notice that most trees survived this fire, proving it was not very hot. In areas where fire is suppressed, large amounts of fuel accumulate, and the fire that eventually occurs will be devastating. Soon we pass a marshy pond on the crest of a moraine and begin the steep 2500-foot descent to Hetch Hetchy. As we wind down the rocky, dusty trail, the forest cover changes to reflect the elevation loss. We leave sugar pine behind, white fir is replaced by Douglas-fir and black oak gives way to canyon live oak. About 600 vertical feet down this hill we round a ridge where we can pause to take in the views of Hetch Hetchy reservoir and the surrounding uplands. Descending farther, we cross a small creek and soon join the service road to Lake Eleanor. The last 2½ miles to the trailhead take one down the steep canyon wall via a series of long switchbacks under canyon live oak and California bay. Cutting switchbacks along this descent has caused severe erosion. Natural erosion is also evident where the last switchback begins next to a large landslide. Here, tall trees have been broken off and carried a long way downslope. Beyond the last switchback the trail from Rancheria Creek joins the road, and we stroll 0.7 mile to the dam.

25   Gianelli Cabin to Y Meadow Lake

TRIP   From Gianelli Cabin to Y Meadow Lake (round trip). Topo map *Pinecrest*. Best mid or late season; 10 miles (16.2 km).

Grade	Trail/layover days	Total recommended days
Leisurely	2/0	2
Moderate	....	....
Strenuous	....	....

HILITES   Except for the short distance from Gianelli Cabin to Burst Rock, this trip is within beautiful Emigrant Wilderness, and the route parallels a segment of the historic Emigrant Trail. En route to Y Meadow Lake, anglers can try their luck on two small but fairly productive lakes, and early-trip views, from Burst Rock, are panoramic.

DESCRIPTION

1st Hiking Day (**Gianelli Cabin** to **Y Meadow Lake**, 5 miles—8.1 km): At Gianelli Cabin (8560')—now only part of the log cabin's base remains—the trail begins in a meadow and ascends a steep slope covered with red fir and silver and lodgepole pine. This segment has been used as a jeep trail, so it is somewhat eroded. The trail tops the ridge at Burst Rock (9161'), a landmark for the old Emigrant Trail, and crosses the Emigrant Wilderness boundary (no motorized vehicles allowed). This vantage point offers excellent views to the north of Liberty Hill, Elephant Rock, the Dardanelles, Castle Rock, and the Three Chimneys. You can see as far as Mt. Lyell on the southeast border of Yosemite Park. As the trail bears east along the ridge, the traveler also has excellent views of the Stanislaus River watershed to the north and the Tuolomne River watershed to the south.

The trail descends gradually to a low saddle overlooking granitic Powell Lake. This small lake offers fair fishing for brook trout in early and late season, and the fine views to the northeast makes this an attractive spot for a lunch break. The trail then crosses a small ridge, descends through a forest of lodgepole, fir, and mountain hemlock, and arrives at the open stretches of meadowy Lake Valley. A faint fisherman's trail (0.7 miles) to Chewing Gum Lake turns south through the meadow. Anglers with a yen will want to try the fair-to-good fishing for brook on this small (5-acre) lake before continuing. From Lake Valley it is 1½ miles across another broad ridge to the turnoff to Y Meadow Lake. Here our route turns south for one winding mile to the fair campsites at the north end of Y Meadow Lake (8600'). Unfortunately, the water level fluctuates so much that the lake cannot support fish life. However, anglers accustomed to cross-country walking may elect to try the waters of Granite Lake (0.7 mile south) for the good fishing for brook (8-13"). There are some poor-to-fair campsites at Granite Lake.

2nd Hiking Day: Retrace your steps, 5 miles (8.1 km).

Gianelli Cabin

26   Gianelli Cabin to Wire Lakes

TRIP   From Gianelli Cabin to Wire Lakes (round trip).
             Topo map *Pinecrest*. Best mid or late season; 24.8
             miles (40 km).

Grade	Trail/layover days	Total recommended days
Leisurely	4/1	5
Moderate	4/0	4
Strenuous	2/1	3

HILITES This round trip penetrates the heart of the
             Emigrant Wilderness as it wends through a
             delightful series of meadows and over high, open
             ridges. Wire Lakes, the destination for this trip, is
             a stepladder set of three memorable high-
             mountain lakes that afford excellent angling and
             several fine choices for secluded camping.

DESCRIPTION (Leisurely trip)

1st Hiking Day: Follow Trip 25 to **Y Meadow Lake,** 5 miles (8.1
km).

2nd Hiking Day (**Y Meadow Lake** to **Upper Wire Lake,** 7.4
miles—11.9 km): First retrace your steps from Y Meadow
Lake to the trail junction of the Gianelli Cabin/Whitesides
Meadow Trail. Here our route turns right (northeast) toward
very large Whitesides Meadow. Travelers should be prepared
for the probability of seeing summer-grazing cattle on these
broad expanses (Forest Service Multiple-Use land program)
but these bovine occupants should not detract too much from
an appreciation of this subalpine grassland. At the east end of
the meadow our route passes the Eagle Pass Trail, and then
ascends the moderately timbered slope at the northeast end.
On this ascent our rough path passes a trail to Upper Relief
Valley and Kennedy Meadow, and another one after 1½ miles
of descent. Then it dips down to ford West Fork Cherry Creek
(sometimes dry in late season) at Salt Lick Meadow (8520′).
From here the trail climbs to a tarn-dotted bench and then

descends past several picturesque tarns to Spring Meadow. Tiny lakes sprinkle the green expanse of the meadow, and early-to-mid season trailpounders will find the grassland areas spiced with lupine, paintbrush and buttercup. Fishermen will find the fishing for brook trout fair-to-good along the tributary (Spring Creek) flowing through Post Corral Canyon. A short mile farther southeast, a signed trail leaves the main trail and winds the remaining 0.4 mile along a ridge to the excellent campsites on the northwest side of upper Wire Lake (8800'). Equally good campsites may also be found at Banana Lake (middle Wire Lake), 0.3 miles southwest on a cross-country route. Fishing on the Wire Lakes is good-to-excellent (with a midseason slowdown) for brook (8-14"). Campers will find any of the several secluded campsites on these high montane lakes an idyllic setting for a base camp.

3rd & 4th Hiking Days: Retrace your steps, 12.4 miles (20 km.).

Marmot

Caroline Winnett

27   Crabtree Camp to Bear Lake

TRIP   From Crabtree Camp to Bear Lake (round trip)
           Topo map *Pinecrest*. Best early-to-mid season; 8
           miles (12.8 km).

Grade	Trail/layover days	Total recommended days
Leisurely	2/0	2
Moderate	....	....
Strenuous	....	....

HILITES   Bear Lake usually is a good bet for an early-season
              trip, when fishing for the rainbow trout that
              inhabit the lake waters is best.

DESCRIPTION

1st Hiking Day (**Crabtree Camp** to **Bear Lake,** 4 miles—6.4 km):
Leaving the moderately forested flats of Crabtree Camp, we
hop Bell Creek, making sure that our canteens are full for the
waterless climb to Camp Lake, and quickly come to a junction
with the Chewing Gum Lake Trail on a sandy bench. Our
route ascends dustily through open mixed conifers, then
contours, undulating gently, south to reach a segment of older
trail. Here we assault a steep, much abused path, fortunately
well-shaded, which levels out under aspen and lodgepole at a
lateral trail to Pine Valley. Open stands of mature Jeffrey
pine, lodgepole pine, black oak, red fir, and Sierra juniper
allow a viewful traverse above deeply forested Pine Valley;
then the trees close in as we follow a red-fir corridor around a
grassy pond and gently ascend to the Emigrant Wilderness
boundary. Four hundred yards later we reach the west end of
shallow, green Camp Lake. This sparsely forested, sorely
trampled lakelet supports a harried population of brook trout.
At a saddle just past Camp Lake, we branch left and go 1 mile
to granitic Bear Lake (7700'). Campsites on the west of this
high, mountain lake have been somewhat vandalized but they
are the best to be had. Swimming in late season is invigor-
atingly good, and fishing on this 30-acre lake is fair for rainbow and brook (7-13").
2nd Hiking Day: Retrace your steps, 4 miles (6.4 km).

Crabtree Camp to Deer Lake

TRIP   From Crabtree Camp to Deer Lake (round trip). Topo map *Pinecrest*. Best mid or late season, 24.8 miles (40 km).

Grade	Trail/layover days	Total Recommended days
Leisurely	6/2	8
Moderate	5/2	7
Strenuous	4/2	6

HILITES   Fine fishing and the protected beauty of the Emigrant Wilderness highlight this round trip. A variety of wildlife is present along this route through three life zones, and the higher ridges offer impressive views of the glaciated terrain.

DESCRIPTION (Leisurely trip)

1st Hiking Day: Follow Trip 27 to **Bear Lake**, 4 miles (6.4 km).

2nd Hiking Day (**Bear Lake** to **Piute Lake**, 5.4 miles—8.8 km): First, retrace your steps to the Crabtree Camp/Deer Lake Trail, where our route turns left (east). From the junction, the steep, dusty trail switchbacks down on deep sand flanked by dense manzanita and ceanothus to an easy ford of Lily Creek. Swinging southeast through a meadow sporting corn lilies, lungwort and groundsel, our path soon comes to a granite headwall, and makes a steep, rocky ascent. Now above most of the trees, we see, in the south, Pine Valley and the chaos of white domes in the Chain Lakes region. A parade of switchbacks leads to a lengthy traverse that passes through meadows south of black-streaked granite outcrops, and we soon reach a pretty lakelet, much larger than shown on the topo map, speckled with Indian pond lilies and backdropped by dancing aspens and lichen-dappled granite. Its clear, shallow waters support a thriving population of yellow-legged frogs.

After a short climb east of this tarn, we survey large Piute Meadow in the east, dome-guarded Toms Canyon in the north, Groundhog Meadow below in the southeast, and, on the eastern horizon, Bigelow Peak and the jutting prominence of Tower Peak. Bone-jarring dynamited switchbacks, esthetically ameliorated by a profusion of wildflowers, lead down to a sidehill traverse in glacial boulders west of Piute Meadow. Keeping to the trees south of the willowed west arm of Piute Meadow, we pass a small campsite; then, where our route bends south to easily cross Piute Creek, there is another, larger site. Only yards after Piute Creek the unsigned Groundhog Meadow spur trail comes in from the south. The dry slabs and lodgepole pines demarcating the lower margin of Piute Meadow are left behind when our path bends upward, switchbacking rockily up the east slope of Piute Creek canyon to a broad saddle southwest of Piute Lake. The trail then descends to the meadowed fringes of tiny (2-acre) Piute Lake (7900′) and the good campsites on the north side. Fishing for rainbow (8-12″) in this shallow lake is fair to good.

3rd Hiking Day (**Piute Lake** to **Deer Lake,** 3 miles—4.8 km): From Piute Lake the trail drops to ford West Fork Cherry Creek and then strenuously ascends a steep, rocky, washed-out section to an overlook just above warm little Gem Lake. Less steep than the previous climb, the trail from Gem to Jewelry Lake is nonetheless a rocky ascent. Our route skirts the north side of the meadow fringes surrounding Jewelry Lake, and anglers will want to try their luck for the fair-to-good fishing for rainbow (to 10″) in the lake and the lagoons around the inlet. From the east end of Jewelry Lake, it is a short mile by rocky, gently ascending trail to the excellent campsites on the north side of Deer Lake (8540′). This long, granite-bound lake has nice meadow fringes on the north side. The forested campsites look out over the lake's island- and rock-dotted surface. Fishing for nice-sized rainbow (8-16″) is good-to-excellent on both the lake and the inlet stream.

4th, 5th and 6th Hiking Days: Retrace your steps, 12.4 miles (20 km).

Gianelli Cabin to Crabtree Camp **29**

TRIP From Gianelli Cabin to Crabtree Camp via Wire and Deer Lakes (shuttle trip). Topo map *Pinecrest*. Best mid or late season, 27.3 miles (44 km).

Grade	Trail/layover days	Total recommended days
Leisurely	5/2	7
Moderate	4/2	6
Strenuous	3/2	5

HILITES This route has proved popular with angler, naturalist, photographer and hiker alike. High, coldwater lakes and streams vie with deep fir forests and alpine meadows for the attention of the visitor. The shortness of the shuttle for this trip makes it a near-loop.

DESCRIPTION (Leisurely trip)

1st and 2nd Hiking Days: Follow Trip 26 to **Upper Wire Lake**, 12.4 miles (20 km).

3rd Hiking Day (**Upper Wire Lake** to **Piute Lake**, 5.5 miles—8.9 km): From upper Wire Lake the traveler has the option of circling to Deer Lake by the longer trail route or descending through the Wire Lakes basin and going cross country to the west end of Deer Lake. The trail route, after retracing the short fisherman's lateral, rejoins the Spring Meadow/Deer Lake main trail and turns south. After a slight climb, the remaining distance to Deer Lake is a steady descent over a forested streamcourse that passes several small, unnamed lakes. At Deer Lake this route passes the Buck Lakes trail and turns right (southwest) toward Jewelry Lake.

The cross-country route from upper Wire Lake to this point first leads southwest to Banana Lake (middle Wire Lake), where all semblance of trail vanishes. The easiest descent from here is to take the clear route through the meadowed

area east of Banana Lake and then descend via the usually dry
streamcourse to the Jewelry Lake/Deer Lake Trail about 0.3
mile west of Deer Lake. The trail from Deer Lake to Jewelry
Lake is a ½-mile rocky descent that brings the traveler to the
pleasant meadow fringes surrounding Jewelry Lake. This
lake has placid lagoons forming its inlet which provide
fair-to-good fishing for rainbow (to 10″). Crossing the inlet
stream, the route descends a rocky trail to warm little Gem
Lake (8240′). From this viewpoint the trail descends steeply to
a ford of West Fork Cherry Creek and then climbs gently to
tiny Piute Lake. Fishing for rainbow (8-12″) in this shallow
lake is fair-to-good.

4th and 5th Hiking Days: Reverse the steps of the 1st and 2nd
hiking days, Trip 28, 9.4 miles (15.1 km).

Gianelli Cabin to Kennedy Meadow **30**

TRIP   From Gianelli Cabin to Kennedy Meadow via Deer and Emigrant Lakes (shuttle trip). Topo maps *Pinecrest, Tower Peak, Sonora Pass*. Best mid or late season; 33.3 miles (53.7 km).

Grade	Trail/layover days	Total recommended days
Leisurely	5/2	7
Moderate	4/2	6
Strenuous	3/2	5

HILITES   This trip journeys through a cross section of the Emigrant Wilderness. The route touches some justly popular base-camping lakes, and from these points the traveler has access to the unusual and exciting surrounding country. Taken at Leisurely pace, this route affords one of the best possible week-long excursions in the region.

DESCRIPTION (Leisurely trip)

1st and 2nd Hiking Days: Follow Trip 26 to **Upper Wire Lake**, 12.4 miles (20 km).

3rd Hiking Day (**Upper Wire Lake** to **Emigrant Lake** via Deer and Buck Lakes, 7.5 miles—12.1 km): The traveler going to Deer Lake has a choice of going by trail or cross country. The trail route entails retracing the short fisherman's trail to its junction with the main trail from Spring Meadow. There our route turns right (south), and descends gently past several unnamed tarns to Deer Lake. The cross-country route goes south through the Wire Lakes basin to Banana Lake (middle Wire Lake), and then veers east a short distance through a meadowed basin. At the end of this meadow a long, usually dry streamcourse descending to the south gives access to the trail

0.3 mile west of Deer Lake (8540'). This is a large, granitoid, meadow-fringed lake offering good-to-excellent fishing for nice-sized rainbow (to 16"), and anglers who have had an early start will want to try these waters.

The trail to Buck Lakes continues east over a low rocky ridge, and then descends steeply to join the Emigrant Lake/Cow Meadow Lake Trail on the west shore of Buck Lakes. At this junction our route turns left (north) along the west side of upper Buck Lake, and follows Buck Meadow Creek as it crosses the long meadow at the lake's north end. Our route then veers east, fords Buck Meadow Creek, and crosses the steep, low ridge separating the Emigrant Lake and Buck Lakes basins. At Emigrant Lake (8800') the trail follows the long north shore to the several good-to-excellent campsites near the inlet. Emigrant Lake is the largest lake (230 acres) in the Wilderness, and is a long-time favorite of fishermen because of the good-to-excellent rainbow fishing (8-18") in its deep waters. Those who prefer stream fishing will find the lagoons near the inlet exciting sport, but the fish are smaller. *4th and 5th Hiking Days*: Reverse the steps of the 2nd and 1st hiking days, Trip 21, 13.4 miles (21.6 km).

Lower Buck Lake   *Luther Linkhart*

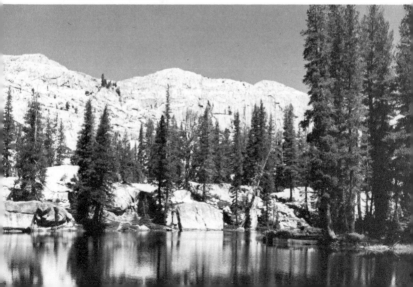

Kennedy Meadow to Gianelli Cabin **31**

TRIP   From Kennedy Meadow to Gianelli Cabin via Brown Bear Pass and Emigrant Meadow, Maxwell, Buck, Wire, and Y Meadow lakes (shuttle trip). Topo maps *Sonora Pass, Tower Peak, Pinecrest*. Best mid or late season, 43.1 miles (69.5 km).

Grade	Trail/layover days	Total recommended days
Leisurely	7/3	10
Moderate	5/2	7
Strenuous	4/2	6

HILITES   After visiting the north side of the Emigrant Wilderness, this route turns south and traverses the beautiful, lake-dotted country of the Cherry Creek watershed. At Emigrant Meadow the trail joints the old Emigrant Trail, and history buffs will have the opportunity of seeing this historic crossing as the pioneers did.

DESCRIPTION (Leisurely trip)

1st and 2nd Hiking Days: Follow Trip 20 to **Emigrant Meadow Lake**, 12.6 miles (20.3 km).

3rd and 4th Hiking Days: Reverse the steps of the 5th and 4th hiking days, Trip 23, 13 miles (21 km).

5th Hiking Day (**Cow Meadow Lake** to **Deer Lake**, 3.5 miles—5.6 km): Leaving Cow Meadow Lake, the trail passes a junction with a trail from East Fork Cherry Creek and then ascends steeply 600 feet amid a dense, predominantly lodgepole forest cover to a junction with the Wood Lake lateral. Lower Buck Lake (42 acres) is a rocky, deep, glacial lake that is separated from upper Buck Lake by a narrow isthmus. Fishing on both lakes for rainbow (to 18″) is good. Our route crosses the isthmus and turns north, where it strikes the Deer Lake Trail.

Here our route turns left (west) and climbs steeply for ½ mile. Then it descends more gently for a mile past the Wood Lake Trail to the excellent campsites on the north side of Deer Lake (8540'). This long lake has the same kind of subalpine meadow fringing as upper Buck Lake. The fine campsites, situated in small stands of lodgepole, look out across the lake's island-dotted surface. Fishing for rainbow (to 16″) is good-to-excellent.

6th Hiking Day (**Deer Lake** to **Y Meadow Lake**, 9 miles—14.5 km): The mileage for this hiking day is calculated on the basis of bypassing Wire Lakes. However, those who elect to visit this charming lake chain (good fishing) should examine the alternative route offered in the description of the 3rd hiking day, Trip 29. From the trail junction at the middle of Deer Lake's north shore, our route climbs north beside an unnamed stream and past a series of inviting tarns. About 1.7 miles from Deer Lake we pass the Wire Lakes Trail going left (west) and then descend a densely forested slope to the east end of Spring Meadow. This meadow is a vast, lakelet-dotted grassland that is lush with buttercups, lupine and paintbrush. One frequently sees cattle grazing here, allowed by the National Forest multiple-use land program. From Spring Meadow the trail crosses a small ridge containing more tarns and then descends moderately-to-steeply through a wooded section to Salt Lick Meadow, where it crosses tiny West Fork Cherry Creek (sometimes dry in late season). Then the route ascend through lodgepole pine and mountain hemlock, passing the first of two trails leading north to Upper Relief Valley and Kennedy Meadow and, 0.6 mile later, an unsigned trail leading south to secluded Toejam Lake. Our trail tops the ridge and then descends to sprawling Whitesides Meadow. At its head we pass another trail to Upper Relief Valley and, soon after, a trail to Cooper Meadow, both leading north. The green expanse of this meadow is broken by the flow of an unnamed tributary of South Fork Stanislaus River. Our trail touches this stream at the meadow's west end, then veers away southwest to the Y Meadow Lake Trail junction. Here we branch left and walk one winding mile to the fair campsites in the timber fringe at the north end of Y Meadow Lake (8600').

7th Hiking Day: Reverse the steps of the lst hiking day, Trip 25, 5 miles (8.1 km).

The North Boundary Experience

Wherever Sierra mountaineers gather there is sure to be talk of the fabulous "North Boundary Country," and there is just cause for this preoccupation. Here Yosemite boasts its least-visited and wildest backcountry. In these glaciated canyons and on these granite crests, five generations of hikers, climbers and horsemen have found the solitude, beauty and challenge they sought. Lying between the Tioga Road (State Highway 120) and the northern edge of the Park, it is a heavily glaciated region of uniform drainage pattern and rounded slopes that appeals to the cross-country wanderer. It is remote because it is large, and because it is isolated by the main Sierra crest on the east and north, and by the Grand Canyon of the Tuolumne on the south.

The topography of this region also contributes to the feeling of solitude that attends trips taken through it. The terrain is split by no fewer than 11 ridge-valley sequences, all running northeast to southwest. A group of hikers can be in one drainage and totally oblivious of another group only one mile away, with a natural wall of glaciated granite in between. Travelers on the famed Pacific Crest Trail are aware of another, equally desirable quality that accrues to the ridge-valley sequence: each ridge encountered and surmounted is sure to reveal a fresh, new valley full of different claims on the visitor's attention.

With the exception of the volcanic and metamorphic rock along much of the eastern escarpment, this is all granite country. Time and evolution are at work here, and mountains are being leveled. You might be misled into thinking that these things are occurring too slowly to be noticed, but the joyous instant a wildflower frantically bursts into bloom is an integral part of the juggernaut process, and the spreading of its petals is as inexorable as the sun's rise, and, in its context, more powerful than an earthquake. One writer put it this way: "Time is the factor. If a butterfly were to brush a wing against the great granite wall of Half Dome in a daily pilgrimage, it would eventually level the mountain." The valleys of the northern part of the Park are full of life that is moving mountains, and if you watch closely you *can* see it happen.

Aside from the remoteness, perhaps the most appealing things about the North Boundary Country is the variety of the plant life. The elevation spread of nearly 9000 feet encompasses almost every kind of Sierran ecological niche. From the digger-pine belt near Hetch Hetchy Reservoir to the whitebark-pined summits of Burro Pass, almost every tree to be seen in the Sierra is represented. Early-summer wildflower displays are nowhere more abundant nor varied, and it is not at all unusual to come across the sunburst yellow of golden brodiaea and the delicate blossom of the alpine-dwelling yellow columbine in the same hiking day. On every hand the hiker sees a vital urgency for life—a living claim for one's right to the sun. Perhaps it is this intense process of life frantically renewing itself in a high alpine meadow that man returns time and again to witness. Both a wildflower and a backpacker cram a lot of living into an all-too-short summer. In all cases it is an affirmative celebration of life, and the backpacker, by his personal witness, is a celebrant.

Trails through the North Boundary Country are, understandably, not as well maintained as trails more heavily used and closer to roads in the Park. However, these neglected paths are ways of solitude where one is sometimes able to walk for long distances without encountering another living soul. Best-known among the North Boundary trails is the Tahoe-to-Yosemite route, which is also a segment of the Pacific Crest Trail. This trail receives the brunt of the traffic. Most of the routes described in this section begin on the east side of the Sierra. The weekend trips flirt with the Sierra crest, but one should plan at least a three-day trip for any serious penetration of the North Boundary Country.

All kinds of reasons are given for trips into wilderness, but the most commonly given is fishing. For the angler who measures any and all wilderness experiences in terms of the fishing opportunities, the North Boundary Country is a frustrating area to consider—frustrating because the options are so many, the fishery so varied, and the scenery so distracting. Living in the waters of this region are eastern brook, rainbow, brown, golden and some cutthroat trout. The most consistent fish-producing streams are Falls Creek in Jack Main Canyon, Rancheria Creek in Kerrick Canyon, Matterhorn Creek in Matterhorn Canyon and Return Creek in Virginia Canyon. Lakes that are annual "hotspots" include Benson, Smedberg, Peeler, the McCabes, and the lakes above Saddlebag Lake. A state fishing license is required within the Park for all persons over 16.

A word about bears

Since backpackers' food is attractive to bears, and all too often easily available, the animals have developed a habit of seeking it and eating it. They patrol popular campsites nightly. As the bears have become more knowledgeable and persistent, backpackers have escalated their food-protecting methods. From merely putting it in one's pack by one's bed at night, and chasing away any bear that came, backcountry travelers switched to hanging the food over a branch of a tree. But bears can climb trees, and they can gnaw or scratch through the nylon line that you tie around a tree trunk. When they sever the line, the food hanging from the other end of the line of course falls to the ground.

To avoid food loss due to line severance, you can learn the *counterbalance* method of "bearbagging." First, tie a small stone to the end of a 30-foot length of nylon line (⅛″ or so in diameter) as a weight to hurl up and over a likely branch. The branch should be at least 16 feet up, and long enough that the line can rest securely at a point at least 6 feet from the tree trunk. When you have the line over the branch, tie a rock that weighs about the same as the food bag to one end of the line. (Instead of a rock, you could tie a bag containing half the food, if you have two appropriate bags.) Now pull the rock up to the branch that the line passes over. Then tie your food bag to the other end of the line, as high as you can conveniently reach, and stuff any extra line into the mouth of the food bag. Now push up on the food bag with just enough force—you hope—that the system will come to rest with the rock and the bag equally high. If they aren't equally high, take a long enough stick, preferably forked, and push up the lower of the two until they are even. If you can reach them standing on tiptoes, they are too low. Try again. Next morning, push up either rock or bag until one descends enough that you can reach it. As a high-tech version of a tree limb, rangers have installed cables up high between two trees at popular campsites in Yosemite. In addition, steel food-storage lockers have been placed at some campsites in the Sierra.

REMEMBER: If a bear does get your food, he will then consider it his, and he will fight any attempts you make to retrieve it. Don't try! Remember also never to leave your food unprotected even for a short while during the daytime.

The Trailheads

O'Shaughnessy Dam (Hetch Hetchy Reservoir). Go east on State Highway 120 4 miles beyond Buck Meadows and turn left at a signed junction. Go 6 miles to another signed junction, turn right and go 6½ miles to Camp Mather and then 9½ more miles to the roadend.

Leavitt Meadow. Go 8 miles east from Sonora Pass on State Highway 108, or 7 miles west from U.S. 395 on the same highway.

Buckeye Roadend. Go 7 miles west from Bridgeport on the Twin Lakes road and turn north for 4 dirt-road miles at the junction signed **Buckeye Campground**. Just beyond Buckeye Creek, turn left and go 1.1 miles, passing through a Forest Service Campground, to the end of the road. Alternatively, leave U.S. 395 3.8 miles north of Bridgeport and drive 6.0 miles to the same roadend.

Twin Lakes. Drive to the end of the paved 13½-mile road marked *Twin Lakes* that branches west from U.S. 395 in downtown Bridgeport. Park at the backpacker parking lot at the entrance to private Mono Village Campground. You must pay $5 in advance at the campground gate.

Green Creek Roadend. Take the dusty dirt road signed *Green Lakes Pack Station* which leaves U.S. 395 4.7 miles south of Bridgeport and 21 miles north of Lee Vining. Go 9½ miles west to the roadend.

Saddlebag Lake. Go 2 miles up a gravel road that branches northwest from State Highway 120 2 miles north of the Tioga Pass entrance to Yosemite.

Glen Aulin Trailhead. From State Highway 120 in Tuolumne Meadows, just east of the bridge over the Tuolumne River, turn west on a dirt road and go 0.3 mile to a parking area near the stables. On crowded days you may have to park immediately off the highway at the Dog Lake trailhead parking lot.

Virginia Lakes Trailhead. From Conway Summit on U.S. 395 go 6 miles on paved Virginia Lakes Road, then ½ mile on dirt road to the campground on the right.

Leavitt Meadow to Fremont Lake   **32**

TRIP   From Leavitt Meadow Campground to Fremont Lake (round trip). Topo map *Sonora Pass*. Best mid or late season; 18 miles (29 km).

Grade	Trail/layover days	Total recom- mended days
Leisurely	2/1	3
Moderate	2/0	2
Strenuous	....	....

HILITES   Along this well-traveled route the traveler is introduced to the contrasts of the North Boundary Country. Here the dark rock thrown up by volcanoes meets the lighter, more typical Sierra batholith granite. Cameras for the photo-bug are a must, and the angler can look forward to good rainbow-trout fishing at Fremont Lake.

DESCRIPTION

1st Hiking Day (**Leavitt Meadow Campground** to **Fremont Lake**, 9 miles—14.5 km): The trail leaves the Leavitt Meadow Campground (7120') via a metal bridge across the West Walker River. Beyond the bridge our trail ascends stiffly for ¼ mile, to a junction just beyond a mountain juniper on the left and a Jeffrey pine followed by a stump on the right. Here we veer right onto a shortcut trail on a sagebrush-covered arid slope. In a few minutes we re-meet the main trail and go right on it, traversing over to the wide valley of Leavitt Meadow. As we ascend gently just above the valley floor, it does not take a great deal of imagination to picture emigrant wagons working their way southwest toward Emigrant Pass, at the headwaters of this river. Close beside the trail are many tall specimens of a bush-tree called mountain mahogany. Despite its dry, tough appearance, the foliage of this desert plant is relished by the local mule-deer population. The plant is particularly striking in the early fall, when the styles of the flowers are white, silky, 3-inch-long plumes growing by the hundreds on each bush.

On this steady ascent we meet three trails, coming in at acute angles, that lead back north to the pack station in Leavitt Meadow. Then, after the meadow disappears from sight, we pass the Poore Lake Trail branching left and continue to the north shore of algae-bottomed Roosevelt Lake, ringed with a sparse fringe of Jeffrey pines. There are some undistinguished campsites on the west side of the lake, and sometimes fishing is good for brook trout to 13″.

Then our trail leads over a granite shoulder and down to the outlet of Lane Lake, nearly a twin of Roosevelt and only a few yards from it. This outlet usually dries up by midsummer, but the dead lodgepole pines southwest of the ford are testimony to flooding earlier in the season. From the ford, the trail ascends briefly southeast and then levels off as it passes several lovely aspen groves, some with lush grass floors even into late season. Just over a mile from Lane Lake we pass a junction with the old trail, no longer maintained, which runs north from Lane Lake near the West Walker River. Past the junction, our trail soon descends to the willow-lined banks of the river, crossing a small but vigorous tributary ⅛ mile before reaching the main stream. We ascend gently near the riverside for ¼ mile through a cool forest of mixed conifers, aspens and cottonwoods, then veer away on a steeper ascent that fords another tributary. The rocky-dusty trail then steepens to surmount a saddle crested with junipers and Jeffrey pines, which offers fine views up the West Walker valley to Forsyth Peak and the Sierra crest. Descending over a sandy trail, our route passes the marked turnoff to Hidden and Red Top lakes, and then resumes its moderate ascent along the east bank of the West Walker River. The rocky stretch of trail alongside the river gives access to many pleasant, granite-bottomed potholes. Here the river tumbles along in a series of small falls and cascades that have carved a narrows through the white granite which typifies the middle of the West Walker River Valley. The upper walls are of barren, metavolcanic rock that ranges the color spectrum from black to reds and yellows.

Where the narrows opens out onto a forest flat, rife with mosquitoes in early season, we come to a junction with the Fremont Lake Trail, just off the Sonora Pass topo map. Turning right, we follow this trail to the riverbank and find a good log crossing less than 100 yards downstream. Across the river are many well-used campsites, and we stroll downstream past several to reach the signed Fremont Lake trail continuation. This we follow westward and ascend steeply to cross a saddle topped with juniper and Jeffrey pine. This saddle offers V'd views south to Tower Peak. The trail then descends gently, passes the trail to Chain of Lakes, and in 100 yards reaches Fremont Lake (8240'). The forest cover around this generous-sized lake is moderate-to-dense lodgepole and juniper, most of it around the south end of the lake. Here in the timber are fair campsites, and fishing for rainbow (to 12") and eastern brook (to 10") is good.

2nd Hiking Day: Retrace your steps, 9 miles (14.5 km).

West Walker River above Leavitt Meadow

33   Leavitt Meadow to Cinko Lake

TRIP   From Leavitt Meadow Campground to Cinko Lake (round trip). Topo maps *Sonora Pass, Tower Peak.* Best mid or late season; 28 miles (45.2 km).

Grade	Trail/layover days	Total recommended days
Leisurely	3/1	4
Moderate	3/0	3
Strenuous	2/0	2

HILITES   This interesting route traces West Fork West Walker River to its headwaters cirque beneath the Sierra crestline. From the sagebrush and Jeffrey pine belt it ascends to the Boreal belt, passing through three ecological zones. Of the several trips in this drainage, this offers one of the best exposures to the geological, topographical and biological features of the country.

DESCRIPTION (Leisurely trip)

1st Hiking Day: Follow Trip 32, to **Fremont Lake**, 9 miles (14.5 km).

2nd Hiking Day (**Fremont Lake** to **Cinko Lake**, 5 miles—8.1 km): After retracing our steps back to the Chain of Lakes junction described in Trip 32, we turn right (south) and ascend steadily near, but out of sight of, Fremont Lake. This ascent steepens as it crosses open, granite-sand slopes with only a few junipers and pines for shade. Near the top of this ascent one has uninterrupted views to the south of Forsyth and Tower peaks, and one encounters his first silver pines of this trip. The first of three large granite domes that tower over the east side of Chain of Lakes comes into view, and the trail crosses to the north of it. Then, on a gently descending path through an increasingly dense forest cover, we pass the marked trail to Walker Meadows and arrive at the first of several tiny, green, lily-padded lakes. These lakes reflect the verdant forest cover that extends to their willow-lined shores, and by late summer their shallow depths teem with the biota that typifies near-stagnant waters. Fair campsites for early and mid season, usable when the water is moving, dot the west sides of all three lakes.

The trail leaves the last and largest of the Chain of Lakes and ascends gently over sand and duff through a moderate forest cover of lodgepole and silver pine past a small, unnamed lake north of Lower Long Lake. A few yards past this lily-padded lake, the trail veers right, around the north side of Lower Long Lake. The "blancoed" rock in the center of the lake is a favorite midday resting place for the sandpipers that inhabit the area. Fishermen seeking the pan-sized rainbow here will enjoy the sandpiper's low, skimming flight, which seems to trim the fringe of rushes. Fair-to-good campsites dot the north and west sides of the lake. More extensive campsites are found a few yards farther up the trail, at Upper Long Lake. The trail jogs around the lower end of Upper Long Lake, fords the intermittent outlet stream and meets the Piute Meadows lateral, going left. Our route turns right past a picturesque tarn to the banks of West Fork West Walker River. Here at another junction our route branches left alongside this tumbling stream. Good campsites dot both sides of the West Fork near the junction, marred only by the cowflops incident to the Multiple-Use grazing permit for nearby Walker Meadows. Occasional hemlocks with their gracefully bowed tops occur along the pleasant, granite-ledged, timber-pocketed ascent from the campsites. Many wildflowers, including shooting star, penstemon, bush lupine, aster, pennyroyal, columbine, goldenrod, heather, false Solomon's seal, Mariposa lily, wallflower, woolly sunflower and fleabane, decorate the stream's edge and complement the cheerful splashing of the nearby stream. This gentle-to-moderate climb continues along the southeast side of the stream to the foot of a large, white granite dome (Peak 10010), where it fords via boulders to the northwest side of the creek. Contrasts of the dark volcanic rock and the white granite underlayment of this part of the Sierra are nowhere more marked than in this valley, and the viewer is assailed with dark battlements of multihued basalt, and sheer escarpments of glacially smoothed batholithic granite. William H. Brewer, head of the Brewer Survey party that passed near here in July 1863, took note of the volcanic surroundings, saying ". . . in the higher Sierra, along our line of travel, all our highest points were capped with lava, often worn into strange and fantastic forms—rounded hills of granite, capped by rugged masses of lava, sometimes looking like old castles with their towers and buttresses and walls, sometimes like old churches with their pinnacles, all on a gigantic scale, and then again shooting up in curious forms that defy description."

This ascent takes the traveler to timberline and to alpine climes as the surrounding forest cover becomes stunted and includes occasional altitude-loving whitebark pines. At a signed junction our route turns southeast along a clear trail to Cinko Lake. This trail fords West Fork West Walker River and passes a charming meadow with a tiny tarn in its upper reaches. Then it makes a brief moderate ascent to the intermittent north outlet of arrowhead-shaped Cinko Lake. There is another outlet on the south side of the lake. The trail emerges at the lake's edge (9200'), adjacent to the north outlet, where there are several good campsites. Fishing for rainbow and eastern brook (to 12") is good.

3rd Hiking Day: Retrace your steps, 14 miles (22.6 km).

Crown Point over Barney Lake

Leavitt Meadow to Dorothy Lake

34

TRIP From Leavitt Meadow Campground to Dorothy Lake (semiloop trip). Topo maps *Sonora Pass, Tower Peak*. Best mid or late seaon; 34 miles (54.7 km).

Grade	Trail/layover days	Total recommended days
Leisurely	6/1	7
Moderate	4/1	5
Strenuous	3/1	4

HILITES Touring the headwaters of the West Fork West Walker River and the headwaters of Cascade Creek and Falls Creek would be an ambitious undertaking in any one trip, but this trip boasts more. Near Dorothy Lake, the culmination of the trip, the visitor can take in the unusual Forsyth Peak "rock glacier."

DESCRIPTION (Moderate trip)

1st and 2nd Hiking Days: (**Leavitt Meadow** to **Dorothy Lake**, 18 miles—29 km). First follow Trip 33 to **Cinko Lake**, 14 miles (22.6 km). From the southeast side of Cinko Lake our trail winds down a lodgepole- and hemlock-clothed hillside to the unpopulated banks of an unnamed stream. Then it climbs slightly, veering east away from the water. A very short, steep descent then takes the hiker to a beautiful lakelet. About ⅛ mile past the lake, we reapproach the stream and then veer away again eastward. In another ⅛ mile the trail crosses this persistent tributary on a wooden bridge, then ascends for a moment, levels off, and passes three snowmelt tarns on the right. Continuing level through a tarn-filled saddle here, our southbound trail soon meets the Dorothy Lake Trail. Here we turn right (south), following the trail on a gentle ascent through a thinning forest cover of lodgepole, hemlock and whitebark pine. One-half mile from the junction we cross

Cascade Creek on a large log near a large east-bank campsite, and in another ⅓ mile ford the outlet of Lake Harriet. After this ford the trail ascends more steeply, and becomes rocky after passing island-dotted Lake Harriet. This ascent levels through a meadowy section and fords the stream joining Stella and Bonnie lakes. Ahead, the low profile of Dorothy Lake Pass is fronted by another moderate, rocky ascent, and the trail then levels past the grassy north arm of Stella Lake. At the northeast end of this arm, a ducked cross-country route to Lake Ruth and Lake Helen departs from our route.

   The long, low saddle on which Stella Lake sits terminates at Dorothy Lake Pass, where there is an excellent view of Dorothy Lake (9400'). To the southeast, the hiker has V-notched views of Tower Peak, and to the south, the granite grenadiers of multi-turreted Forsyth Peak dominate the landscape. From the pass, the trail descends steadily over a rocky slope that is the territory of numerous conies and marmots. As the trail skirts the north side of this beautiful lake, it winds through lush grass and willow patches with spots of color provided by bush lupine, shooting star, elephant heads, goldenrod, paintbrush, whorled penstemon, aster, fleabane, pussy paws and false Solomon's seal. This stretch of the north shore was not so lush when the first recorded explorer of this lake walked here. Lt. N. F. McClure, of the 4th Cavalry, came this way in 1894 noting, "Grazing here was poor, and there had evidently been thousands of sheep about." The trail passes three windy campsites along the north shore before arriving at the good campsites at the west end of the lake. Fishing for rainbow and occasional eastern brook is good-to-excellent except during a midsummer slowdown. This lake makes an excellent base-camp location for exploring and fishing the surrounding lakes in the upper Cascade Creek basin, and for viewing the Forsyth Peak "rock glacier."

   This phenomenon can be viewed from the unnamed lake south of Dorothy Lake. Seen from here, it is a prominent "river" of rock flowing in a long northwest-curving arc. This arc begins on the northeast face of Forsyth Peak, then curves down the easternmost ravine and points its moving head toward Dorothy Lake. Composed of coarse rock that tumbled from Forsyth Peak's fractured face, it hides an underlayment of silt, sand and fine gravel, and it depends upon ice caught between larger boulders for its mobility.

3rd Hiking Day (**Dorothy Lake** to **Fremont Lake Trail Junction**, 8 miles—12.9 km): First retrace the steps of the previous hiking day as far as the Cinko Lake Trail. Then continue to descend on the north side of tumbling Cascade Creek. Switchbacks are needed to convey the hiker down past the cascades of this namesake creek. Near the bottom of this descent the forest, now including stately red firs, becomes thicker. As the trail nears the West Walker River, the moderate descent levels, and then the route fords near an old corral. Beyond the wading ford is a **Y** junction, and here our route turns left (downstream). The trail continues north along the east side of the West Walker River, fords an unnamed tributary of the river, and skirts a large meadow before beginning a gentle-to-moderate ascent. The sand-and-duff trail then crosses a saddle and descends to ford Long Canyon Creek. About ¼ mile beyond this stream is the Fremont Lake Trail junction, and we take this trail across the river to the campsites passed on the first hiking day. Alternatively, one may continue downstream on the east side of the river to other good campsites. Fishing in the deeper holes of this section of the river is good for rainbow (to 11″).

4th Hiking Day: Reverse the steps of most of the 1st hiking day, Trip 32, 8 miles (12.9 km). (If your car is above the pack station, turn left on the trail that goes west through a grassy flat just before the final small descent to the campground, and wade the river to reach the highway.)

Dorothy Lake and "rock glacier" on Forsyth Peak

35   Leavitt Meadow to Tower Lake

TRIP   From Leavitt Meadow Campground to Tower Lake (semiloop trip, part cross country). Topo maps *Sonora Pass, Tower Peak*. Best mid or late season; 40 miles (64.4 km).

Grade	Trail/layover days	Total recommended days
Leisurely	7/2	9
Moderate	5/2	7
Strenuous	4/2	6

HILITES   The cross-country segment of this trip makes it a choice for experienced backpackers only. The strenuousness of the route guarantees the walker a proportionate measure of solitude, and views of the alpine crestal country seldom seen by anyone except the cross-countryer.

DESCRIPTION (Moderate trip)

1st and 2nd Hiking Days: Follow Trip 34 to **Dorothy Lake**, 18 miles (29 km).

3rd Hiking Day (**Dorothy Lake** to **Tower Lake**, 5 miles—8.1 km): From the campsites at the west end of Dorothy Lake, retrace the steps of the previous hiking day to Stella Lake, where the ducked cross-country route to Lake Ruth rounds the northeast end of the lake. This route ascends over a rock-and-grass ledge system along the east side of the intermittent stream joining Stella Lake and Lake Ruth, and arrives at the outlet end of Lake Ruth. Here, nestled in the sparse whitebark-pine fringe of the lake, are good campsites that make a fine alternative to the more crowded environs of Dorothy Lake. The route from the outlet skirts the east side of the lake for a short distance and then ascends a long, gentle swale to the southeast. Several small melt-off tarns mark the crossover point to the Lake Helen drainage. Keeping to the south side of this large, granitic, circular lake, the route fords the tiny but noisy southwest inlet, and then crosses the rocky slope directly south of the lake.

At the southeast inlet our route fords and ascends moderately to a lovely grass bench. The remaining ascent to the obvious saddle in the southeast crosses steeper sections, and route-picking is best accomplished on the left (north) side of the cirque wall. This steep pitch brings one to a sparsely dotted whitebark-pine saddle offering incomparable views. Included in the views to the north and west are, from north to west, Wells Peak, White Mountain, Sonora Peak, Stanislaus Peak, Leavitt Peak, Kennedy Peak, Relief Peak and Forsyth Peak. To the east and southeast the view encompasses, from east to south, Flatiron Butte, Walker Peak, Buckeye Ridge, the Kirkwood Creek drainage, Grouse Mountain, Hunewill Peak, Hawksbeak Peak, Kettle Peak, Cirque Mountain and Tower Peak. From the summit of this saddle one can also see most of the lakes of the Cascade Creek drainage, as well as Tower Lake at the foot of Tower Peak. Tower Peak, the most spectacular peak of the North Boundary Country but not the tallest, is the goal of most climbers in this region. Visible from most of the drainages to the south, it has served mountaineers as a landmark for more than a hundred years.

Descending from the saddle on the southeast side entails crossing rock and scree to a rocky bench, and thence a grass-and-ledge system to a small lakelet just north of Tower Lake. The route then rounds the south nose of a granite ridge to the willowed outlet of Tower Lake, where it fords to the fair campsites, centered in the only stand of timber found here on the east side of the outlet (9600'). There is fair-to-good fishing for the golden trout (to 11") that inhabit this lake. Good alternative campsites can be found ½ mile down the outlet stream.

4th Hiking Day (**Tower Lake** to **Fremont Lake Trail Junction**, 9 miles—14.4 km): From Tower Lake the trail descends over a rocky slope close to the north side of the outlet stream from Tower Lake. This steep, rocky descent affords a view of a dramatic avalanche chute that slices the slope on the northeast side of Kirkwood Creek canyon. To be rear, back toward Tower Peak, the view is dominated by the climactic, phalluslike northern extension of Tower Peak. This classic white-granite pinnacle soon obliterates views of Tower Peak itself, and it stands as mute testimony to the obdurate granite's resistance to glacial erosion. The rocky descent soon reaches timberline, where hemlock and lodgepole pine appear, and then refords the outlet stream in a willowed section at the confluence of the Tower Lake outlet and the tiny stream draining the glacier at the foot of the granite column to the south. This new section of trail from Tower Lake keeps to the east side of the creek as it descends gently over duff and rock, and fords an unnamed tributary.

Beyond the ford, the new trail rejoins the old trail, winding through a dense forest cover of lodgepole and hemlock. Then the trail refords Tower Lake's outlet stream and ascends above the narrowing canyon. These narrows show almost vertical granite walls, between which the stream becomes a plummeting ribbon. Ahead, the valley of the West Walker River can be seen through the trees, and a short, easy descent over a duff trail soon brings us to a trail junction just north of the confluence of the Tower Lake outlet and Kirkwood Creek. Our route turns right, fords the West Walker River, and then skirts the oxbows of the river where it serpentines through Upper Piute Meadows. At the north end of the meadows the sandy trail passes a turnoff to Piute Cabin, a Forest Service trail-maintenance station, and then veers away from the river as it continues to descend gently. The cattle in Upper Piute Meadows are part of the Forest Service's "Multiple Use" administrative concept. Cowflops have been reported as far away as the head of Thompson Canyon—and it may be logically assumed that they were a result of allowing grazing here. After jogging around a marshy section, the trail again comes within sight of the river, and then joins the trail from Dorothy Lake. From the junction we proceed as described in the 3rd hiking day, Trip 34.

5th Hiking Day: Reverse the steps of most of the 1st hiking day, Trip 32, 8 miles (12.9 km).

Upper Piute Meadows

Leavitt Meadow to Buckeye Creek **36**

TRIP From Leavitt Meadow Campground to Buckeye Roadend (shuttle trip). Topo maps *Sonora Pass, Tower Peak, Matterhorn Peak*. Best early or mid season, 39.9 miles (64.2 km).

Grade	Trail/layover days	Total recommended days
Leisurely	7/2	9
Moderate	5/2	7
Strenuous	4/1	5

HILITES Using two major eastside drainages this trip circumnavigates Walker Mountain and Flatiron Ridge, and is about evenly split between high country and lower, forested areas. This is a superlative choice for the novice who has a couple of shorter trips behind him, and who is looking for a longer trip with some of the challenge of cross-countrying.

DESCRIPTION (Moderate trip)

1st, 2nd and 3rd Hiking Days: Follow Trip 35 to **Tower Lake**, 23 miles (37.0 km).

4th Hiking Day (**Tower Lake** to **Buckeye Forks**, 7.5 miles—12.1 km): First, descend to Upper Piute Meadows as described in the 4th hiking day, Trip 35. Just below the confluence of Kirkwood Creek and the creek draining Tower Lake, ford to the northeast side of the stream and turn right, up Kirkwood Creek. Here at the southernmost extension of Upper Piute Meadows our route ascends moderately through a dense forest cover of lodgepole and occasional silver pine that sees the inclusion of hemlock near the top of the climb. This route passes below the spectacular avalanche chute noted on the previous hiking day. On a moderate ascent that steepens as it turns east and then northeast, the trail rises to the saddle marking the divide between the Walker River and Buckeye Creek. The startling eminence of Hawksbeak Peak to the south vies for the traveler's attention with the rich volcanic reds and blacks of the slopes to the north. After reaching a small pond at the headwaters of Kirkwood Creek, the trail descends moderately on duff and rocky surfaces to the head of North Fork Buckeye Creek. This descent through a sparse-to-moderate forest cover of lodgepole, hemlock, and occasional whitebark and silver pine crosses back and forth over the splashing creek. Then, in a final steep descent, the trail drops to "Buckeye Forks," where it meets the trail descending from Buckeye Pass to the south.

Here at the forks is a meadow-set snow-survey cabin of log-tenon construction. It is believed that this well-made cabin was constructed in 1928, and is the oldest U. S. Snow Survey shelter. When built, the cabin was surrounded by open meadow, which has since been overgrown with the ubiquitous lodgepole and willow. This dense growth is undoubtedly due to the strong evolutionary contribution of the nearby colony of beavers. As is clearly seen just downstream, these beavers have repeatedly flooded this section between Buckeye Forks and The Roughs, and the consequent buildup of sediments and high water table were conducive to forest reproduction. However, what the beaver giveth he also taketh away. Were this dense forest to be flooded again, these healthy trees would be drowned. That happened downstream, where the bleached white ghost snags make skeletal reminders of the beaver's potent niche in the evolutionary web. Of the mammals, excepting man, the beaver is far and away the greatest single alterer of the natural environment.

There are good campsites near the old cabin, and fishing in Buckeye Creek is good for rainbow and eastern brook (to 9″). *5th Hiking Day* (**Buckeye Forks** to **Buckeye Roadend**, 9.4 miles—15.1 km): From the cabin, the trail continues to descend steadily over alternating duff, sand and rock. On each side, gnawed and fallen aspen show the beaver's dietary prefer-ences, but despite this rodent's industrious efforts (some naturalists would say "because of it") the forest cover along the creek is dense, and it serves as a foraging grounds for all manner of birdlife, including flickers, chickadees, juncos, robins, Williamson's sapsuckers, hummingbirds and nuthatches.

As the canyon narrows between high, glacially polished granite walls, the trail enters the section known as The

Roughs. Here the sometimes swampy trail winds along the left bank of Buckeye Creek, overshadowed by sheer, rounded granite to the north and polished spires to the south. Good campsites can be found in The Roughs. The first one is one mile from the forks, and there is another ¼ mile farther. Then, ¼ beyond, we make a steep 200-yard ascent over black medasedimentary shale to a juniper-topped saddle and the boundary of the Hoover Wilderness. From just beyond the saddle views down Buckeye Canyon are spectacular. The lush grasslands of Big Meadow provide a soft counterpoint to the ruggedness of Flatiron and Buckeye ridges.

A few hundred steep yards down beyond the saddle, we ford the vigorous creek that drains the basin between Ink Rocks and Hanna Mountain, and the tumultuous sounds of the cascades above and below the ford furnish soul-satisfying background music for a fine rest stop. From this viewpoint the trail descends over a rocky, exposed slope on a long traverse to rejoin the trail shown on the topo map just upstream from the confluence of Buckeye Creek and the tributaries draining the slopes of Hunewill and Victoria peaks. This steady descent is the last of the precipitous terrain, and the remainder of the walk is over long, gradual slopes covered with sagebrush, mountain mahogany, bitterbrush and mule ears. Occasional clumps of aspen occur where the trail crosses a tributary or where it veers close to Buckeye Creek, and they provide welcome shade on a hot mid-summer afternoon. In these well-watered sections the traveler also encounters colorful clumps of monkey flower, goldenrod, lupine, shooting star, paintbrush and penstemon.

Big Meadow itself is a charming two-mile-long grassland replete with Belding ground squirrels and morning-feeding deer. At one time, around 1870, this meadow rang with the sounds of axes and the whirring of a sawmill blade. Here the Upper Hunewill mill operated to provide mining timber. Near the fence at the bottom of the meadow, the observant passerby can make out the signs of an abortive effort to construct a flume to carry water from Buckeye Creek to Bodie.

We pass through a gate in this fence and immediately head right, downhill, for the ford of Buckeye Creek, marked by two posts about 6 feet tall, about 30 yards downstream from the fence. This ford can be difficult in early season. From the creek our trail leads up a small ridge and then undulates over several more ridges, generally within sight of the stream. Beyond a viewpoint for seeing a beaverdam, the trail traverses along a hillside clothed by many head-high aspen trees and many flowers (in season), including scarlet gilia, with its red, trumpet-form blossoms. After crossing two little runoff rills, we can look through the trees down upon a large meadow, which we skirt on a level trail under aspen, juniper, red-fir and lodgepole-pine trees. About ½ mile farther we cross the tip of a tongue of that meadow, and an unmapped stream that flows late into the summer. Soon the trail becomes a two-track abandoned vehicle way, and we stroll through a sagebrush field squeezed between the lodgepole pines that border the creek and a large stand of aspen trees on the nose of a ridge that protrudes onto the canyon bottom.

The next section of trail passes through alternating green meadows and gray sagebrush fields, with constant good views of the towering north and south walls of Buckeye Canyon. Past one last, fairly large meadow we come to a fence with both a hiker's gate and a stock gate, where we begin the last mile of this 5-day journey under the shade of Jeffrey and ponderosa pines, red firs and quaking aspens. This last mile is a gentle downhill stroll that ends at a parking area just up-canyon from a Forest Service campground.

37   Twin Lakes to Peeler Lake

TRIP   From Twin Lakes to Peeler Lake (round trip). Topo map *Matterhorn Peak*. Best mid or late season; 16 miles (25.8 km).

Grade	Trail/layover days	Total recommended days
Leisurely	....	....
Moderate	2/1	3
Strenuous	....	....

HILITES   Despite a stiff 2500-foot climb, this trip makes a fine choice for the city-weary hiker with a "long weekender" trip-selection problem. An early start will allow the hiker to enjoy the morning freshness on the steeper uphill parts, and to be in camp soon enough for a pleasurable swim or some afternoon angling. Peeler Lake, as a destination, is a delightfully unique Sierra experience in that one camps literally on top of the mountain chain, for this lake pours its waters down both sides of the Sierra.

DESCRIPTION

1st Hiking Day (**Twin Lakes** to **Peeler Lake**, 8 miles—12.9 km): This trip begins in the Mono Village Campground at the west end of Twin Lakes. (There is a fee for parking on the private property here.) First, follow signs saying *Barney Lake* through the campground to find the wide, level, shaded trail. Travelers setting out in the fall season should take a few minutes at the outset for a side trip to view the colorful Kokanee salmon spawning in the shallows of Robinson Creek south of the campground.

Beyond the campground our sandy trail winds through a moderate-to-dense forest of Jeffrey pine, juniper, lodgepole pine, aspen and cottonwood along Robinson Creek. In late summer, cottony catkins from the cottonwood trees here litter the initial section of trail, leaving the ground surface the gray-white of spring snow. Crossing several small tributaries, the trail then ascends gently, and within ¾ mile encounters the first fir trees, but the forest cover soon gives way to a sagebrush-covered, gently sloping bench, from where one can see the great headwall of the valley in the west. As one makes his way up this open bench through thigh-high sagebrush, rabbitbrush, chamise and mule ears, one has unobstructed views of Victoria, Hunewill and Robinson peaks on the right, and some ragged teeth of the Sawtooth Ridge on the left. About halfway up this bench the trail passes a "ghost forest" of drowned trees caused by beaver dams downstream. Beavers still share this fine Sierra stream with us. On the right, somnolent marmots are likely to be seen dozing among piles of scree that flow from the feet of the avalanche chutes scarring Victoria Peak; on the left, the dramatic, unbroken granite wall of Blacksmith Peak at the top of Little Slide Canyon dominated the view. A sign here proclaims this area as part of the Hoover Wilderness. On the left, Robinson Creek becomes a willow-lined cascade that is frequently heard but seldom seen. About ½ mile into the wilderness, the ascent resolves into switchbacks that ford several small tributaries. In their moist banks one encounters monkey flower, monkshood, red columbine, swamp onion and shooting star scattered among clumps of bracken fern. Along the drier stretches of trail the severity of the rock is alleviated by colorful patches of Indian paintbrush, Mariposa lily, scarlet gilia, yarrow milfoil, whorled penstemon, pussy paws, streptanthus and goldenrod.

After the ascent levels out, the trail veers south, fords another tributary, and arrives at the outlet point of arrow-shaped Barney Lake. Anglers wishing an interlude of fair-to-good fishing for eastern brook and a rainbow trout will want to tarry around the deeper east and northeast shores of this 9-acre gem. The alternatives for the nonfisherman are equally attractive. He may elect to take a cool, quick dip, or merely to lie on the sandy beach and watch the play of the local water ouzels. (If you camp here, you must camp at least 200 feet from the lake.)

The remainder of the trail to the top of the watershed is not marked on the topo map, but is patently clear on the scene. This trail skirts the west side of the lake in a steady, long, hot ascent that takes one onto the canyon wall well above the "ghost forested" delta inlet of Barney Lake. Once above the wetter sections of the delta, the trail descends to a wildflower-decorated ford of Robinson Creek. Here amid the willows can be found lavendar swamp onion, red columbine, orange tiger lily and yellow monkey flower. The moderate forest cover now shows the transition to higher climes with the introduction of hemlock and some silver pine. About ¼ mile upstream the trail refords Robinson Creek, and after fording the outlet creek from Peeler Lake just above its confluence with Robinson Creek, it rises abruptly by steep, rocky switchbacks. Leveling off somewhat, it then comes to a bench junction with the Crown Lake Trail. This junction is ¼ mile northwest of Robinson Lakes (the two tiny lakes downstream from Crown Lake). Here our route turns right and ascends moderately for about ½ mile near the south outlet from Peeler Lake, and then steeply up the draw just northeast of the lake, to reach this outlet. Beautiful Peeler Lake (9500') sits astride the Sierra crest, contributing water to Robinson Creek on the east and Rancheria Creek on the west. Large (about 60 acres), it has abrupt, rocky shores, and the deep-blue color characteristic of deeper Sierra lakes. There are good-to-excellent campsites almost all around the lake, though some are within 200 feet of the lake, where camping is now forbidden. The best campsites lie on the east shore, reached by leaving the trail where it starts to descend to cross the south outlet. Fishing for eastern brook and rainbow trout (to 14") is sometimes good.
2nd Hiking Day: Retrace your steps, 8 miles (12.9 km).

Twin Lakes to Crown Lake 38

TRIP From Twin Lakes to Crown Lake (round trip). Topo map *Matterhorn Peak*. Best early, mid or late season; 16 miles (25.8 km).

Grade	Trail/layover days	Total recommended days
Leisurely	....	....
Moderate	2/1	3
Strenuous	....	....

HILITES Like the previous trip, this one entails considerable "up," but it is still a good two-day trip selection. This route follows Robinson Creek all the way to Crown Lake, and in its course exposes the traveler to some of the finest east-side scenery available anywhere along the Sierra. Crown Lake itself is set in the heart of the Sierra crest, and consonant with its name, it forms a royal diadem of blue in a regal setting of forest greens.

DESCRIPTION

1st Hiking Day (**Twin Lakes** to **Crown Lake**, 8 miles—12.9 km.): First follow Trip 37 to the junction of the Peeler and Crown Lake trails. From this junction our route leads south, undulating gently between large outcroppings of glacially polished granite. As the trail ascends moderately below Robinson Lakes (unlabeled on the topo map; they are the lakes downstream from Crown Lake) it winds through one near-pure stand of hemlock—unusual for this part of the Sierra. Robinson Lakes are two small, shallow, placid lakes with a sparse forest cover of lodgepole pine, silver pine and hemlock, separated by an isthmus. The trail rounds the south side of the larger Robinson Lake, fords Robinson Creek, and turns south on a steady ascent. Just below Crown Lake we reford the creek and then switchback up to the good campsites

(9500′) just downstream from the lake along the outlet, where there are excellent views of Kettle Peak and Crown Point. Fishing for rainbow and some eastern brook (to 9″) is fair. The fishery of Crown Lake is unusual in that it is one of the few Sierra lakes claimed by the Department of Fish and Game to be self-sustaining.

2nd Hiking Day: Retrace your steps, 8 miles (12.9 km.).

Sierra Crest over Crown Lake

Twin Lakes to Upper Piute Creek **39**

TRIP

From Twin Lakes to Campsites, Upper Piute Creek (round trip). Topo map *Matterhorn Peak*. Best mid or late season; 23 miles (37.1 km).

Grade	Trail/layover days	Total recommended days
Leisurely	....	....
Moderate	4/1	5
Strenuous	3/1	4

HILITES

This trip is a satisfying one for the hiker who has viewed the Sawtooth Ridge from the north side only. Following Robinson Creek nearly to the crest of the Sierra, this route circles the west end of the Sawtooth Ridge, and then drops down into the scenic upper reaches of Piute Creek. For those who appreciate spectacular mountain scenery of alpine character, this trip is a must.

DESCRIPTION (Moderate trip)

1st Hiking Day: Follow Trip 38 to **Crown Lake**, 8 miles (12.9 km).

2nd Hiking Day (**Crown Lake** to **Campsites, Upper Piute Creek,** 3.5 miles—5.6 km.): From Crown Lake's outlet the trail ascends along the west side, offering fine views of the meadowed inlet. The ascent soon steepens as the trail begins a series of short, rocky switchbacks that terminate just east of Crown Point, Here the trail levels out in a willowed meadowy area with several small lakelets, and meets the Snow Lake Trail just beyond. Our route turns left (south), fords the stream draining Snow Lake, and climbs over an easy talus-and-scree pile. This rocky ascent levels briefly within sight of another small lakelet; then the trail cuts across a bench and ascends steeply by rocky switchbacks. In most years there is a large snowbank across this slope well into summer, and one should exercise some caution here. After one more bench this ascent terminates at a tundra-topped saddle on the divide north of Slide Mountain. Here sparse whitebark pine and hemlock stoop to alpine climes, and the traveler taking a breather at this unnamed pass is likely to hear the scolding of a disturbed cony.

From this pass the trail stepladders down through a series of sandy tundra pockets, serpentining its way north and then east before beginning the long traverse down to Piute Creek. This traverse strikes timberline just below the cross-country turnoff to Ice and Maltby lakes, which is at the ford of the stream draining the swale that gives access to Ice Lake. Fishermen will find the excellent fishing for eastern brook in these two lakes worth the side trip. On the lodgepole and hemlock that line the trail, one will encounter the historic **T** blaze typical of the older trails in Yosemite National Park—a sign emblazoned on these trails by the U.S. Cavalry in the early part of the century, when it was their responsibility to patrol the Park.

This hiking day terminates at the campsites upstream from the signed turnoff to the cross-country route down Slide Canyon, located on Piute Creek (9600′) along the first ½ mile after the trail comes within sight of the creek. Fishing for eastern brook (to 8″) is fair. This location makes a fine base-camp location for exploratory trips down Slide Canyon or over into Matterhorn Canyon, and it is a traditional base camp for climbers making ascents of Matterhorn Peak and other climbs along the Sawtooth Ridge.

3rd and 4th Hiking Days: Retrace your steps, 11.5 miles (18.6 km.).

Switchbacks on Crown Lake Trail

Twin Lakes to Buckeye Creek   **40**

TRIP From Twin Lakes to Buckeye Roadend (shuttle trip via Peeler Lake and Buckeye Pass). Topo map *Matterhorn Peak*. Best mid or late season; 22.4 miles (36.0 km).

Grade	Trail/layover days	Total recommended days
Leisurely	4/1	5
Moderate	3/1	4
Strenuous	3/0	3

HILITES This circle trip around Buckeye Ridge visits nearly the entire gamut of Sierran ecology, from the sagebrush-scrub of the east side to the subalpine grassland of Kerrick Meadow. In between, it winds through pure stands of hemlock, past water-loving clumps of quaking aspen and amidst windblown, gnarled whitebark pine. In its ecological variety it is indeed an "everything trip for everyone."

DESCRIPTION (Moderate trip)

1st Hiking Day: Follow Trip 38 to **Peeler Lake**, 8.0 miles (12.9 km).

2nd Hiking Day (**Peeler Lake** to **Buckeye Forks**, 5.0 miles—8.0 km): From Peeler Lake the trail descends along the lake's west outlet, crossing and recrossing this outlet as it flows down into the marshy upper reaches of Rancheria Creek in Kerrick Meadow. In the meadow, we meet the Kerrick Canyon Trail, turn right (north) on it, and ascend a gentle slope above the north end of the meadow. A moderate forest cover of mostly pines lines the rest of the gently ascending sand-and-duff trail to the summit of Buckeye Pass. This pass (9580′) in a small, lodgepole-encroached meadow is on the Park boundary.

Then the duff trail drops down the northeast side of the pass, and soon fords the infant rill of Buckeye Creek. From here to the next ford, this descent skirts a series of charmingly meadowed steps on the northwest side of the creek. These pockets of grasslands have rich gardens of flowers whose full, splashy colors invite the passerby to linger and enjoy the aster, goldenrod, paintbrush, penstemon, shooting star, larkspur, lupine, buttercup, columbine and monkey flower. Owls hunt these meadows at night, and the daytime traveler should keep a lookout for large convoctions of agitated birdlife. At the core of such gatherings, frequently, is a large owl seeking protection in dense foliage.

The series of meadows terminates at a ford where the trail crosses to the east side of the creek. About ¼ mile beyond this ford is a snowcourse, and from it an unmaintained trail takes off over the ridge bound for Barney Lake. For the next ½ mile our trail continues to descend moderately through an area where the trees are much avalance-broken, and then we jump across an unnamed tributary that tumbles down from Hunewill Peak. In another ½ mile we reach the first of several fair and good campsites located at places where the trail periodically touches the stream. Then a steep descending section followed by two less steep inclines bring us to the flat where the North and South Forks of Buckeye Creek conjoin. In this quiet flat we cross the South Fork on a log and 200 yards farther on wade the North Fork. There are good campsites in the vicinity of a snow-survey cabin here, and the junction with the main east-west trail is just beyond. Fishing in the forks for rainbow and brook (to 9″) is good.

3rd Hiking Day: Follow the 5th hiking day, Trip 36, 9.4 miles (15.1 km).   (Just 1.1 miles down the road toward Bridgeport a side road goes south across Buckeye Creek, but if you go straight ahead 0.4 mile and then park in a used-looking area beside the road, you can walk a few yards downhill to Buckeye Hot Springs. Here, right beside the singing brook, you can soak away the trip's dirt in a natural hot spa.)

Twin Lakes to Kerrick Meadow

TRIP   From Twin Lakes to Kerrick Meadow (semiloop trip via Crown and Peeler lakes). Topo map *Matterhorn Peak*. Best mid or late season; 22.5 miles (36.3 km).

Grade	Trail/layover days	Total recommended days
Leisurely	5/1	6
Moderate	3/1	4
Strenuous	3/0	3

HILITES   To use a business metaphor, this trip gives a great return for a minimum investment. From the outset this route is enveloped in magnificent scenery. Along Robinson Creek, the skyline and the immediate surroundings are those of rugged grandeur, consonant with the physical expenditure of effort required on the uphill. As the trip circles Crown Point, it "levels out" both in physical terrain and in emotional impact. The ruggedness gives way to sweeping meadows and rounded summits, providing the traveler an opportunity to absorb some of the impact of this land of contrasts.

DESCRIPTION (Moderate trip)

1st Hiking Day: Follow Trip 38 to **Crown Lake**, 8 miles (12.9 km).

2nd Hiking Day (**Crown Lake** to **Peeler Lake**, 6.5 miles—10.5 km): Rounding the rocky west side of Crown Lake, the trail rises out of the lake basin by steep, rocky switchbacks that offer fine views back of the clear blue lake. This ascent levels out as it crosses a granite-flanked saddle and meets the Rock Island Pass Trail just west of a lakelet in a sandy-meadowed section, with several small lakelets and tarns hidden in willows near the trail. Our route turns right (southwest) and begins a long, steadily traversing climb toward Snow Lake. This traverse gives way to switchbacks midway up the hill, and jogs southwest under Crown Point before resuming its southward course on more switchbacks by a little stream. Looking back from the top of this climb, we have fine views to the east of the soldier-tipped summit of Kettle Peak and the west end of the Sawtooth Ridge (called Blacksmith Peak). Snow Lake itself, like Peeler Lake to the north, is a crestal lake perched atop a divide, but in angling circles it is best known for its fishery of golden trout. As the trail rounds the rocky north edge of the lake, we see the meadowy lake fringes, which are most extensive at the southwest end. Here the meadows extend from the lake's edge to the low-profiled saddle called Rock Island Pass (10,150'), a few hundred yards southwest of the lake.

From Rock Island Pass the trail descends into the Rancheria Creek drainage. The descent witnesses a change from sparse whitebark pine to a conglomerate forest of lodgepole, hemlock and silver pine. After traversing above a sandy meadow, the T-blazed trail here rises sharply over a sandy ridge and then drops moderately on switchbacks through dense forest cover to Kerrick Meadow and a ford of Rancheria Creek.

On the northwest side of the ford, the trail meets the Kerrick Canyon Trail, where our route turns right and ascends gently up Kerrick Meadow. Rancheria Creek winds its oxbowing way through these sandy grasslands, and on the right we can see large crestal sand accumulations indicating where the living stream has moved across the meadow floor, leaving its spoor. The meadow bottlenecks briefly into a canyon narrows, where the creek tumbles over a silver cascade, and then opens into a beautiful, open, wetter section near the headwaters. In the middle of this marshy section the trail fords one arm of the creek, and then continues on to meet the unsigned Peeler Lake Trail at the meadow's head, where our route turns right (east). From this junction the trail crosses the open meadow and winds through a broken, moderate forest cover of lodgepole. This route crisscrosses back and forth over the west outlet stream from Peeler Lake and arrives at the good campsites along the west shore of this large and beautiful lake (9500'). These campsites offer fine views to the east of Cirque Mountain, Kettle Peak and Crown Point, and the deep waters near the west shore offer fine bank fishing for eastern brook and rainbow (to 14").

3rd Hiking Day: Reverse the steps of the 1st hiking day, Trip 37, 8 miles (12.9 km).

Twin Lakes to Hetch Hetchy   **42**

TRIP From Twin Lakes to O'Shaughnessy Dam via Bear Valley (shuttle trip). Topo maps *Matterhorn Peak, Tower Peak, Hetch Hetchy Reservoir.* Best mid or late season; 43.8 miles (70.7 km).

Grade	Trail/layover days	Total recommended days
Leisurely	8/2	10
Moderate	6/1	7
Strenuous	5/0	5

HILITES This trip passes through the heart of the largest roadless area in the lower 48. After crossing the crest on the northern boundary of Yosemite, this route takes in a very large part of the Park before ending near its western boundary, 5700 feet lower. Few trans-Sierra crossings are less traveled or more scenic.

DESCRIPTION (Moderate trip)

1st Hiking Day: Follow Trip 37 to **Peeler Lake,** 8 miles (12.9 km).

2nd Hiking Day (**Peeler Lake** to **Arndt Lake,** 5 miles—8.1 km): Leaving Peeler Lake beside the west outlet, the trail drops down gently as it crosses back and forth over the outlet stream. This descent soon leaves the moderate forest cover and enters the north edge of Kerrick Meadow. At the head of this open, rank grassland the trail meets the Buckeye Pass Trail, where our route turns left (south) and begins a long, gentle descent. The trail on the west side of twisting Rancheria Creek is a narrow, sandy track lined with a wildflower collage of shooting star, penstemon, paintbrush, aster, goldenrod, buttercup, lupine, Douglas phlox, and pussy paws. In a timber-lined bottleneck, the meadows narrow briefly and then reopen. On the left one can see sand banks that were stranded when the oxbowing stream altered course sometime in the geologic past. The broad grasslands are alive with the scurrying and piping of alarmed Belding ground squirrels.

The trail then passes the Rock Island Pass Trail and continues to descend to a second timbered narrows. This brief stretch of lodgepole pine opens to yet another long meadow that is flanked on the southwest by the granite heights of Price Peak. On the descent through this meadow the canyon starts to narrow, and where the trail starts a gentle 200-yard ascent, our route leaves the trail.

Our short cross-country segment strikes out southward, fords Rancheria Creek, and ascends beside the tundra-lined outlet of Arndt Lake. A good route to the north shore of hidden Arndt Lake is via the saddle in the granite just east of where the outlet leaves the lake.

One will find good campsites at the outlet and around the north shore of Arndt Lake (9240'). Those with a tolerance for cool mountain water will enjoy the swimming off the granite that drops into this lake. Views of the polished granite domes flanking the south and east sides of the lake are soul-satisfying, and beckon the explorer to further investigation and discovery.

3rd Hiking Day (**Arndt Lake** to **Bear Valley Lake,** 7 miles— 11.3 km): From Arndt Lake our route retraces the cross-country segment of the previous hiking day to the Kerrick Canyon Trail, and then continues down through a narrow, rocky canyon. The unseamed white granite canyon walls in this narrows show the glacial polish, smoothing and sculpting that reflect the geologic history of the canyon. Rancheria Creek on the left bumps and splashes down through a series of fine potholes offering swimming and fishing spots. Like all the older trails in the Park, this one is **T**-blazed, indicating that it was once a U.S. Cavalry patrol route—a route blazed when the Army was responsible for the integrity of the Park lands.

The sparse-to-moderate forest cover of whitebark, hemlock and lodgepole pine in the narrows gives way to another meadow as the trail continues to descend. This meadow is surrounded by several magnificent examples of glacial domes—all unnamed. The clean, sweeping lines of the dome to the west are particularly impressive, and the passerby cannot help but feel the awesome power of the natural forces that created it. Near the foot of the meadow, the trail fords to the east side of Rancheria Creek, where it hugs the sheer, water-stained granite wall. Both the trail and the creek make an exaggerated **Z** before straightening out on a westward course and reaching the Pacific Crest Trail. Beyond this junction, our route begins a steep switchbacking ascent up the south wall of Kerrick Canyon. Winding back and forth through a moderate forest cover of lodgepole pine, silver pine and hemlock, the trail near the top affords superlative views to the north and northeast.

A short distance beyond the lip of Kerrick canyon we come to Bear Valley Lake (9200'). There are excellent campsites near the outlet of this beautiful lake. Though fishless, this lake warms up enough by mid-summer to provide excellent swimming. Notwithstanding its name, Bear Valley has few bears. Of course it only takes one to eat your food, so, even in this remote spot it is best to store your supplies properly.

4th Hiking Day (**Bear Valley Lake** to **Pleasant Valley,** 5.5 miles—8.9 km): From Bear Valley Lake our trail crosses the outlet and descends a canyon to the southwest. After a short descent we cross the creek and turn south, passing a small lake. Beyond the lake we climb over a low moraine and descend to a meadow, signed BEAR VALLEY ELEV. 9400' To the south is a saddle 700 feet above, to which we shall climb. After skirting this meadow on either side, we pick up the trail again and wind up through willow thickets, crossing a small, overgrown stream. Our trail, often muddy in places, is well appointed with wildflowers, including Sierra gentian, lupine and shooting star. Soon the ground becomes drier as we pass a grove of large hemlocks before the last, steep 200 feet to the saddle. From here we can look north over the heavily glaciated granitic landscape of northern Yosemite. To the south is a gently sloping valley that has seen glaciation only in the distant past, if at all. Much of our route to Rancheria Creek will now be through an island of forested, unglaciated upland, on Rancheria Mountain. We follow the faint, ducked trail, descending gently along an open grus-covered hillside above a small creek. Soon we swing south, drop down a sagebrush-covered hill and cross that creek. You may notice sharp boundaries between vegetation types by the creek. This indicates porous soil that drains very well, and grabbing a handful reveals mostly grus—granules of weathered granite. Such an accumulation could not develop here without a very prolonged absence of glaciation.

Beyond the creek we descend a hillside covered with tall wheatgrass and reach another small creek. Now we enter dense forest, and a short descent brings us to a wet, meadowy flat, beyond which we cross an indistinct moraine. After another short descent we arrive at a small, marshy lake. If you want to avoid the 1200-foot descent into and the return climb out of Pleasant Valley, you can camp at this mosquito haven. The sojourn would not be without its rewards, as the lake may contain mallards when you're there and the surrounding forest supports juncos, chickarees and deer. From the lake we descend past an aspen flat to a broad, red-fir-covered saddle, where we meet the trail to Pleasant Valley. Turning south onto it, we descend gently and then steeply, as the trail winds down the side of Piute Creek canyon. Emerging from timber, we get good views up-canyon toward Sawtooth Ridge, while below us we can see some of the lakes around Pleasant Valley. To the south is the chasm of the Grand Canyon of the Tuolumne, flanked by Double Rock and Colby Mountain. The grade eases until we enter a gully and descend it to the forested floor of Pleasant Valley (6850'). Good campsites can be found along Piute Creek, and both the nearby lakes and the creek provide good fishing for rainbow trout.

5th Hiking Day (**Pleasant Valley** to **Rancheria Creek,** 11.8 miles—19 km): Though this day begins with an 1800-foot climb, the remainder is a 4000-foot descent of Rancheria Mountain to Rancheria Creek. First retrace your steps of the previous hiking day to the junction with the trail to Hetch Hetchy. Turning left, we ascend the dry slopes of Rancheria Mountain and gain its broad ridge. From the top of this ascent you can climb up volcanic talus to the left and enjoy the wonderful views from the actual summit of Rancheria Mountain. From there you can see Sawtooth Ridge, Piute Creek canyon, Mt. Dana, the Tuolumne River canyon and the Cathedral Range. Heading southwest, we descend gently through open forest of silver pine and red fir, cross a dry hillside, and enter the lush meadows around the headwaters of an unnamed creek. Among the lodgepole pines along the creek are Bigelow sneezeweed, yarrow milfoil and elephant heads. Beyond the creek we cross over a low, dry hill that is covered with pussy paws and laced with gopher holes. Then we swing near a small creek, descend an eroded stretch of trail, and arrive at a campsite by the creek we crossed earlier. This may be the last water before Rancheria Creek, and it is a lovely spot to tank up before the upcoming 3000-foot descent.

Past the creek, the forest cover changes in response to lower elevation; we leave lodgepole pine behind and enter a white fir forest. After a series of switchbacks the grade eases as we pass through an alder thicket and enter drier environs inhabited by a sparse forest of Jeffrey pine, incense-cedar, sugar pine and white fir. Drought-tolerant ceanothus and manzanita dot the hillside between trees as we descend past a seasonal stream and climb over the east shoulder of LeConte Point. The last 1400-foot descent to Rancheria Creek begins gently, and we get our first views of Hetch Hetchy Reservoir and Kolana Rock. Soon we begin a long series of switchbacks, where we see large numbers of black oak and perhaps a few of its associate, the California gray squirrel. When we arrive at the gorge above Rancheria Falls, we may or may not find a bridge across the creek. If there is no serviceable bridge, then crossing the creek *above the falls* can be extremely difficult and dangerous except during very low water. Beyond the creek we descend a rocky hillside past the trail to Tiltill Valley, and after ⅓ mile the trail levels off in a forested flat. Here we turn left onto a spur trail and walk over to the shaded creekside camping area below Rancheria Falls. Both bears and people frequent this area, so tend your supplies accordingly.

6th Hiking Day: Reverse the steps of the 1st hiking day, Trip 48, 6.5 miles (10.5 km).

43 Twin Lakes to Benson Lake

TRIP From Twin Lakes to Benson Lake (round trip). Topo maps *Matterhorn Peak, Tower Peak*. Best mid or late season; 37.2 miles (59.8 km).

Grade	Trail/layover days	Total recom- mended days
Leisurely	9/3	12
Moderate	6/3	9
Strenuous	4/2	6

HILITES This long trip penetrates to the heart of the North Boundary Country. In its course it surmounts the Sierra crest and traces a westside watershed to the Shangri-la basin of Benson Lake. Because of its moderate climes and its remote location, this lake is a favorite layover spot for parties traversing the Pacific Crest Trail, and its popularity is well founded.

DESCRIPTION (Moderate trip)

1st and 2nd Hiking Days: Follow Trip 42 to **Arndt Lake**, 13 miles (21 km).

3rd Hiking Day (**Arndt Lake** to **Benson Lake,** 5.6 miles—9 km): Proceed to the Kerrick Canyon Trail junction as described in the third hiking day, Trip 42. At this junction our route turns left (south) and ascends steadily by switchbacks through a moderate forest cover of hemlock. At the top of the first rise Piute Mountain comes into sight, and the trail levels briefly as it wends past a tiny snowmelt tarn. The trail then resumes climbing steeply through an increasingly sparse forest cover of lodgepole, hemlock and silver pine to Seavey Pass (9150').

From the glacially polished granite setting of Seavey Pass the trail drops past another stately rockbound tarn just below the pass, and finally plummets down over steep, eroded pitches alongside a riotous unnamed stream that feeds the Benson Lake alluvial fan. This descent is rocky going, requiring a "grunt and bear it" attitude of the downhill-weary traveler, alleviated only by the fine views of Volunteer Peak across Piute Creek and of the splashing waterfall springing from the ridge south of Piute Mountain.

Where the trail levels out on the valley floor, it crosses the sandy alluvial sediments, and witnesses some drastic changes in the flora. The initial contact with the valley floor, with its solitary-standing specimens of Jeffrey pine towering amid gooseberry, gives the traveler the impression of sandy aridity. But within a few yards, the atmosphere changes as the trail becomes immersed in bracken fern, overflow freshets and dense forest. The trail is sometimes difficult to follow because of the rank growth and quagmire conditions of the valley floor. Two trails cut through this fertile area to Benson Lake. One, unmarked, turns right just after you enter the valley floor. The other departs just before the ford of Piute Creek. This lateral winds along the northwest bank of Piute Creek through fields of corn lily and bracken fern, with occasional clumps of tiger lily and swamp onion, to the good campsites along the east shore of the lake (7600'). Fishermen can look forward to good fishing for rainbow and eastern brook trout (to 14"). Except in mosquito season, this lake makes a fine spot for a layover day.

4th, 5th and 6th Hiking Days: Retrace your steps, 18.6 miles (29.9 km).

Benson Lake

44 Twin Lakes to Smedberg Lake

TRIP From Twin Lakes to Smedberg Lake (semiloop trip via Peeler Lake, Arndt Lake, Benson Lake, Smedberg Lake, Matterhorn Canyon and Burro Pass). Topo maps *Matterhorn Peak, Tower Peak*. Best mid or late season; 49.6 miles (79.8 km).

Grade	Trail/layover days	Total recommended days
Leisurely	11/3	14
Moderate	8/3	11
Strenuous	5/2	7

HILITES Making a grand loop through the center of the North Boundary Country, this trip traces three major watersheds, visits six major lakes, and views the finest scenery in the region. Layover days taken on this long route provide the opportunity of visiting any of the nearby lakes, over a dozen, or making side trips into any one of several other watersheds. It is a long trip with many stiff climbs that make it advisable for the hiker to first prepare himself by taking one or more shorter trips.

DESCRIPTION (Moderate trip)

1st, 2nd and 3rd Hiking Days: Follow Trip 43 to **Benson Lake**, 18.6 miles (29.9 km).

4th Hiking Day (**Benson Lake** to **Smedberg Lake**, 4.5 miles—7.2 km): There is an old saying among those who have visited Benson Lake, "Everywhere from that hole in the ground is up," and one contemplating this hiking day must agree. Retracing our steps over the short lateral to the main trail, the route then fords Piute Creek and begins a long, steep climb through a moderate forest cover of lodgepole laced with occasional silver pine. Criss-crossing back and forth over the outlet stream from Smedberg Lake, the trail then circles beneath the steep west facade of Volunteer Peak, and finally crosses over the shoulder of this peak past the first of two trail junctions to Pate Valley. On the north side of Volunteer Peak the trail drops to the south shore of Smedberg Lake (9220'), where excellent campsites may be found all along the south shore and along the southeast inlet about 200 yards from the lake. Fishing for rainbow and occasional eastern brook (to 13") is excellent. As a layover point this picturesque, island-dotted lake makes a fine central location for excursions to nearby Surprise and Sister Lakes.

5th Hiking Day (**Smedberg Lake** to **Matterhorn Canyon,** 6.5 miles—10.5 km): From the narrow valley holding Smedberg Lake, the trail is a steady climb to Benson Pass. It first follows up an inlet of Smedberg Lake on a southeast, meadowed course, then swings east on a stepladdering climb through moderate, then sparse, forest cover to an upper meadow above the main drainage feeding Smedberg Lake. After this brief respite the trail resumes its steep, rocky, upward course to Benson Pass (10,139'). The last climb is over a heavily eroded surface through sparse whitebark pine and hemlock. Excellent views to the northeast present themselves at the pass, and one can see Whorl Mountain, Twin Peaks, some of the pinnacles making up the Sawtooth Ridge, and the granite divide between Matterhorn Creek and Piute Creek.

The trail leaves Benson Pass on a descent that is steep, level and steep again as it drops to Wilson Canyon. Then the downgrade is gradual along the banks of Wilson Creek to the lip of Matterhorn Canyon. In this section the trail winds back and forth over Wilson Creek through an increasingly dense forest cover of lodgepole, with occasional whitebark pine near the top and silver pine near the bottom. Finally, the path is steep again to the floor of Matterhorn Canyon. On the canyon floor, Matterhorn Canyon Creek is a meandering stream flowing alternately through willowed meadows and stands of lodgepole mixed with silver pine. Our trail turns north and follows the stream a mile, then fords it to several campsites 200 yards downstream from the junction with the trail to Tuolumne Meadows. These canyon campsites (8480') boast several fine swimming holes just upstream in granite potholes. Fishing for eastern brook and rainbow trout (to 12") is good.

6th Hiking Day (**Matterhorn Canyon** to **Campsites, Upper Piute**

Creek, 8.5 miles—13.7 km): From these campsites our route goes northeast and leaves the Pacific Crest Trail behind. The route ascends moderately through alternately sandy and rocky sections. On both sides of the canyon, glaciated gray granite shoulders drop to the valley floor, and the black water-staining on their broad surfaces, particularly on Quarry Peak, makes eerie configurations. In a wet, muddy section where the trail fords several small tributary runoffs, it winds through wildflower displays that include false Solomon's seal, lupine, elephant heads, monkey flower, paintbrush, goldenrod, aster, fleabane, buckwheat and Mariposa lily. The trail then fords to the west side of Matterhorn Canyon Creek and then refords to follow the east bank through the latter part of the canyon narrows and well beyond. About ½ mile above a meadow it refords back to the west side.

From this ford the trail keeps to the west side of the creek, winding through meadow and tundra sections on a moderate ascent. Ahead, the pointed tops of Finger Peaks come into view, and later the massive granite of Whorl Mountain and Matterhorn Peak. Scattered lodgepole and hemlock trees dot the trail as it progresses up to the sky-parlor meadows of the upper basin. Some clumps of trees hold campsites (their protected location is testimony to the wind that often sweeps through the canyon), and the tree clumps are interspersed with stretches of grassland laced with sagebrush and willow.

The trail passes the last stand of trees, and ascends steadily on a long traverse below Finger Peaks. Views, across the barren upper basin, of Whorl Mountain are awesome, and its rugged massiveness contrasts sharply with the delicate wildflowers found underfoot as one nears Burro Pass. Here, scattered among sparse whitebark pines, one enjoys the spots of color provided by primrose, scarlet penstemon, wallflower and Douglas phlox. The final climb to the divide is accomplished via rocky switchbacks that terminate on the low saddle of Burro Pass (10,560'). Fine views of both the Matterhorn and Piute Creek canyons are to be had, but overshadowing all are the soldier-topped summits of the Sawtooth Ridge to the north.

The first recorded crossing of this pass was made by Lt. N. F. McClure in 1894. Today's traveler can compare his observations of the pass and its surroundings with those of McClure, who said, "The route now led for five miles through little meadows on each side of the stream, until a comparatively low saddle was seen to the left of us and near the head of the canyon. Investigating this, I found it was a natural pass. The scenery here was truly sublime. I doubt if any part of the main chain of the Sierras presents a greater ruggedness . . ."

As the trail descends on the north side of the pass, it affords fine views of the tiny, barren lakes at the foot of Finger Peaks. The basin of the pass is usually wet, and sometimes covered with snow, thereby making route-picking an instinctive matter. Here Piute Creek is a far cry from what was seen two hiking days ago. A mere stripling of a stream, it tinkles through meadow grass, and the traveler fords to the north side by an easy step. Belding squirrels pipe one's passage through the grassy tundra stretches, and the call of marmots on the nearby scree is a cacophonous accompaniment to the gentle descent into the moderate forest cover of lodgepole and hemlock. This hiking day ends at the good campsites (9600') found along that stretch of Piute Creek where the trail touches the creek banks northeast of Finger Peaks. Here fishing for eastern brook (to 8") is fair.

7th and 8th Hiking Days: Reverse the steps of Trip 39, 11.5 miles (18.5 km).

Up the Robinson Creek Trail

45   Green Creek to East Lake

TRIP   From Green Creek Roadend to East Lake (round trip). Topo map *Matterhorn Peak*. Best early, mid or late season; 7 miles (11.2 km).

Grade	Trail/layover days	Total recommended days
Leisurely	2/0	2
Moderate	....	....
Strenuous	....	....

HILITES   This is a fine beginner's weekend hike. East Lake offers one of the most colorful backdrops for a camping scene to be found in any wilderness. The trilogy of Gabbro, Page and Epidote peaks is composed of rocks varying in hue from vermilion reds to ochre, and these colors are set in metavolcanic blacks for contrast. Nearby Nutter, Gilman and Hoover lakes offer good fishing to supplement the angling in East Lake, and the general spectrum of scenery along the trail rounds out a rich diet indeed.

DESCRIPTION

1st Hiking Day (**Green Creek Roadend** to **East Lake**, 3.5 miles—5.6 km): The trailhead is just beyond the Green Lakes Pack Station at road's end. Amid moderate-to-dense Jeffrey, juniper, lodgepole and aspen forest cover, the trail ascends gently to a small step-across spring runoff. A ground cover of sagebrush, mule ears, serviceberry, western blueberry, wild lilac, lupine, wallflower, paintbrush, pennyroyal and buckwheat lines the trail in the initial drier stretches, and along the wetter spots one finds tiger lily, penstemon, shooting star, monkshood, monkey flower, columbine, rein-orchid and aster. The ascent then becomes steeper as it crosses an easy rocky ridge, and finally it begins a long series of steady switchbacks.

Crossing several intermittent runoff tributaries coming

down from Monument Ridge, the trail keeps to the northwest side of West Fork Green Creek. While the creek itself is never out of hearing, it is often obscured visually by the sheath of willows that line its bank. Ahead, on the left, one can make out Gabbro Peak, and on the right the stream that falls from the hanging valley containing West Lake. Added to the wildflowers to be seen along the trail here are iris, corn lily, cow parsnip, stickseed, gooseberry, Douglas phlox and pussy paws.

The trail then climbs another dry slope by moderately ascending switchbacks to a junction just before Green Lake where the right fork leads to campsites on Green Lake and to West Lake. Anglers may wish to tarry here for the good fishing for rainbow and eastern brook (to 14″). Green Lake is large (about 50 acres), with a rocky west shore and a steep southeast shore. A mixed timber cover of lodgepole, hemlock and occasional silver pine surrounds most of the lake except for the meadowed inlet delta.

Our route, the left fork, fords West Fork Green Creek just below the lake and makes a long dogleg to the south before turning east to ford the outlet stream from East Lake. This outlet stream is a vigorous watercourse that follows the natural ravine shown on the topo map just north of East Lake. The trail makes a long loop away from the stream and then veers back to a second ford. The ascent is sometimes steep as it continues on to the meadowed outlet of East Lake. Fair-to-good campsites (9440′) can be found around the outlet just below the flood-control dam, and on the north shore. Fishing for rainbow trout on this 75-acre lake is good. This lake makes a fine base-camp location for forays to nearby Nutter, Gilman and Hoover lakes.

2nd Hiking Day: Retrace your steps, 3.5 miles (5.6 km).

46 Green Creek to Tuolumne Meadows

TRIP From Green Creek Roadend to Tuolumne Meadows (shuttle trip). Topo maps *Matterhorn Peak, Tuolumne Meadows.* Best mid or late season; 26.2 miles (42.2 km).

Grade	Trail/layover days	Total recommended days
Leisurely	4/1	5
Moderate	4/0	4
Strenuous	3/0	3

HILITES Three quarters of this scenic route travels remote sections of Yosemite National Park that are not frequented by day walkers. The solitude-seeker will find the quiet of upper Virginia Canyon to his liking, and the fisherman wanting a variety of lake and stream fishing for rainbow and eastern brook will pronounce this trip ideal.

DESCRIPTION (Moderate trip)

1st Hiking Day: Follow Trip 45 to **East Lake**, 3.5 miles (5.6 km).
2nd Hiking Day (**East Lake** to **Lower Virginia Canyon**, 9 miles—14.5 km): From the outlet of East Lake the trail ascends above the lake's waters as it rounds the east shore, affording superlative views of Gabbro, Page and Epidote peaks foregrounded by the deep blue of East Lake. The trail drops briefly across the gentle ridge separating East Lake from the tiny lakelets to the east, and then veers away from East Lake on an ascending traverse before descending gently to the meadow-fringed shores of Nutter Lake. Through a sparse forest cover of lodgepole and hemlock, the trail then climbs above the west shore of beautiful Gilman Lake, passing a lateral trail down to it. Flanked by the steep west face of

Dunderberg Peak, and foregrounded by a meadow and timber cover, this lake is a favorite of photographers. Fishermen may also wish to linger—the better to sample the good fishing for rainbow.

From the Gilman Lake lateral our trail ascends past several small tarns, fords the stream joining Gilman and Hoover lakes, and then rises steeply to the bench holding Hoover Lakes. These two alpine lakes are set between the dark rock of Epidote Peak and the burgundy-red rock of the magnificent unnamed mountain to the southeast (see cover photo). They are considerably colder than the lakes below, and they have been planted with eastern brook trout. The trail skirts the southeast side of the first, fords the stream between them, and passes by the northwest side of the second. After fording the inlet, it ascends steeply along the stream joining Hoover Lakes with Summit Lake. This rocky ascent through a thinning forest cover of lodgepole and occasional hemlock and whitebark pine meets the unsigned Virginia Lakes Trail on a small bench, where our route turns right (northwest). This moderate ascent fords the aforementioned stream and arrives at aptly named Summit Lake (10,160′). Like Peeler Lake to the north, Summit Lake contributes water to both sides of the Sierra. It sits atop the crest in a **V**′d notch between the dark rock of Camiaca Peak and a lighter ridge extending north from Excelsior Mountain.

The trail skirts the north side of Summit Lake to the Sierra crest and then switchbacks steeply down the west slope. Looking back toward Summit Lake, we can see clearly that the glaciers which had their beginnings below Camiaca Peak on both the east and the west sides met at the present site of Summit Lake. Across the cirque basin of upper Virginia Canyon, the rounded eminence of Grey Butte and the sharply nippled tops of Virginia Peak and Stanton Peak dominate the views to the west. The descent levels out before it fords Return Creek and continues down-canyon. Recent avalanches have made obvious incursions into the sparse forest cover of lodgepole, aspen and occasional red fir and hemlock, and have left broken stubs on every hand.

The trail then fords several tributary streams as it keeps to the west side of Return Creek on a long, moderate descent to a junction with the Pacific Crest Trail. At this junction our route turns left, fords Return Creek, and arrives at some good campsites (8600′) in the granite ledge system on the east side of the creek. Fishing for eastern brook and rainbow is fair to good.

3rd Hiking Day (**Lower Virginia Canyon** to **Glen Aulin**, 8 miles—12.9 km): The trail from the campsites near the ford continues southwest along the banks of Return Creek and fords McCabe Creek before beginning the steep ascent of the canyon wall. This gentle descent along Return Creek passes the stream's beautiful bedrock-granite cascades. Dropping into deep, clear potholes, the creek has carved and sculpted the bedrock into smooth, mollescent lines that invite the traveler to run his hands across them. Columbine clustered amid lupine and whorled penstemon add color to the green mats of swamp onion and gooseberry near the ford. (In late season fill your canteen at McCabe Creek, for there is no more water until Glen Aulin.) Beyond this ford the trail begins long switchbacks across a slope moderately forested with fine specimens of silver pine, lodgepole and occasional red fir. These rocky switchbacks terminate at the McCabe Lake Trail junction, where our route turns right and descends gently over a duff surface. Birdlife abounds through the moderate-to-dense forest cover of red fir, lodgepole and silver pine, and the hiker is very likely to see chicadees, juncos, warblers, flycatchers, woodpeckers, bluebirds, robins and evening grosbeaks in these precincts.

A short ¾ mile beyond the last junction, close under Point 9186, you may find water even in late season. Then your route declines gently through cool, moist forest to a fairly large meadow east of Elbow Hill. After threading a course through a few stands of pines, you emerge in an even larger meadow—about 2 miles long, although the trail does not trace all 2 miles of it. At a stream fork shortly beyond a *very* large boulder to your west, you may find water even in late season. Then the trail climbs over a saddle in a low, forested ridge and gently descends for about ½ mile. Over the next mile, always near Cold Canyon creek, the level, rutted path passes many possible campsites in pleasant meadowy areas studded with small lodgepole pines.

From this camping region a series of easy switchbacks accomplish about half the descent to the Tuolumne River, and where the trail re-reaches the creek there is another good campsite. On the final rocky downhill mile to the river, you catch glimpses of Tuolumne Falls and White Cascade, and their roar carries all the way across the canyon.

Finally, you reach "civilization" at the Glen Aulin High Sierra Camp. Within sight of the camp you pass the Tuolumne River Trail westbound, and in 15 yards come to the little spur trail that crosses Conness Creek on a bridge to the camp. Very meager supplies are sometimes available here. The backpacker campsites just upstream from the "lodge" are very popular with bears, and you would be less likely to have ursine visitors at one of the campsites a mile or two before you reach Glen Aulin—though it would be no guarantee.

4th Hiking Day (**Glen Aulin** to **Tuolumne Meadows,** 5.7 miles— 9.2 km).

From Glen Aulin the trail crosses the Tuolumne River on a low steel bridge, from which one has excellent views of White Cascade and the deep green pool below it. In a few minutes we reach the May Lake Trail, ascending west, and continue our steep climb to gain the height of White Cascade and Tuolumne Falls. The trail passes a fine viewpoint below the falls, and if the light is right, you'll get a great photograph. Above the falls, the river flows down a series of sparkling rapids separated by large pools and wide sheets of clear water spread out over slightly inclined granite slopes.

Soon the trail crosses the river for the last time, on a boulders-and-steel bridge, and then climbs a little way above the gorge the river has cut here. Across the stream one can easily make out basaltic "Little Devils Postpile," the only volcanic formation anywhere around here. Then we descend to larger, polished slabs near the river, and follow a somewhat ducked route across them for about a mile beside the beckoning waters. When trail tread resumes, we soon cross the three branches of Dingley Creek, which may be dry in late season, and stroll along a "levee" built to raise the trailbed above the flood level here. About ½ mile of almost level walking in cool forest brings the long-distance trekker to the Young Lakes Trail junction, and then he touches the northwest edge of his destination, Tuolumne Meadows. Soon after, we cross three branches of Delaney Creek, the last being the only one of consequence. Just beyond this ford, a trail veers left, bound for the Tuolumne Meadows Stables. We instead veer right and ascend a long, dry, sandy ridge. From the tiny reeded lakes on top of this ridge, the trail drops gently down through meadowed pockets and stands of lodgepole pine to Soda Springs, once a drive-in and then a walk-in campground, but since 1976 closed to camping.

From the effervescent springs, in their dilapidated enclosure, the trail follows a closed-off dirt road east above the north edge of Tuolumne Meadows, the largest subalpine meadow in the Sierra Nevada. The spiring summits of the Cathedral Range across the meadow provide challenging vistas as we stroll the last, level ¾ mile to a parking lot beside State Highway 120, the Tioga Road.

47 Green Creek to Virginia Lakes

TRIP   From Green Creek Roadend to Virginia Lakes
              Campground (shuttle trip). Topo map *Matterhorn
              Peak*. Best mid or late season; 10 miles (16.1 km).

| | Trail/layover | Total recom- |
Grade	days	mended days
Leisurely	2/1	3
Moderate	2/0	2
Strenuous	....	....

HILITES This **U**-shaped trip circles around Kavanaugh
             Ridge and Dunderberg Peak, and in its passage
             touches 14 alpine and subalpine lakes. Scenery
             along this route is mostly of the open alpine
             variety, and the route is a fine sampling of the
             majestic Sierra crest. For the beginner or for the
             experienced back-country traveler, this trip is an
             excellent choice for a weekend excursion.

DESCRIPTION

1st Hiking Day: Follow Trip 45 to **East Lake**, 3.5 miles (5.6 km).

2nd Hiking Day (**East Lake** to **Virginia Lakes Campground**, 6.5
miles—10.5 km): Proceed to the Virginia Lakes Trail junction
as described in the 2nd hiking day, Trip 46. At this junction
our trail turns left (southeast) and climbs steeply up a series of
switchbacks that overlook the Hoover Lakes in the valley of
East Creek below. Beyond these zigzags we reach a sloping,
willowed bowl surrounded by many snowbanks into late season. Then, under a small red cliff, the trail switchbacks up
again, to cross the northern of the two streams in this two-
headed canyon. Again the way steepens, and at frequent rest
stops you can see the small white petals of Douglas phlox and
the purple trumpetforms of Davidson's penstemon. There are

even a few specimens of a yellow flower hardly ever found below 10,000 feet: alpine gold. Finally we cross the divide at 11,000 feet, where the red rocks of the crest on our right contrast with the somber dark grays of Black Mountain straight ahead.

The trail ahead has been altered slightly from that shown on the topo map, now being located farther south where it drops down the tundra steps of Frog Lakes. In Frog Lakes and in the willowed stream between them, anglers will find fair fishing for eastern brook and rainbow trout. Just north of Cooney Lake the new trail and that shown on the topo map once more coincide. This lake, with its willowed inlet and its precipitous outlet, contains thriving populations of eastern brook and rainbow.

Continuing the moderate descent over a rocky ledge system, the trail winds down through sparse clumps of whitebark pine past a mining claim, and then fords the willowed outlet stream of Moat Lake. In the wetter stretches here, wildflower fanciers will delight in the lush clumps of columbine, swamp onion and shooting star. Under the steep, avalanche-scarred south face of Dunderberg Peak, the second-highest peak in the North Boundary Country, the trail slopes down on a rocky traverse to the outlet of Blue Lake. The broken talus and scree to the north are a haven for marmots and conies, whose scats and hay harvests can be found on and between the rocks next to the trail. Like Cooney Lake, Blue Lake has a fishery of eastern brook and rainbow trout. Past Blue Lake the descending trail is within sight of one more tiny, unnamed lake. Soon the trail splits and ramifies, and even some roads appear, but route-finding is not a problem, because following any of them will in about ¼ mile bring you to Virginia Lakes Campground (9760').

48 Hetch Hetchy to Rancheria Creek

TRIP From O'Shaughnessy Dam (Hetch Hetchy Reservoir) to Rancheria Creek (round trip). Topo map *Hetch Hetchy Reservoir*. Best early season; 13 miles (21 km).

Grade	Trail/layover days	Total recommended days
Leisurely	2/0	2
Moderate	....	....
Strenuous	....	....

HILITES Early season is the ideal time to view the falls along this route, and eager opening-day anglers will find the good fishing along Rancheria Creek a satisfying clumination to a fine trip.

DESCRIPTION

1st Hiking Day (**O'Shaughnessy Dam** to **Rancheria Creek,** 6.5 miles—10.5 km): From the trailhead at the south end of the dam, the thunder from the discharge pipe accompanies the traveler as he crosses this 600-foot-long piece of concrete. Although 8 miles of the Grand Canyon of the Tuolumne River were put under a reservoir for the sake of San Francisco's water supply, the actual intake for the aqueduct is 17 miles downstream in a relatively ordinary part of the canyon.

The first 0.7 mile of our route is on the service road (no longer used by vehicles, and badly deteriorated) to Lake Eleanor (part of San Francisco's water project). Once across the dam, the road passes through a long tunnel, beyond which it winds along the hillside above Hetch Hetchy's high-water mark. Views across the reservoir include, from the left, Tueeulala Falls (seasonal), Wapama Falls, Hetch Hetchy Dome and Kolana Rock. Soon the road begins a gentle, shaded ascent through canyon live oak, incense-cedar, Douglas-fir, California bay, California grape, big-leaf maple and poison oak. As our route swings east and achieves a more southerly and drier position, trees become scarce. After we turn right onto the signed trail to Rancheria Creek, there are Digger pines and live oaks for shade. The trail winds along a sunny bench where glacial polish and glacial erratics remind us that at times during the Pleistocene Epoch glaciers up to 60 miles long—the longest in the Sierra—flowed down this canyon.

After crossing seasonal Tueeulala Falls creek, we descend to the bridges over Falls Creek. During high runoff this creek can be impassable, as the bridges may be under water or washed out. In early season Wapama Falls will cover these bridges with spray. Beyond the creek our fly-infested trail climbs onto a meadowy ledge system where we have an airy view of the water below. In spring, wildflowers dot the meadows here and you can see monkeyflower, paintbrush and Sierra onion. This hike usually boasts a great variety of wildlife, and commonly seen animals include alligator lizard, Steller's jay and California ground squirrel.

Beyond the ledges our trail makes a long descent to cascading Tiltill Creek, which we cross on a bridge. From here we climb onto the low ridge separating Tiltill Creek and Rancheria Creek. About ¾ mile beyond the bridge, the trail enters a shaded flat where a spur trail (right) leads to streamside campsites ¼ mile below Rancheria Falls. Please be careful here as the area is heavily used and bears are persistent. Fishing in Rancheria Creek is poor-to-good for rainbow trout (to 10″).

2nd Hiking Day: Retrace your steps (6.5 miles—10.5 km).

Hikers near O'Shaughnessy Dam

49   Hetch Hetchy to Tiltill Valley

TRIP   From O'Shaughnessy Dam (Hetch Hetchy Reservoir) to Tiltill Valley (round trip). Topo maps *Lake Eleanor, **Hetch Hetchy Reservoir***. Best early season; 18.6 miles (30 km)

Grade	Trail/layover days	Total recommended days
Leisurely	4/0	4
Moderate	3/0	3
Strenuous	2/0	2

HILITES   Like the previous trip, this route tours the northern edge of Hetch Hetchy Reservoir. Across the lake the views of Kolana Rock and the sheer granite walls of the Grand Canyon of the Tuolumne provide a majestic accompaniment. The contrasting intimate serenity of Tiltill Valley is a pleasant terminus to this early-season trek.

DESCRIPTION (Leisurely trip)

1st Hiking Day: Follow Trip 48 to **Rancheria Creek**, 6.5 miles (10.5 km).

2nd Hiking Day (**Rancheria Creek** to **Tiltill Valley**, 2.8 miles—4.5 km): From the junction of the Pate Valley/Tiltill Valley trails above the campsites, the trail to Tiltill Valley climbs steeply for a full 1200 feet up to a timber-bottomed saddle. As the trail descends on the north side of the saddle, it traverses a pine forest with a sprinkling of incense-cedar and black oak. When this duff trail emerges at the east end of Tiltill Valley, it meets a trail to Tilden Canyon and Benson Lake. The valley is a long meadow which in early spring is usually quite wet and boggy at the east end. Lodgepole pine fringes the meadow, and the valley is flanked by polished outcroppings of granite and by brush-covered slopes. The trail crosses to the north side of the meadow and winds west to the excellent campsites just south of the Tiltill Creek ford (5600'). These camping places, located in an isolated stand of lodgepole and sugar pine, afford excellent views in both directions down the meadows. Campers have an uninterrupted vantage point from which to watch the large variety of wildlife that make this meadow their home. Fishing on Tiltill Creek for rainbow (to 10″) is excellent in early season.

3rd and 4th Hiking Days: Retrace your steps, 9.3 miles (15 km).

Rancheria Falls

50   Saddlebag Lake to McCabe Lakes

TRIP   From Saddlebag Lake to Lower McCabe Lake
               (round trip). Topo map *Tuolumne Meadows*. Best
               mid or late season; 11 miles (17.8 km).

Grade	*Trail/layover* days	*Total recom-* mended days
Leisurely	3/0	3
Moderate	2/1	3
Strenuous	....	....

HILITES   Alpine from beginning to end, this trip crosses the
               Sierra crest between the east end of Shepherd
               Crest and North Peak. High tundra meadows,
               sparkling clear-water lakes and weathered white-
               bark pines are hallmarks of this loftily routed
               excursion. Although the route is not marked as a
               trail on the topo map, there is sometimes a well-
               worn trace and sometimes adequate duck-on-
               the rock markings to delineate the route. This is
               a good trip selection for both intermediate and
               advanced backpackers.

DESCRIPTION (Moderate trip)

1st Hiking Day (**Saddlebag Lake** to **Lower McCabe Lake,** 5.5
miles—8.9 km): Saddlebag Lake (10,087'), caught in the
barren alpine basin between the Tioga Crest and the main
Sierra divide, is one of the largest lakes of the North Boundary
Country. About 340 acres in area, it is a long lake to walk
around, and hikers may elect to use the boat-taxi that runs the
length of the lake from Saddlebag Lake Resort. Rates are
reasonable, and the service convenient. Those who wish to
walk should take the mining road that leaves from the east
end of the resort area, rounds the south end of the lake, and
then skirts the rocky, open northeast side. At various times
dating back to the 1880s, it provided access for the numerous

mining ventures that occupied the basin above Saddlebag Lake and nearby Lundy Canyon. One claim is still registered as active.

To the east, the gently rounded summits of the Tioga Crest dip to Dore Pass, and hikers with a little imagination can see and hear the struggling men and animals of the winter of 1882 as they "snaked" and hauled 16,000 pounds of mining machinery across this pass on balky skid sleds. Bound for Bennettville, the sleds were lowered to the edge of Saddlebag Lake and run across on the thick midwinter ice.

Near the northwest end of the lake, the mining road meets a short trail leading up from the boat-taxi dock, and through a sparse forest cover of stunted lodgepole pine it continues west to the north shore of Greenstone Lake. This rocky lake is backgrounded by the glacier-footed crest of Mt. Conness, and its cold waters hold cutthroat and eastern brook trout. The road then winds gently up through swales in the buckling fields of glacially smoothed granite and past several small tarns to Wasco Lake. The wonderful variety of alpine flora along this gentle ascent sees the appearance of the whitebark pine in the sparse forest cover. Among the profuse wildflowers are primrose, heather, paintbrush (several varieties), wallflower, monkey flower, penstemon, corn lily, Douglas phlox, alpine columbine and aster.

The road then descends along the gullied stream flowing into Steelhead Lake, and at the south end of Steelhead Lake the cross-country route we will follow branches left around the west side of Steelhead Lake. Crossing granite ledges, the route fords Mill Creek, and then veers west around the small, unnamed lake to the northwest. At this point, anglers may wish to sample the golden trout fishing at Cascade Lake before going on. The steep rock-and-grass-ledge ascent of the crest begins as our route turns northwest beside a flower-lined inlet stream. The course of this tiny rill bends northward, and our route follows it faithfully to the small, unnamed lake it drains, locally called Secret Lake.

Pausing at Secret Lake to survey your route up the head-wall, you have three choices. Adept mountaineers can attack the wall directly, preferably keeping just to the right of the black, lichen-stained vertical streak on the headwall. Hikers who want to put out some extra effort to achieve certainty and lack of steep exposure can arduously pick their way up the scree north of Secret Lake to the lip of what looks like—but isn't—a lake basin. From there, they will traverse slightly upward to their left, under the solid face of the east end of

Shepherd Crest, to the low point on the headwall divide. Probably most people choose the third way: From the south side of Secret Lake walk directly up the increasingly steep headwall until, about halfway up, you come to a long ledge that slopes slightly up to the south. Many ducks mark this route, but they are not always easy to see. About 200 yards south up this ledge, you leave it and follow ducks almost directly up to the ridgecrest. Once on it, follow it north to the low point of the divide to find the ducked route descending on the west side of the ridgecrest.

Excellent views northwest from the ridgecrest include Tower Peak and Saurian Crest. Descending from this ridge, a steep, eroded trail follows the gully northeast of upper McCabe Lake. This section levels out near some small tarns, and our route continues to the north shore of upper McCabe Lake. (One could camp here in a small stand of whitebark pines.) Turning west along the shore, we ford the outlet and then strike out for the low, rock-cairned saddle due west of the outlet. Beyond this saddle, the best route drops past snowmelt tarns not shown on the topo map and then winds down through a dense forest cover of lodgepole, whitebark pine and hemlock to the east shore of beautiful lower McCabe Lake (9850′). The best campsites on the lake are near the outlet. Fishing for eastern brook (to 12″) is excellent.

2nd Hiking Day: Retrace your steps, 5.5 miles (8.9 km).

Peak 11282 over Nelson Lake

Saddlebag Lake to Tuolumne Meadows 51

TRIP
From Saddlebag Lake to Tuolumne Meadows via Lower McCabe Lake, Cold Canyon and Glen Aulin (shuttle trip). Topo map *Tuolumne Meadows*. Best mid or late season; 20.4 miles (32.9 km).

Grade	Trail/layover days	Total recommended days
Leisurely	4/1	5
Moderate	3/1	4
Strenuous	3/0	3

HILITES
Some hikers may choose this trip for its easy shuttle, but the country that this route tours should be adequate reason in itself. The variety of a trip that is part cross country, part on trail and part over water should appeal to the most jaded mountaineer's appetite. This route does that and more. Crossing the Sierra crest above upper McCabe Lake, the trip traverses the long meadows of Cold Canyon, and finishes by touring the splashing cascades and roaring falls of the Tuolumne River.

DESCRIPTION (Moderate trip)

1st Hiking Day: Follow Trip 50 to **Lower McCabe Lake**, 5.5 miles (8.9 km).

2nd Hiking Day (**Lower McCabe Lake** to **Glen Aulin**, 9.2 miles—14.8 km): From the campsites at the outlet of lower McCabe Lake the trail descends along the west side of the stream through a moderate-to-dense forest cover of hemlock, lodgepole, whitebark and silver pine and occasional red fir.

The trail between lower McCabe Lake and the place where it veers west is usually very wet and swampy, a soggy condition hospitable to the fields of corn lily that line the way. As the trail veers west it becomes drier, and most of the timber near the trail is lodgepole pine. Flowers indigenous to better-drained soils are found along this section of trail, including wallflower, Douglas phlox, lupine, buckwheat, aster and pussy paws. The descent becomes gentle as the trail passes through a "ghost forest" caused by the needleminer moth and crosses an unnamed tributary of McCabe Creek before reaching the junction with the Virginia Canyon Trail. At this junction our route turns left (west) and continues to Glen Aulin as described in the third hiking day, Trip 46.

3rd Hiking Day: Follow the 4th hiking day, Trip 46, 5.7 miles (9.2 km).

White Cascade near Glen Aulin

National Park Service

Saddlebag Lake to Twin Lakes **52**

TRIP From Saddlebag Lake to Twin Lakes via Lower McCabe Lake, Matterhorn Canyon, Burro Pass, Upper Piute Creek and Crown Lake (shuttle trip). Topo maps *Tuolumne Meadows, Matterhorn Peak.* Best mid or late season; 34.5 miles (55.6 km).

Grade	Trail/layover days	Total recom- mended days
Leisurely	8/2	10
Moderate	5/2	7
Strenuous	4/2	6

HILITES Of the many crestal routes throughout the Sierra, this is one of the most exciting. The scenery is wild and rugged, the six watersheds visited provide excellent fishing, and the route touches some of the most remote country of Yosemite National Park. Most of the campsites mentioned below are situated in central locations that invite side trips, and the visitor is advised to allow enough layover days for such trips.

DESCRIPTION (Moderate trip)

1st Hiking Day: Follow trip 50 to **Lower McCabe Lake**, 5.5 miles (8.9 km).

2nd Hiking Day (**Lower McCabe Lake** to **Matterhorn Canyon**, 9 miles—14.5 km): This is the longest hiking day of the trip, and the prudent hiker will get an early start. From the outlet of Lower McCabe Lake the trail descends to the Virginia Canyon Trail junction as described in the 2nd hiking day, Trip 51. At this junction our route turns right and descends down the steep switchbacks into Virginia Canyon. The trail along these switchbacks is **T**-blazed, and the deep layers of bark that have built up around these blazes give the passerby an indication of this trail's age. Blazed by the U.S. Cavalry under the acting superintendency of Captain Abram Epperson Wood in the 1890s, this trail was once used for access to the more remote portions of the North Boundary Country. As the intimidated sheepmen who had been encroaching on Park lands moved their herds northward, it became necessary for the Army caretakers to widen the area of their patrols. The traveler of today, like the mounted cavalryman of yesterday, may pause in wonder at the magnificent specimens of red fir and silver pine along this descent.

The trail descends nearly to Return Creek before turning northeast to ford McCabe Creek. Near the ford are magnificent examples of water-sculpting on the granite bedrock of Return Creek, and this bedrock is bordered with colorful patches of columbine, tiger lily and shooting star.

A short way beyond the ford of McCabe Creek the trail passes a packer campsite and there fords to the north side of Return Creek, where it meets the Summit Pass Trail. Our route turns left (southwest) and ascends moderately across the easy juniper-crowned divide to Spiller Canyon. One's first views of Spiller Creek are those of open granite bedrock, over which Spiller Creek splashes in a series of lovely chutes and miniature falls. The trail ascends along the creek for about ¼ mile and then fords it.

Through a moderate forest cover that now includes hemlock, the trail then climbs by steady switchbacks. At the hairpin turns one has fine views up Spiller Canyon all the way to the sky-parlor meadows at its headwall, and south across Return Creek to North Peak and Mt. Conness. The trail descends briefly through a long, dry, sandy meadow, and then ascends again over a grassy saddle. From the saddle, the trail dips gently to beautiful Miller Lake. Foregrounded by a large green meadow, the sparkling waters of this small lake tempt the traveler to stop and rest, but drama lies right around the bend.

From Miller Lake the rutted trail bends north, up a grassy swale to a timbered saddle. The views from this saddle burst upon the traveler as he is suddenly confronted with the chasm of Matterhorn Canyon and the distant teeth of the Sawtooth Ridge. This viewpoint marks the beginning of a long, switchbacking descent into Matterhorn Canyon, until finally the rocky trail levels off in the sand of the meadowed junction with the Matterhorn Canyon Trail (8480'). There are good campsites in the meadow and more just upstream. Fishing for eastern brook (to 12") is good in Matterhorn Canyon creek, and the granite potholes upstream from the junction provide fine swimming in late season.

3rd, 4th and *5th Hiking Days*: Follow the 6th, 7th and 8th hiking days of Trip 44, 20 miles (32.2 km).

Ragged Peak over Young Lake

53 Tuolumne Meadows to Young Lakes

TRIP From Tuolumne Meadows to Young Lakes (semi-loop trip). Topo map *Tuolumne Meadows*. Best mid or late season, 15.1 miles (24.3 km).

Grade	Trail/layover days	Total recommended days
Leisurely	....	....
Moderate	2/1	3
Strenuous	2/0	2

HILITES The three Young Lakes, cupped under soaring Ragged Peak, offer a large selection of campsites, some in heavy woods and some at timberline. These camps provide a base for exciting excursions into the headwaters of Conness Creek and for climbing Mt. Conness itself.

DESCRIPTION

1st Hiking Day (**Glen Aulin TH** to **Young Lakes**, 8.2 mi.—13.2 km): The first part of this trip follows the Glen Aulin "highway," a heavily traveled path from Tuolumne Meadows to the High Sierra Camp down the Tuolumne River. From the parking area west of State Highway 120 we stroll down a dirt road, pass a locked gate that bars autos, and continue west along the lodgepole-dotted flank of Tuolumne Meadows, with fine views south across the meadows of Unicorn Peak, Cathedral Peak and some of the Echo Peaks. Approaching a boulder-rimmed old parking loop, we veer right and climb slightly to the now-closed Soda Springs Campground. Once this campground was the private holding of John Lembert, namesake of Lembert Dome. His brothers, who survived him, sold it to the Sierra Club in 1912, and for 60 years Club members enjoyed a private campground in this marvelous subalpine meadow. But in 1972 the Club deeded the property to the National Park Service so that everyone could use it.

From the Soda Springs the sandy trail undulates through a forest of sparse, small lodgepole pines, and then descends to a boulder ford of Delaney Creek. Immediately beyond the ford we hop a branch of Delaney Creek, then hop another in 300 yards. Soon our trail almost touches the southwest arm of Tuolumne Meadows before ascending to the signed Young Lakes Trail. From the junction we ascend slightly and cross a broad expanse of boulder-strewn, grass-pocketed sheet granite. An open spot affords a look south across broad Tuolumne Meadows to the line of peaks from Fairview Dome to the steeplelike spires of the Cathedral Range. After crossing the open granite, our trail climbs a tree-clothed slope to a ridge and turns up the ridge for several hundred yards before veering down into the meadowy, bouldery, shallow valley of Dingley Creek, an easy ford except in early season. In the first mile beyond this small creek, we jump across its north fork and wind gently upward in shady pine forest carpeted with a fine flower display even into late season. Groundsel, daisies, lupine, squawroot and gooseberries all are colorful, but one's admiration for floral beauty concentrates on the delicate cream flower cups of Mariposa lily, with one rich brown spot in the throat of each petal. Near the ridgetop, breaks in the lodgepole forest allow us glimpses the whole Cathedral Range.

On the other side of the ridge a new panoply of peaks appears in the north—majestic Tower Peak, Doghead and Quarry peaks, the Finger Peaks, Matterhorn Peak, Sheep Peak, Mt. Conness, and the Shepherd Crest. From this viewpoint a moderate descent leads to a ford of a tributary of Conness Creek, where more varieties of flowers decorate the green banks of this icy, dashing stream. Soon our downwinding trail reaches the Dog Lake Trail junction, where we veer left and descend into thickening hemlock forest. On a level stretch of trail we cross another branch of Conness Creek, and then switchback ¼ mile up to a plateau from where the view is fine of the steep north face of Ragged Peak.

After passing a meadow which was the fourth Young Lake before it filled in with stream sediments, we descend to the west shore of lower Young Lake (9850'). There are both primitive and well-developed campsites along the north shore of this lake. More secluded campsites may be found on middle Young Lake by following the trail east from the ford of the lower lake, and forking right at a junction 400 yards beyond. From the middle lake you can go up the inlet to the upper lake (10,200'), which is the most attractive but also the most exposed. Fishing on the Young Lakes is fair-to-good for brook trout (to 12").

2nd Hiking Day (**Young Lakes** to **Glen Aulin TH**, 6.9 mi.—11.1 km): After retracing our steps to the Dog Lake Trail junction, we turn left onto the southwest spur of Ragged Peak and ascend a sandy, boulder-scattered slope under a moderate lodgepole-and-hemlock forest cover. As the trail ascends, the trees diminish in density and change in species, to a predominance of whitebark pine, the highest-dwelling of subalpine trees. From the shoulder of Ragged Peak the trail descends through a very large, gently sloping meadow. This broad, well-watered expanse is a wildflower garden in season, laced with meandering brooks. Paintbrush, lupine and monkey flower in the foreground set off the great views of the entire Cathedral Range, strung out on the southern horizon.

Near the lower edge of the meadow we cross the headwaters of Dingley Creek, and then descend, steeply at times, some 300 feet through a moderately dense forest of lodgepoles and a few hemlocks. Then the trail levels off and veers east on a gently rolling course through more lodgepole forest where the sandy soil sprouts thousands of prostrate little lupine plants. Beyond is a very large level meadow where the reddish peaks of Mts. Dana and Gibbs loom in the east, Delaney Creek meanders lazily through the grass, and Belding ground squirrels pipe away. The Delaney Creek ford is difficult in early season; shallower fords may be found upstream. Beyond the creek, you will find the trail about 20 yards upstream from the main ford. After crossing a little ridge, our route drops once more toward Tuolumne Meadows. Lembert Dome, the "first ascent" of so many visitors to Tuolumne Meadows, can be glimpsed through the trees along this stretch of trail. The trail levels slightly before it meets the 0.1 mile lateral to Dog Lake. Then it passes a junction with a trail that leads east along the north side of Lembert Dome, and fords Dog Lake's outlet. The 560-foot descent from here is terribly dusty as it switchbacks down close under the steep west face of Lembert Dome. At the bottom of the deep dust, the trail splits into three paths. The right one leads to the stables, the left one to the parking area where we started.

Southern Yosemite/Devils Postpile

This region's topography is varied and complex, ranging from the yawning chasm of Yosemite Valley to the snowy heights of the Sierra crest's peaks, some over 13,000 feet. In profile this section ascends in a long, gentle slope, increasing in height and power until it climaxes at the white-peaked crest. It then drops away suddenly, in an escarpment, to Mono and Long valleys. The more gradual western slope is wrinkled into a complex of lesser crests and valleys that roughly parallel the north-south main crest, and this corrugated surface is broken by the networks of the three major rivers of the area: the Tuolumne, the Merced, and the San Joaquin.

Southern Yosemite National Park provides the grandest scenery in this region. But if Yosemite is first in grandeur, the Devils Postpile area, including the spectacular Ritter Range, is a close second. Combined, these two regions afford some of the best backpacking country in the world.

In all, Yosemite offers the traveler over 700 miles of trail, a figure that does not include the outside-the-Park portions of trails originating in the Park. Because of the number of people traveling the Yosemite backcountry, the Park Service has now instituted a policy of allowing camping with fires only at designated camping spots (and no fires above 9600 feet) and wilderness permits are required. Forest Service fire permits are required for trips outside the Park. (See the chapter on wilderness permits.) The credit for the well-maintained trails of this area belongs to trail crews of the U.S. Forest Service and of the National Park Service. Backpackers in Yosemite soon become familiar with the i tree blaze of the Forest Service and with Yosemite's distinctive T. The T blaze was first used when the U.S. Calvary administered the Park.

The general landforms of the southern Yosemite and Devils Postpile regions are similar because both were created by mountain-building forces followed by erosion by glaciers and rivers. However, anyone who hikes the backcountry of southern Yosemite and of the Ritter Range will see the marked differences between the two areas. In Yosemite, one is

struck with the gargantuan scale of the landscape. Vast
expanses of solid white granite give a sense of colossal
immobility. By contrast, the dark heights of the Minarets of
the Ritter Range appear almost like chocolate icing—
decorative and ephemeral. The difference between the two
areas is in the type of rock, the Yosemite high country being
primarily massive, resistant granites, and the Ritter Range
being mostly metamorphosed volcanic rocks, alternating with
some metasedimentary layers. The softer rock of metamorphosed volcanic origin was more easily quarried by the ice and
water, allowing the more delicate and fragile sculpting.

This dramatic landscaping is the product of many inunda-
tions by glaciers, and evidences of these ancient ice fields are
readily seen along trails in both Yosemite and the Devils
Postpile/Ritter Range country. The size of some of these glaciers is hard to imagine, for, combined, they covered hundreds
of square miles. The most impressive was the great Tuolumne
glacier, emanating from the region of Mt. Lyell and Mt. Dana,
which carved and polished the present Tuolumne and Tenaya
basins. Incredible as it may seem, the Tenaya basin was
scoured by an incidental overflow from the primary Tuolumne
basin glacier, which was a *mer de glace* that once filled the
Grand Canyon of the Tuolumne to its brim! The top of the
Devils Postpile, a fascinating columnar basaltic formation,
offers mute testimony to the awesome power of the shearing
action of these glaciers. Feeder glaciers, like the ones that
carved Echo Creek canyon, Triple Peak Fork canyon, Chain
Lakes basin and Shadow Creek canyon, are responsible for
much of the scenery described in the following trips. Huge
deposits of rocky glacial debris called moraines compose significant parts of the landscape (e.g., the lateral moraines
along the descent from Clouds Rest to Little Yosemite Valley).
Other glacial manifestations that backpackers will see include domes, U-shaped valleys, glacial polish, erratics (boulders left by receding ice fields), striae (grooves) and hanging
valleys (the valleys out of which leap the falls of Yosemite
Valley are classic examples).

Man on this scene seems almost an afterthought. The first
men were the Indians of the Mono and Ahwahneechee tribes.
Primarily peaceful, seminomadic peoples, they hunted and
fished the idyllic Yosemite and Mono regions long before
white men came. Virtually all that remains to mark their
occupancy of the land are place names. They carried on some
trade and social intercourse with each other—the primary
trade route was via Tuolumne Meadows and the present

Sunrise Trail—but for the most part they remained isolated.

The Mariposa Battalion of 1851 was the first white party to penetrate the Yosemite Valley, but the trapper Joseph Walker first crossed the Park and saw the Valley as early as 1833. From 1848 until the 1860s gold fever brought white men into the Sierra in swarms. By 1853 Lee Vining had made prospecting forays into the Mt. Dana country, and by 1859 a temporary boomtown grew up around Dogtown on what is now U.S. 395 near Conway Summit. After the discovery of the fabulous Comstock Lode east of Lake Tahoe, gold fever subsided in the Yosemite/Devils Postpile region, except for a brief flurry caused by the abortive excitement of the Tioga Mine near Tioga Pass, and it had all but died by the turn of the century. This speculative mine, although it never opened or mined a ton of ore, was responsible for the building of the Tioga Road.

In Yosemite Valley a burgeoning tourist trade arose, centering about the natural wonders of the Valley. In 1864 President Lincoln signed an Act of Congress giving Yosemite over to the care of the State of California in the form of a public-land grant. Galen Clark, who established Clark's Station, the current site of Wawona, was appointed Yosemite's first guardian, and he served in this capacity until 1879. In 1890 Yosemite was made a National Park, the grant to be administered by the U. S. Cavalry. This Army administration lasted until 1916, when the National Park Service was established. Short as it was, this interim period of U. S. Army administration based at Wawona saw many "firsts" in the Park. Its boundaries were patrolled to keep out infringing cattle- and sheepmen; fish were introduced to high-country lakes and streams (the new strains included golden, brook, brown, cutthroat, Dolly Varden and grayling); and an exploration and trail-blazing program was carried out that created trails still used today. This was an exciting pioneer period, and today's backpacker can glean a taste of its fascination by visiting the Pioneer Yosemite History Center at Wawona.

Anglers will find that this region abounds in "hot fishing spots." Some of them are the Merced River east of Little Yosemite Valley, the Royal Arch Lake-Chilnualna Lakes area and the Chain Lakes basin. Today four species of trout— rainbow, brook, brown and golden—make up the primary fishery of this area, although an occasional catch will be made of a hybrid or a cutthroat. Nearly all the lakes and streams of the high country have been planted in the past, but a new policy in Yosemite National Park calls for no more planting there. The effects of this policy remain to be seen.

Fishing on the lakes is best during the first three weeks after the ice has cleared (from late June to the end of July, depending on the altitude) and during the last few weeks of the season before the first snows (late September to mid October). After the streams clear up, fishing is generally good all summer long. Usually they clear up by early July; however, this date can be affected by late rains and by the ground cover on the particular stream's watershed.

Flies are preferred to bait by most backpackers for reasons of sport, esthetics and weight, and the clear waters of the high-country lakes and streams behoove the angler to use fine leader material and a wary approach. Experienced backpacking fishermen use a light-action fly rod (3-5 sections) strung with tapered line and leader. Novice anglers find that a spinning rod with a bubble-fly combination or a metal wobbler is easily mastered, and is effective against blustery afternoon winds on lakes.

Anglers should keep only the fish they will eat. A fishing trip's success is never measured solely by the number of pounds in the creel.

NOTE: Bears are now a problem in the Devils Postpile area as well as in Yosemite.

The Trailheads

Gibbs Lake Trailhead. Go 1.3 miles south from the junction of U.S. 395 and State Highway 120 just south of Lee Vining, turn right on the road signed *Horse Meadow*, and go 2.1 miles up it.

Tuolumne Meadows Campground. Turn south off State Highway 120 in Tuolumne Meadows east of the store and drive up the road nearest the river.

Tuolumne Meadows Lodge. Following State Highway 120 in Tuolumne Meadows, drive ½ mile east from the bridge over the Tuolumne River, turn right on a paved road, and go ¾ mile to the roadend parking lot to let your passengers out. You must park at one of the two backpackers' parking lots along this road.

Tioga Road Trailhead. Go 0.5 mile west of the Visitors Center in Tuolumne Meadows, or 0.5 mile east of the west end of the meadows.

Tenaya Lake. Park in the lot at the west end of Tenaya Lake on State Highway 120 in Yosemite, where signs indicate the Walk-in Campground.

Agnew Meadows. Go 9 miles west from U.S. 395 through Mammoth Lakes and over Minaret Summit. Turn right 2.7 miles from Minaret Summit and go ¼ mile to a parking area. There is an overflow parking area just beyond it. You may have to park just before Minaret Summit and take a shuttle-bus.

Devils Postpile. Go 9 miles west from U.S. 395 through Mammoth Lakes and over Minaret Summit. Turn right 6.7 miles from Minaret Summit to go 0.35 mile to a parking area at the spur road's end. You may have to park just before Minaret Summit and take a shuttlebus.

Glacier Point. Drive 9.3 miles up State Highway 41 from Yosemite Valley, turn left, and drive 15.5 more miles to a parking lot at road's end.

Happy Isles. Take the Yosemite Valley shuttle bus to Happy Isles, or park at Camp Curry and hike along a trail 1 mile southeast to Happy Isles.

Bridalveil Creek. Drive 9.3 miles up State Highway 41 from Yosemite Valley, turn left, drive 7.6 more miles to the Bridalveil Campground road, branching right, and follow this road through the campground to the southeast end of it.

ChiquitoCreekTrailhead. From the north shore of Bass Lake, drive northeast 20 miles up Beasore Road 434 (which becomes Road 5S07) to Globe Rock. There, turn left and drive 2.4 miles up Road 5S04 to a signed trailhead atop a small, flat ridge area.

Granite Creek Campground. From the north shore of Bass Lake, drive northeast 20 miles up Beasore Road 434 (which becomes Road 5S07) to Globe Rock, then continue 9.8 miles along your road to the Minarets road, which goes south 52 paved miles to the town of North Fork. Still on Road 5S07, you reach the Clover Meadow Ranger Station in 1.7 miles, then continue past it for 0.5 mile to Road 4S57. Branch right on this road and follow it 1.0 mile to a hikers' parking area in Granite Creek Campground. Road 4S57 may be undrivable as late as early July.

Fernandez Trailhead. From the north shore of Bass Lake follow Beasore Road 434 (which becomes Road 5S07) 20 miles east to Globe Rock. Continue on 5S07—the main road—for 8.0 miles, past Bowler Group Camp. Then, 100 yards beyond Ethelfreda Creek, veer left onto Road 5S05 toward the Fernandez Trailhead. This road climbs steadily for 2.3 miles to a turn-around loop at the trailhead.

54 Horse Meadow to Gibbs Lake

TRIP   From Horse Meadow to Gibbs Lake; round trip.
             Topo map *Mono Craters*. Best mid or late season; *8 miles* (12.8 km).

Grade	Trail/Layover days	Total recommended days
Leisurely	2/0	2
Moderate	....	....
Strenuous	....	....

HILITES The destination of this trip is a little-known lake in Ansel Adams Wilderness on the dramatic east slope of the Sierra east of Yosemite Park. It's a great place to find peace and quiet, and for serious anglers there is a chance to catch some beautiful golden trout.

DESCRIPTION

1st Hiking Day (**Horse Meadow** to **Gibbs Lake**, 4 miles—6.4 km): Ordinary cars will have to park 2.1 miles up the dirt road from U.S. 395 in a little meadow that has a grove of aspen trees and a stream that runs until August. More mountain-worthy cars can ascend another mile to upper Horse Meadow.

We leave the lower meadow and climb steeply, leveling off at a fork where we go right. Soon we pass upper Horse Meadow on our right, which is bounded on the north by the gigantic right lateral moraine of Lee Vining Canyon.

Past the upper meadow the road forks, and 0.1 mile up the left fork is a small parking area below a locked USFS gate. Beyond the gate we climb steeply up an old road on a north-trending ridge, to an overlook of Lee Vining Canyon, far below. Continuing the steep climb, we walk through mixed forest eligible for cutting and pass a road leading left (east). Just beyond a deer hunter's camp we come to a water ditch and then a sign heralding the wilderness ahead. From the ditch, the road ascends gently for ¼ mile and then mercifully ends. From the roadend, a trail takes off up a dry ravine that lies over a little ridge east from Gibbs Canyon creek. Then it crosses the ridge and dips down near the stream, where recent blazes mark the trail. We ascend through a cool forest of lodgepole, whitebark and silver pine, with an occasional mountain hemlock and with much Labrador tea along the creek, to the signed border of Ansel Adams Wilderness. Here, perhaps, one will feel a distinct relief that autos and the rest of civilization are locked out beyond the invisible gate Congress erected here in 1963.

The remaining gentle climb to Gibbs Lake proceeds through moderate-to-dense forest near Gibbs Canyon creek, as we catch glimpses through the trees of the great Sierra crest dead ahead. There are fair-to-good campsites south of the outlet and west of the inlet of emerald-green Gibbs Lake (9500'). For the adventurous camper, an easy if steep route to Kidney Lake goes up the forested south side of the stream, and the expansive views of Mono Lake and the mountains around it are worth the climb. Most of the shore of this lake is barren, but some whitebark pines at the east end provide shelter for a primitive camp.

2nd Hiking Day: Retrace your steps, 4 miles (6.4 km).

Gibbs Lake

55   Tenaya Lake to Sunrise Camp

TRIP   From Tenaya Lake Walk-In Campground to Sunrise High Sierra Camp (round trip). Topo map ***Tuolumne Meadows***. Best mid or late season; 11.4 miles (18.4 km).

Grade	Trail/layover days	Total recommended days
Leisurely	2/1	3
Moderate	2/0	2
Strenuous	....	....

HILITES Although this route is very popular, being within the Yosemite High Sierra Camp network, the superb, unusual scenery of the high country makes this trip a must. The spectacular topography of the Tenaya canyon and of the serrated northwestern end of the Cathedral Range combine to overcome the most strident objections of the solitude-seeker.

DESCRIPTION

1st Hiking Day (**Tenaya Lake Walk-in Campground** to **Sunrise Camp**, 5.7 miles—9.2 km): From the campground parking lot (8149′) the trail crosses the outlet of Tenaya Lake and skirts the meadowy edge of the walk-in campground. For a mile the trail winds south through moderate forest cover interrupted by small meadows where the quiet early-morning hiker will probably see browsing mule deer. The first part of this trail is lush with wildflowers as late as July, and one can expect to see blooming lupine, aster, larkspur, brodiaea and buttercup. Just past the stream from Lower Sunrise Lake the ascent begins to steepen, and soon it becomes a long series of rocky switchbacks up a slope clothed with pine and hemlock. From these switchbacks one can see the highway and can hear passing autos, but these are infinitesimal compared to the polished granite expanses of Tenaya Canyon. The Indian name for Tenaya Creek, Py-wi-ack ("Stream of the Shining Rocks"), was quite apt, for this canyon exhibits the largest exposed granite area in Yosemite, and its shining surfaces are barren except for sporadic clumps of hardy conifers that have found root in broken talus pockets.

Where the trail begins to rise, the long, gradual slope falling from the promontory called Clouds Rest comes into view in the south. This slope is a 4500-foot drop, one of the largest continuous rock slopes in the world. The traveler who feels sated by the panorama will find a different world to wonder at, right at his own boot-clad feet, for these slopes grow dozens of wildflower species, among them pussy paws, penstemon, paintbrush, lupine, streptanthus, aster, larkspur, brodiaea and buttercup. Finally the switchbacks end and the trail levels as it arrives at a junction with the lateral trail to Sunrise camp. Turning left (east), we stroll on a nearly level path under a sparse forest cover of pine and fir until the trail dips for about ¼ mile to the first Sunrise Lake. After passing the west side of the lake on a trail fringed with red mountain heather, we cross the outlet and ascend gradually northeast. Then the trail levels off and wanders roughly north through a sparse lodgepole forest. The second Sunrise Lake comes into view on the left, but we veer east and climb away from it, paralleling its inlet some distance from the cascading water. The few trees here are not enough to block our views of granite domes all around. Then our trail skirts the south side of the highest Sunrise Lake and begins a gradual ascent by crossing the lake's inlet stream.

Continuing southeast, we cross a little saddle and descend gradually almost straight south from the upper lake. After passing most of the hogback lying east of us, we swing northeast and switchback down to a bench overlooking spacious Long Meadow. There are fair campsites or, if advance reservations have been made, one may enjoy the luxury of a hot shower, a hot meal and a made-up bed at the High Sierra Camp (9320') nearby.

2nd Hiking Day: Retrace your steps, 5.7 miles (9.2 km). Alternatively, you could retrace the steps of Trip 57, 8.5 miles (13.7 km).

56   Tioga Road to Lower Cathedral Lake

TRIP   From Trailhead on the Tioga Road (Tuolumne Meadows) to Cathedral Lake (round trip). Topo map *Tuolumne Meadows*. Best mid or late season; 7.8 miles (12.6 km).

Grade	Trail/layover days	Total recom-mended days
Leisurely	2/0	2
Moderate	....	....
Strenuous	....	....

HILITES   Used since the time of the Indians, this trail offers some of the finest views of the Tuolumne Meadows region. Two large granite domes, Fairview and Medlicott, and the foremost landmark of the area, Cathedral Peak, line this route. Because of the relatively short mileage and the high-country scenery, this round trip is an excellent beginner's selection.

DESCRIPTION

1st Hiking Day (**Trailhead on Tioga Road** to **Cathedral Lake**, 3.9 miles—6.3 km): From the parking area (8560') on the Tioga Road, we follow a gently ascending trail that is quite objectionably dusty except after rainy sprinkles. (After this initial section the trail itself is not bad at all, and the panoramic views more than make up for the early unpleasantness.) A few steps from the trailhead our route crosses the Tenaya Lake/Tuolumne Meadows Trail and then begins to climb more steeply. After ½ mile of ascent under a welcome forest cover, the trail levels off and descends to a small meadow that is boggy in early season. From here we can see the dramatically shaped tops of Unicorn Peak and The Cockscomb, and the apparent granite dome in the south is in reality the north ridge of Cathedral Peak, whose steeples are out of sight over the "dome's" horizon.

The trail cruises gently up and down through more little meadows set in hemlock forest and then dips near a tinkling stream whose source, we discover after further walking, is a robust spring on a shady set of switchbacks. Beyond this climb our tread levels off on the west slope of Cathedral Peak and makes a long, gentle, sparsely forested descent on sandy underfooting to a junction with the spur trail to lower Cathedral Lake, where our route turns right. Periodically the traveler has westward views of another granite sentry left by the glacial ice, Medlicott Dome, and one can easily discern the difference between the rounded, polished tops of the domes and the jagged crest of Cathedral Peak. The domes were completely covered by the ice, whereas the top few hundred feet of Cathedral Peak stood above the grinding glacier, and hence was not rounded and smoothed by the ice.

From the junction, a ⅔-mile stroll across stream-braided meadows leads to the shores of lower Cathedral Lake (9320'). Fishing is poor for rainbow and brook (to 9″) but swimming is good. The views more than make up for the shortcomings, however, for from here Polly Dome, Cathedral Peak, Echo Peaks, Medlicott Dome and Unicorn Peak provide a rugged glacial setting.

2nd Hiking Day: Retrace your steps, 3.9 miles (6.3 km).

Tuolumne Meadows *National Park Service*

57 Tioga Road to Sunrise Camp

TRIP   From Trailhead on the Tioga Road (Tuolumne
              Meadows) to Sunrise High Sierra Camp (round
              trip). Topo map *Tuolumne Meadows*. Best mid or
              late season; 18.4 miles (29.6 km).

Grade	Trail/layover days	Total recommended days
Leisurely	4/1	5
Moderate	3/1	4
Strenuous	2/1	3

HILITES   The Sunrise Trail, of which this is the first leg, is a
              justly famous and popular route. Superlative
              views confront the traveler at every summit and
              oftentimes in between—views of whole ranges in
              the distance as well as spectacular peaks nearby.

DESCRIPTION (Leisurely trip)

1st Hiking Day: Follow Trip 56 to **Cathedral Lake**, 3.9 miles (6.3
km).

2nd Hiking Day (**Cathedral Lake** to **Sunrise High Sierra Camp**,
5.3 miles—8.5 km): First retrace the steps of the 1st hiking
day to the Sunrise Trail at the foot of Cathedral Peak. Here our
route turns right (south) and ascends gently to upper
Cathedral Lake, a few yards to the right of the trail. Though
camping is prohibited here, one may enjoy a stop for a snack
and a swim. Our trail then skirts the east side of the lake and
ascends to Cathedral Pass, where the excellent views include
Cathedral Peak, Tresidder Peak, Echo Peaks, Matthes Crest,
the Clark Range farther south and Matterhorn Peak far to the
north. Beyond the pass is a long, beautiful swale, the
headwaters of Echo Creek, where the midseason flower show
is alone worth the trip. Our path traverses up the east flank of
Tresidder Peak on a gentle climb to the actual high point of
this trail, at a marvelous viewpoint overlooking most of
southern Yosemite Park. The inspiring panorama includes
the peaks around Vogelsang High Sierra Camp in the

southeast, the whole Clark Range in the south, and the peaks on the Park border in both directions farther away. Then our high trail switchbacks quickly down to the head of the upper lobe of Long Meadow, levels off, and leads down a gradually sloping valley dotted with little lodgepole pines to the head of the second, lower lobe of l-o-n-g Long Meadow. Passing a junction with the trail down Echo Creek, this route continues its meadowy descent to the fair campsites along the stream at the south end of the meadow, past Sunrise High Sierra Camp, which is near the south end of the meadow, almost out of sight off to the west of the trail.

3rd and 4th Hiking Days: Retrace you steps, 9.2 miles (14.8 km).

Upper Cathedral Lake, Cathedral Peak

58   Tioga Road to Merced Lake

TRIP   Trailhead on the Tioga Road to Merced Lake via
               Echo Creek (shuttle trip). Topo maps *Tuolumne
               Meadows, Merced Peak*. Best mid or late season;
               34.2 miles (55.1 km).

Grade	Trail/layover days	Total recom- mended days
Leisurely	5/1	6
Moderate	4/1	5
Strenuous	3/0	3

HILITES   This looping excursion out of Tuolumne Meadows
               samples everything the Cathedral Range has to
               offer, from sweeping vistas at 10,000-foot passes to
               the deeply glaciated Merced River canyon to
               forested side streams with secluded campsites. For
               anglers there are lakes large and small, mead-
               owed creeks, and huge river pools.

DESCRIPTION (Leisurely trip)

1st Hiking Day: Follow Trip 56 to **Cathedral Lake**, 3.9 miles (6.3
km).

2nd Hiking Day (**Cathedral Lake** to **Echo Creek Crossing**, 9.0
miles—14.5 km): First, follow Trip 57 to the trail junction in
Long Meadow. Here we turn left (east) on the signed Echo
Creek Trail and ford the Long Meadow stream on boulders.
The trail quickly switchbacks up to the top of the ridge that
separates this stream from Echo Creek and then descends
through dense hemlock-and-lodgepole forest toward the
Cathedral Fork of Echo Creek. Where our route approaches

this stream, we have fine views of the creek's water gliding down a series of granite slabs, and then the trail veers away from the creek and descends gently above it for more than a mile. Even in late season this shady hillside is watered by numerous rills that are bordered by still-blooming flowers. On this downgrade the trail crosses the Long Meadow stream, which has found an escape from that meadow through a gap between two large domes high above our trail.

Then our route levels out in a mile-long flat section of this valley where the wet ground yields a plus of wildflowers all summer but a minus of many mosquitos in early season. Beyond this flat "park," the trail descends a more open hillside, and where it passes the confluence of the two forks of Echo Creek, we can see across the valley the steep course of the east fork plunging down to its rendezvous with the west fork. Finally the trail levels off and reaches the good campsites just before a metal bridge over Echo Creek (8100'). Fishing in the creek is good for rainbow and golden trout to 10".

3rd Hiking Day (**Echo Creek Crossing** to **Merced Lake**, 4.9 miles—7.9 km): After crossing the bridge over Echo Creek, our trail leads down the forested valley and easily fords a tributary stream, staying well above the main creek. This pleasant, shaded descent encounters fibrous-barked juniper trees and then tall, brittle red firs as it drops to another metal bridge 1 mile from the last one. Beyond this sturdy span, the trail rises slightly and the creek drops precipitously, so that we are soon far above it. Then our sandy tread swings west away from Echo Creek and traverses down a hillside where views are excellent of Echo Valley, a wide place in the great Merced River canyon below. Our trail passes a junction with the High Trail, which leads west to the Sunrise Trail, and then descends south to a green-floored forest of mixed conifers threaded by a tinkling all-year stream and decorated with a brilliant array of mountain wildflowers.

Then a last series of switchbacks span the descent to the floor of Echo Valley, where we meet and turn left (east) on the Merced River Trail. After crossing several forks of Echo Creek on wooden bridges, we pass a burn area where a 1966 fire killed most of the mature trees. But already new, small lodgepoles grow by the hundreds, and the grassy valley floor is extensively decorated with the blue flowers of lupine and the white blossoms of yarrow and yampah. Leaving Echo Valley, the trail leads up immense granite slabs. In places, the path is an elevated dirt strip on the slabs held in place between two parallel rock walls; in other places the route is simply indicated by two rock borders on the slabs.

At the hairpin angle of a set of switchbacks, the trail comes very close to the cascading Merced River, and a breather stop here will allow the traveler to drink in the sights and sounds of this dramatic part of the river—a long series of chutes, cascades, falls, cataracts and pools that are all due to the glacier which roughened up the formerly smooth bed of the Merced River. Above this turbulent stretch, the trail levels off beside the now-quiet river and arrives at the outlet of Merced Lake (7216'). This large lake has a High Sierra Camp at its east end, where the only presently legal campsites are. You can buy a few provisions at the small store, or even rent a rowboat to try your luck for rainbow and brown trout to 9". Be sure to bearproof your food.

4th Hiking Day (**Merced Lake** to **Emeric Lake**, 5.6 miles—9.0 km): The first short mile of this day's hike follows an almost level, wide, sandy path under a green forest canopy of fir and pine, juniper and aspen. Immediately beyond a bridge over roaring Lewis Creek we arrive at the Merced Lake Ranger Station (emergency services available in summer) and beside it find the Lewis Creek Trail, leading north. Quickly the ascent up this cobbled trail becomes steep, and it remains so for a panting half-mile-plus. Fortunately, Sierra junipers and Jeffrey pines cast plenty of morning shade. The trail levels momentarily as we pass a fine viewpoint for taking pictures of Merced Lake, far below, and Half Dome, due west. One more cobbled, steep climb leads to a junction with the Fletcher Creek Trail, and we turn left onto this path. Several switchbacks then descend to a wooden bridge over Lewis Creek. From here the trail enters more open hillside as it climbs moderately on a cobbled path bordered by proliferating bushes of mountain whitethorn and huckleberry oak. Just past a tributary ½ mile from Lewis Creek, we have fine views of cataracts and waterfalls on Fletcher Creek where it rushes down open granite slopes dotted with lodgepole pines. The trail then passes very close to the creek before veering south and climbing, steeply at times, on the now-familiar cobbling placed by trail crews. Here one has more good views of Fletcher Creek chuting and cascading down from the notch at the base of a granite dome before it leaps off a ledge in free fall. The few solitary pine trees on this otherwise blank dome testify to nature's extraordinary persistence.

At the notch, our trail levels off near some nice but illegal campsites, and then soon passes a side trail to Babcock Lake. From this junction the sandy trail ascends steadily through a moderate forest cover just east of Fletcher Creek. After a mile this route breaks out into the open and begins to rise more steeply via rocky switchbacks. From these zigzags one can see nearby in the north the outlet stream of Emeric Lake—though not the lake itself, which is behind a dome just to the right of the outlet's notch. Leaving the trail, we cross Fletcher Creek, follow up this outlet and stroll along the northwest shore of Emeric Lake (9370′) to the excellent campsites midway along this shore. Fishing is often good for rainbow trout to 12″. Sometimes windy, this lake was nevertheless so still one night that one could see the Milky Way clearly reflected in it.

5th Hiking Day (**Emeric Lake** to **Tuolumne Meadows**, 10.8 miles—17.4 km): This is the longest hiking day on this trip, but the ascent is not too severe and it comes at the beginning. From Tuolumne Pass at the crest of the Cathedral Range, the rest is downhill.

After circling the head of Emeric Lake and crossing the inlet stream without benefit of trail, we find a trail at the northeast corner of the lake, at the base of a granite knoll. This trail leads east-northeast for 0.6 mile to an **X** junction in the valley of Fletcher Creek. Taking the left branch up the valley, we follow a rocky-dusty trail through the forest fringe of the long meadow that straddles Fletcher Creek. This trail climbs farther from the meadow and passes northwest of a bald prominence that sits in the center of the upper valley of Fletcher and Emeric creeks, separating the two. Topping a minor summit, the trail descends slightly and then winds levelly past a long series of lovely ponds that are interconnected in early season. Then, immediately beyond an abandoned section of old trail, there is a lakelet 100 yards in diameter that would offer good swimming around late August. Just beyond it, the old trail veers sharply right, and our rutted meadow trail, going left, ascends to the top of a little swale with another good swimming pond and reaches an overlook above Boothe Lake. Our trail contours along this meadowy hillside about 50 vertical feet above the lake, passing a junction with a rutted use trail down to the lake. About ¼ mile farther we reach west Tuolumne Pass and a junction with the trail to Vogelsang High Sierra Camp, from where we retrace most of the steps of Trip 64.

59   Tioga Road to Tenaya Lake

TRIP   Trailhead on the Tioga Road to Tenaya Lake via Cathedral Pass, Echo Creek and Sunrise Creek (shuttle trip). Topo maps *Tuolumne Meadows, Merced Peak*. Best mid or late season; 25.6 miles (41.2 km).

Grade	Trail/layover days	Total recommended days
Leisurely	4/1	5
Moderate	4/0	4
Strenuous	3/0	3

HILITES   The first and last parts of this trip are along favorite and well-used trails, but in the middle we follow a little-used stretch of trail in the heart of Yosemite's spectacular glaciated highlands. Views of the immense domes and deep-cut canyons will impress the traveler's eye forever.

DESCRIPTION (Leisurely trip)

1st and 2nd Hiking Days: Follow Trip 58 to the **Echo Creek crossing**, 12.9 miles (20.8 km).

3rd Hiking Day (**Echo Creek Crossing** to **Sunrise Creek**, 5.1 miles—8.2 km): First follow the third hiking day, Trip 58, to the junction of the Echo Creek and High trails above the Merced River. Here our route turns right (west) and climbs rockily several hundred feet before leveling off above the immense Merced River canyon. This trail segment was part of the route from Yosemite Valley to Merced Lake until a path up the canyon was constructed in 1931. Before that, the steep canyon walls coming right down to the river near Bunnell Point, the great dome to our southwest, had made passage impossible. Finally a trail was built that bypasses the narrowest part of the canyon by climbing high on the south wall, and the trail we are now on fell into relative disuse.

With fine views of obelisk-like Mt. Clark in the south, we descend gradually for ½ mile over open granite in a setting that is sure to give you a feeling of being above almost everything. Then the trail passes a stagnant lakelet and ascends to even better viewpoints for appreciating the grandeur of the glaciated granitic wonder of nature spread out before you. It takes time to grasp the immensity of Mt. Clark, Clouds Rest, Half Dome, Mt. Starr King, Bunnell Point, and the great unnamed dome across the canyon west of it. Our continuing ascent then rounds a ridge and veers north into a forest of handsome Jeffrey pines. Here the trail levels off, and it remains level for a mile of exhilarating walking through Jeffreys, lodgepoles and red firs which shade patch after patch of vivid green ferns and a complement of multihued floral displays. Still in forest, we descend slightly to meet the John Muir Trail, go right on it for 150 yards to the Forsyth Trail, and then go left up it 150 yards to the fair campsites on Sunrise Creek (8080'). Fishing in this enticing stream is only fair for small rainbow and brook trout.

4th Hiking Day: Reverse the steps of the 1st hiking day, Trip 61, 7.6 miles (12.2 km).

Looking up the Merced River Canyon

60   Tioga Road to Yosemite Valley

TRIP   From Trailhead on the Tioga Road (Tuolumne
              Meadows) to Yosemite Valley via the Sunrise
              Trail (shuttle trip). Topo maps *Tuolumne Meadows,*
              Merced Peak, Yosemite. Best mid or late season;
              21.8 miles (35.0 km).

Grade	Trail/layover days	Total recom- mended days
Leisurely	4/0	4
Moderate	3/0	3
Strenuous	2/0	2

HILITES The Sunrise Trail route from the Meadows to the
             Valley (a segment of the John Muir Trail) is one of
             the Park's most famous and most used knapsack
             routes. Its reputation is an honest one, for these
             miles contain a magnificent range of flora and
             fauna, and the trail surveys some of the Park's
             best-known landmarks. This is a fine trip for the
             beginning knapsacker who has a couple of shorter
             trips under his (or her) belt, and has a taste for
             more.

DESCRIPTION (Leisurely trip)

1st and 2nd Hiking Days: Follow Trip 57 to **Sunrise High Sierra
Camp**, 9.2 miles (14.8 km).
3rd Hiking Day (**Sunrise High Sierra Camp** to **Sunrise Creek**, 5.1

miles—8.2 km): The trail from Sunrise High Sierra Camp continues south through Long Meadow, undulating gently below the eastern crest of Sunrise Mountain. After climbing to a forested saddle over a mile past the meadows, the trail parallels the headwaters of Sunrise Creek, descending steeply by switchbacks down a rocky moraine. This moraine is the largest of a series of ridgelike glacial deposits in this area, and the gigantic granite boulders along their sides testify to the power of the *mer-de-glace* that once filled Little Yosemite Valley and its tributaries. One such "erratic," about the size of a compact car, was found poised on the side of Moraine Dome to the southwest, and geologists have determined that it came from the slopes of the peaks at the northwest end of the Cathedral Range. The current belief is that there were at least three and possibly four ice ages that covered the country with glaciers. Because of the glacial moraines, the forest cover—mainly lodgepole pine—occurs in splotchy, broken stands. On the descent of the moraine, where Sunrise Creek is in a gully on the left, a remarkable flower display will tempt one to stop and try to identify a species or two. At the foot of the morainal descent, the trail crosses Sunrise Creek, and then descends on a westward course to the fair campsites on Sunrise Creek (8080') 150 yards up the Forsyth Trail from our trail's junction with it. Fishing on Sunrise Creek is poor-to-fair for rainbow and brook (fry).

4th Hiking Day (**Sunrise Creek** to **Yosemite Valley**, 7.5 miles—12.0 km): First retrace your steps 150 yards south to the first junction. Back on the John Muir Trail, our route continues southwest on a gradual descent, passing the High Trail to Merced Lake. Our trail is bounded on the north by the Pinnacles, on the south ridge by the Clouds Rest eminence, and on the south by Moraine Dome. Francois Matthes, in an interesting "detective story" written in the form of a geological essay (Professional Paper 160), discusses Moraine Dome extensively. He deduced, using three examples (one was the "erratic" cited above), that the moraines around the dome were the product of at least *two* glacial ages—a notion contrary to the thinking of the time. The morainal till of the last glacial age characterizes the underfooting of our descent into Little Yosemite Valley. A mile from the last junction is a ford of Sunrise Creek in a red-fir forest whose stillness is broken by the creek's gurgling and by the occasional screams of Steller jays. In another mile we pass the trail to Clouds Rest, and about ½ mile from there, the lateral to Half Dome (about 4 miles round trip). From this junction our shady path switchbacks down through a changing forest cover that comes to include some stately incense-cedars with their burnt orange, fibrous bark.

There are improved campsites on Sunrise Creek at the foot of the descent, and more numerous ones along the Merced River south of the river trail. A summer ranger is on duty near the trail junction. This is prime bear territory, so be sure to secure your food.

From here, reverse the steps of the 1st hiking day, Trip 81, to Yosemite Valley.

Half Dome from Glacier Point

Tenaya Lake to Yosemite Valley **61**

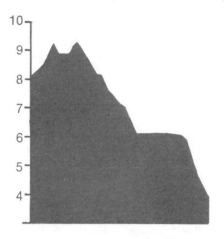

TRIP
From Tenaya Lake Walk-in Campground to Yosemite Valley (shuttle trip). Topo maps *Tuolumne Meadows, Merced Peak, Yosemite*. Best mid or late season; 15.1 miles (24.2 km).

Grade	Trail/layover days	Total recommended days
Leisurely	2/1	3
Moderate	2/0	2
Strenuous	....	....

HILITES
Through an elevation change of over 5000 feet (mostly down hill) this route covers most of Yosemite's spectrum of life zones. Views from various points above Tenaya Canyon are breathtaking in their panoramic scope. By contrast, a different kind of appreciation is evoked when walking alongside the serene waters of the Merced River as it serpentines across the floor of Little Yosemite Valley. The ever-changing nature of a river is a high point of this trip—slides, cascades, and earth-shaking waterfalls add exclamation points. This route is a fine selection for the intermediate backpacker who has never had a taste of Yosemite's varied backcountry.

DESCRIPTION

1st Hiking Day (**Tenaya Lake Walk-In Campground** to **Sunrise Creek**, 7.6 miles—12.2 km): First, follow Trip 55 to the junction of the trail going east to Sunrise Camp. From the junction, our trail makes a 320-foot descent on switchbacks, rises over a talus-swollen little ridge, and drops beside a pleasant-looking lakelet. The lightly forested hillside ahead leads up to three unnamed streams that we cross in quick succession. This watery slope is boggy till midseason, and the plentiful groundwater nourishes rank gardens of wildflowers throughout the summer. Leveling off beyond the streams, our trail meets the 2-mile trail to the summit of Clouds Rest. Hikers with plenty of energy may take this short lateral to this lofty prominence. Views from Clouds Rest are among the most spectacular in the Sierra, including a 4500-foot continuous granite slope stretching all the way down to Tenaya Creek and rising on the other side—the largest exposed granite area in the Park.

From the Clouds Rest junction, the trail meanders over sandy, level terrain for ½ mile, detouring around many fallen trees, before it starts its plunge down toward Sunrise Creek. This switchbacking descent is a little tough on the knees but in repayment the green fir-and-pine forest is a classic of its kind, and occasional views down into the Merced River Canyon are sweeping in their range. Finally our trail approaches a stream, parallels it for almost ½ mile, fords it and then fords Sunrise Creek to the fair campsites on the creek (8080'). Fishing for rainbow and brook (fry) is poor-to-fair.

2nd Hiking Day: Follow the 4th hiking day, Trip 60, 7.5 miles (12.0 km).

Tuolumne Meadows to Nelson Lake **62**

TRIP   From Tuolumne Meadows Campground to Nelson Lake (round trip). Topo map *Tuolumne Meadows*. Best mid or late season; 11.8 miles (19.0 km).

Grade	Trail/layover days	Total recom- mended days
Leisurely	....	....
Moderate	2/1	3
Strenuous	....	....

HILITES   This interesting and varied route visits the scenic Elizabeth Lake basin and then crosses the serrated Cathedral Range to Nelson Lake. No trail route offers finer views of those geologic wonders called Unicorn Peak and the Cockscomb. Open, meadow-fringed Nelson Lake makes a pleasantly fitting end to this exciting trip, and anglers can look forward to good brook-trout fishing on the placid waters of this alpine gem.

DESCRIPTION

1st Hiking Day (**Tuolumne Meadows Campground** to **Nelson Lake**, 5.9 miles—9.5 km): To reach the trailhead, walk to the Group Camping Section of the Tuolumne Meadows campground, where the signed trail begins across from a masonry building. In a few hundred feet we cross the Tenaya Lake/Lyell Canyon Trail and then continue a steady southward ascent. The shade-giving forest cover is almost entirely lodgepole pine as the trail crosses several runoff streams that dry up by late summer. More than a mile from the start, our route veers close to Unicorn Creek, and the music of this dashing, gurgling, cold-water stream makes the climb easier. When the ascent finally ends, the hiker emerges at the foot of a long meadow containing Elizabeth Lake, at the foot of striking Unicorn Peak.

Past Elizabeth Lake, the meadow gives way to a moderately dense forest cover of lodgepole interspersed with mountain hemlock, and the trail climbs, steeply, then moderately, and steeply again. A few hundred feet before you reach the ridge crest, you come to a late-lingering snowbank where the trail splits. If you go left, you will pass through a narrow gully between granite walls. If you go right, you will walk up a bare granite-sand slope. I recommend that if you have a full pack, you take the right trail going to Nelson Lake and the left one returning, because of some steep places on the left trail just beyond the crest.

Because of the close proximity of the Cockscomb, about 1 mile due west, the hiker has excellent views of that knifelike spire from just beyond the left pass. Well-named by Francois Matthes, this slender crest bears clear marks of the highest level reached by the ice of the last glacial episode. Its lower shoulders reveal the rounded, well-polished surfaces that betray glacial action, while its jagged, sharply etched crest shows no such markings. Further evidence of glacial action may be clearly seen on the steep descent into the head of long, typically **U**-shaped Echo Creek valley. The shearing and polishing action of the ice mass that shaped this rounded valley is evident on the cliffs on the west side.

About ⅓ mile from where the trail split, and several hundred yards beyond the crest, the forks come together again on a steep, tree-dotted, ravined hillside. As our route descends along winding, clear, meadowed Echo Creek for about 2 miles, the valley floor is lush with wildflower growth. During midseason the passerby can expect to see Davidson's penstemon, Douglas phlox, groundsel, red heather, lupine and swamp whiteheads. At the end of the second large meadow in this canyon, our trail leaves Echo Creek and veers east up a low, rocky ridge, undulating through sparse forest. One is almost at Nelson Lake (9636') before he can see his destination, meadow-fringed at the foot of imposing granite Peak 11282. Good campsites may be found on the southeast and southwest sides. Anglers will find the lake's waters good fishing for brook trout (7-11").

2nd Hiking Day: Reverse your steps, 5.9 miles (9.5 km).

Tuolumne Meadows to Lyell Canyon **63**

TRIP
From Tuolumne Meadows Lodge to Lyell Base Camp (round trip). Topo map *Tuolumne Meadows*. Best early, mid or late season; 17.4 miles (28.0 km).

Grade	Trail/layover days	Total recommended days
Leisurely	2/0	2
Moderate	....	....
Strenuous	....	....

HILITES
Alpine meadows have a fascination that claims the trail traveler, whether he be novice or hoariest veteran. Campers' descriptions of favorite camping places invariably favor the forested western fringe of a remote meadow (your camp gets the first warming sunlight there). The meadows of Lyell Canyon are the stuff of which such memories are built. Idyllic from beginning to end, this long, gentle grassland with its serpentining river is a delight to travel.

DESCRIPTION

1st Hiking Day (**Tuolumne Meadows Lodge** to **Lyell Base Camp**, 8.7 miles—14.0 km): The trailhead is in the Tuolumne Meadows Lodge grounds, southwest of the office-dining room. The route goes about 100 yards to the Dana Fork of the river, and crosses it on a bridge. Then this segment of the John Muir Trail leads over a slight rise and descends to the Lyell Fork, where there is a substantial double bridge. The meadows above this bridge are among the most delightful in all the Sierra, and anytime you happen to be staying all night at the lodge or nearby, they are a wonderful place to spend the last hour before dinner. Mts. Dana and Gibbs fill the eastern horizon, catching the late sun, and the river has good fishing for brown trout.

About 50 yards past the bridge we meet the trail that comes up the river from the campground, turn left (east) onto it, and skirt a long, lovely section of the meadow. This re-routed trail is relatively new, established because of extensive trail wear and subsequent erosion of the old route. Re-routing is one of several far-sighted Park Service policies that have been adopted to allow areas in the wilderness a "breather"—a chance to recover from overuse. Going through a dense forest cover of lodgepole pine, our route passes the trail that ascends south to Tuolumne Pass and Vogelsang High Sierra Camp, and then fords Rafferty Creek. This ford may be difficult in early season, but you may find a log 200 yards down stream.

From this point on, the trail traverses alternating meadowed and forested sections as it veers southward, and the silent walker may come upon grazing deer in the meadows and an occasional marmot that has ventured from the rocky hillside on the right. Fields of wildflowers color the grasslands from early to late season, but the best time of the year for seeing this color is generally early-to-mid season. From the more open portions of the trail, one has excellent views of the Kuna Crest as it slopes up to the southeast and the river itself has delighted generations of mountain photographers. Our route then passes a trail branching southwest to Evelyn Lake and Tuolumne Pass. There are fair campsites around this junction. Beyond this junction the trail fords Ireland Creek (difficult in early season), passes below Potter Point, and ascends gently for 2 miles to the fair campsites at Lyell Base Camp (9040'). Fishing is fair for brook trout. This base camp, surrounded on three sides by steep canyon walls, marks the end of the meadowed sections of Lyell Canyon, and is the traditional first-night stopping place for those touring the John Muir Trail beginning at Tuolumne Meadows.

2nd Hiking Day: Retrace your steps, 8.7 miles (14.0 km).

Mt. Lyell above Lyell Canyon

Tuolumne Meadows to Vogelsang   **64**

TRIP   **Tuolumne Meadows Lodge** to **Vogelsang High Sierra Camp** (round trip). Topo map *Tuolumne Meadows*. Best mid or late season, 15.4 miles (24.8 km).

Grade	Trail/layover days	Total recommended days
Leisurely	2/1	3
Moderate	2/0	2
Strenuous	....	....

HILITES   Vogelsang Camp has the most dramatic setting of all the famous High Sierra Camps. Located right under the somber north face of Fletcher Peak, it has an authentic alpine atmosphere. Many nearby lakes offer exciting side-trip possibilities for anglers, swimmers and picnickers.

DESCRIPTION

1st Hiking Day (**Tuolumne Meadows Lodge** to **Vogelsang High Sierra Camp**, 7.7 miles—12.4 km): First, follow Trip 63 to the John Muir Trail-Rafferty Creek Trail junction. Here our route turns right and immediately begins the toughest climb of this entire trip. Even so, the grade is moderate as often as it is steep, the trail is fairly well shaded by lodgepole pines, and the length of the climb is well under a mile. Then, as the ascent decreases to a gentle grade, we pass through high, boulder-strewn meadows that offer good views eastward of reddish-brown Mts. Dana and Gibbs, and gray-white Mammoth Peak. Soon the trail dips close to Rafferty Creek, and since this stream flows all year you can count on refreshment here. Then the nearly level trail passes above an orange snowcourse marker in a large meadow below and continues its long, gentle ascent through a sparse forest of lodgepole pines unmixed with a single tree of any other species. About ⅓ mile beyond a stream that dries up in late summer, we ford another that also does in some years and immediately veer right at a junction where the abandoned old trail up the long meadow veers left. Our relocated trail up a cobbly hillside was built to allow the damaged meadow below to recover from the pounding of too many feet—people's and, especially, horses'.

Finally the exclusive lodgepole pines allow a few whitebark pines to join their company, and these trees diminish the force of the winds that often sweep through Tuolumne Pass. Through breaks in this forest one has intermittent views of cliff-bound, dark-banded Fletcher Peak and Peak 11799 in the south. Then our path leaves the green-floored forest and leads out into an area of bouldery granite outcroppings dotted with a few trees. Around this granite and past these trees we wind down to the west side of saucer-shaped Tuolumne Pass, a major gap in the Cathedral Range. Taking the signed trail to Vogelsang here, we follow a rocky-dusty path up a moderately steep hillside below which Boothe Lake and its surrounding meadows lie serene in the west. Finally, our trail reaches the top of this climb, and suddenly we see the tents of Vogelsang High Sierra Camp (10,180') spread out before us. A few snacks may be bought here, or dinner or breakfast if you make a reservation. There are good campsites by Fletcher Creek just beyond the camp, but remember the bears that live here are always interested in your food.

2nd Hiking Day: Retrace you steps, 7.7 miles (12.4 km).

Looking north from Tuolumne Pass

Tuolumne Meadows to Emeric Lake 65

TRIP From Tuolumne Meadows Lodge to Emeric Lake via Vogelsang, Lewis Creek and Fletcher Creek; semiloop trip. Topo maps *Tuolumne Meadows, Merced Peak*. Best mid or late season; 28.8 miles (46.3 km).

Grade	Trail/layover days	Total recommended days
Leisurely	4/1	5
Moderate	3/0	3
Strenuous	2/0	2

HILITES With Tuolumne Pass as the neck of the noose, this trip "lassos" Vogelsang Peak by dashing down the valley of Lewis Creek and then cruising back up the valley of Fletcher Creek. In addition to the spectrum of views of this fine peak, the traveler will constantly have good vistas of many parts of the Cathedral Range, and for anglers there is good fishing in both creeks and at Emeric Lake.

DESCRIPTION (Leisurely trip)

1st Hiking Day: Follow Trip 64 to **Vogelsang High Sierra Camp**, 7.7 miles (12.4 km).

2nd Hiking Day (**Vogelsang High Sierra Camp** to **Florence Creek**, 4.3 miles—6.9 km): Taking the Vogelsang Pass Trail from the camp, we descend slightly to ford Fletcher Creek on boulders and then begin a 550 foot ascent to the pass. The panting hiker is rewarded, as always in the Sierra, with increasingly good views. Fletcher Peak rises grandly on the left, far north is Mt.

Conness, and Clouds Rest and then Half Dome come into view in the west-southwest. The trail skirts above the west shore of Vogelsang Lake as we look down on the turfy shores and the large rock island of this timberline lake. Nearer the pass, views to the north are occluded somewhat, but expansive new views appear in the south: from left to right are Parsons Peak, Simmons Peak, Mt. Maclure, the tip of Mt. Lyell behind Maclure, Mt. Florence and, in the south, the entire Clark Range, from Triple Divide Peak on the left to Mt. Clark on the right.

From the windswept pass the trail rises briefly northeast before it follows steep switchbacks down into sparse lodgepole forest where many small streams provide moisture for thousands of lupine plants, with their light blue, pea-family flowers. The singing of the unnamed outlet stream from Gallison Lake becomes clear as the trail begins to level off, and then we reach a flat meadow through which the stream slowly meanders. There is a fine campsite beside this meadow, though wood fires are illegal here. Proceeding down a rutted, grassy trail for several hundred yards, we come to a brief, steep descent on a rocky path that swoops down to the meadowed valley of multi-braided Lewis Creek. In this little valley in quick succession we boulderhop the Gallison Lake outlet and then cross Lewis Creek on a log. In a few minutes we pass the steep ½ mile lateral to Bernice Lake. The shady trail winds gently down east of the creek under a moderate overhead canopy of lodgepole pine mixed with some hemlock, crossing a little stream about ½ mile from the last ford. Then, after almost touching the creek opposite a steep, rusty west canyon wall, the trail veers away and crosses another small tributary stream as it winds through dense hemlock forest to the good campsites beside Florence Creek (9200'). This year-round creek cascades down to the camping area over steep granite sheets, and the water sounds are a fine sleeping potion at bedtime. Fishing in Florence and Lewis creeks is good for brook trout to 12".

3rd Hiking Day (**Florence Creek** to **Emeric Lake**, 6.0 miles—9.6 km): Leaving the densely shaded hemlock forest floor, our trail descends a series of lodgepole-dotted granite slabs, and Lewis Creek makes pleasant noises in a string of chutes not far away on the right. Then, where the creek's channel narrows, the traveler will find on his left a lesson in exfoliation: granite layers peeling like an onion. One is more used to seeing this kind of peeling on Yosemite's domes, but this fine example is located on a canyon slope. As the bed of Lewis Creek steepens to deliver the stream's water to the Merced River far below, so does the trail steepen, and our descent to middle altitudes reaches the zone of red firs and silver pines. After dipping beside the creek, the trail climbs away from it to a junction with the High Trail, which leads south along the rim of the Merced River canyon.

From this junction the Lewis Creek Trail, now out of earshot of the creek, switchbacks down moderately, sometimes steeply, under a sparse cover of red fir, juniper, and lodgepole and silver pine for 1 mile to a junction with the Fletcher Creek Trail. We turn right onto this trail and follow the latter part of the 4th hiking day, Trip 58, to Emeric Lake.

4th Hiking Day: Follow the 5th hiking day, Trip 58, to **Tuolumne Meadows**, 10.8 miles (17.4 km).

Mt. Clark above Emeric Lake

66 Tuolumne Meadows to Lyell Fork

TRIP From Tuolumne Meadows Lodge to Lyell Fork, Merced River, via Vogelsang, Lewis Creek, return via Fletcher Creek, Babcock Lake, Boothe Lake; semiloop trip. Topo maps *Tuolumne Meadows, Merced Peak*. Best mid or late season, 40.3 miles (64.9 km).

Grade	Trail/layover days	Total recommended days
Leisurely	7/1	8
Moderate	6/1	7
Strenuous	4/0	4

HILITES Every beginning backpacker sooner or later wants to try his newfound skills on a challenging trip of some length. This excursion in Yosemite Park is made to order for him: long mileage but not too long; tough climbs, but manageable ones; lonely stretches, but two popular campsites in between. And it's all wrapped up in some of the best scenery in Yosemite National Park.

DESCRIPTION (Moderate trip)

1st and 2nd Hiking Days: Follow Trip 65 to **Florence Creek**, 12.0 miles (19.3 km).

3rd Hiking Day (**Florence Creek** to **Lyell Fork**, 7.4 miles—11.9 km): First, follow the 3rd hiking day, Trip 65, to the junction of the High Trail and the Lewis Creek Trail, and turn left. The ascent from here is a tough, unrelieved 1000 vertical feet, but fortunately most of it is in shady forest of red fir and silver and lodgepole pine. Near the top, where the grade is a little less steep, the panting hiker is also shaded by altitude-preferring whitebark pines. At about 9000 feet, views to the west and north grow expansive, and one can make out Half Dome, Clouds Rest, the Cockscomb and Unicorn Peak. After crossing a ridge, our sandy path descends into a meadow long since invaded by lodgepole trees and reaches an all-year stream where you can refill your body's cooling system depleted by the long climb. Beyond this easy ford the High Trail lives up to its name as it traverses a broad bench about 10,000 feet above sea level. A second all-year stream, larger than the last, can present slight fording problems in early season. Then the trail climbs again, away from the lip of the main canyon, until it veers south back to the lip at a spectacular viewpoint for studying the headwaters of the Lyell Fork (in the east) and the Merced Peak Fork (in the south) of the Merced River. One could spend many days in these vast, trailless headwaters without seeing another human being.

From this overlook the trail descends a bit steeply in places to a third all-year stream, an easy boulderhop, and then continues down to the cascading, chuting Lyell Fork (9080'). The last segment of trail before the stream, over granite slabs, is a little hard to follow, but the route leads where you would expect it to. The campsites at the ford are poor, but good ones lie 150 yards downstream, where the chutes and rapids flowing over the sculpted granite bedrock are fine visual attractions and provide good music to sleep by. There are also good campsites ½ mile upstream, a better base if you are going to explore the remote lake basins at the headwaters of the Lyell Fork. Fishing in the Lyell Fork is good for brook trout to 11".

4th Hiking Day (**Lyell Fork** to **Babcock Lake**, 9.1 miles—14.7 km): First, retrace your steps to the Lewis Creek Trail and turn left (south). From this junction the Lewis Creek Trail, now out of earshot of the creek, switchbacks down moderately, sometimes steeply, under a sparse cover of red fir, juniper, and lodgepole and silver pine for 1 mile to a junction with a trail that comes steeply up from the main canyon floor. We turn right on this trail and follow several switchbacks down to a bridge over tree-shaded Lewis Creek. From here the rocky trail enters more open hillside as it climbs moderately on a cobbled path bordered by clumps of mountain whitethorn and huckleberry oak. Just past a tributary ½ mile from Lewis Creek we have fine views of cataracts and waterfalls on Fletcher Creek where it rushes down open granite slopes dotted with lodgepole pines. The trail then passes very close to the splashing creek before veering northeast and climbing, steeply at times, on the now-familiar cobbling placed by trail crews. Here one has more good views of Fletcher Creek chuting and cascading down from the notch at the base of a granite dome before it leaps off a ledge in free fall. The few solitary pine trees on this otherwise blank dome are mute testimony to nature's extraordinary persistence.

At the notch our trail levels off near some nice but illegal campsites and soon arrives at the trail to Babcock Lake. Turning left (north) we ford Fletcher Creek (difficult in early season) and follow a winding trail ⅓ mile west to narrow, granite-bound Babcock Lake (8983′). There are fine campsites all around this forested lake, and fishing is good for brook trout to 10″.

5th Hiking Day (**Babcock Lake** to **Boothe Lake**, 4.4 miles—7.1 km): After retracing our steps to the Fletcher Creek Trail, we turn left (north). From this junction the sandy trail ascends steadily through a moderate forest cover just east of the verdant banks of rollicking Fletcher Creek. After a mile, the trail breaks out into the open and begins to rise more steeply via rocky but shaded switchbacks. These zigzags lead to another notch between two granite domes, and upon reaching this notch the slogging traveler suddenly achieves a wonderful panorama. A long, barely sloping, lush meadow stretches several miles ahead, and it is flanked on both sides by soaring, snow-streaked peaks. Down this meadow flows Fletcher Creek, meandering from pool to trout-holding pool. Here one has the feeling of being in truly high country, and the distance passes easily as we stroll to an **X** junction with trails to Emeric Lake and Vogelsang. From this junction follow part of the 5th hiking day, Trip 58, to the overlook of Boothe Lake (9900′) and then leave the trail to find the good campsites on the south side of the lake.

6th Hiking Day (**Boothe Lake** to **Tuolumne Meadows Lodge**, 7.4 miles—11.9 km): First, hike briefly cross country back to the trail you left at the end of the previous hiking day. From that point, near broad Tuolumne Pass, hike up to the junction in the pass, and then retrace most of the steps of Trip 64.

Tuolumne Meadows to Triple Peak Fork 67

TRIP From Tuolumne Meadows Lodge to the Triple Peak Fork of the Merced River via Vogelsang, Lewis Creek, return via Washburn Lake, Fletcher Creek, Emeric Lake. Topo maps *Tuolumne Meadows, Merced Peak*. Best mid or late season; 51.0 miles (82.1 km).

Grade	Trail/layover days	Total recom- mended days
Leisurely	8/1	9
Moderate	7/0	7
Strenuous	4/0	4

HILITES The headwaters of the Triple Peak Fork of the Merced River are about as far as one can get from civilization, so this is a trip for those who feel they encounter too many people on most of their hikes. Their opportunity to view most of the High Sierra from the southern border of Yosemite is won by a long walk through grand high country.

DESCRIPTION (Moderate trip)

1st, 2nd and 3rd Hiking Days: Follow Trip 66 to the **Lyell Fork of the Merced River**, 19.1 miles (30.7 km).

4th Hiking Day (**Lyell Fork** to **Triple Peak Fork**, 6.9 miles—11.1 km): This day's hike starts off strenuously up switchbacks on the south wall of the Lyell Fork canyon. As we progress slowly up the rocky path, views open up to reward us for our struggle. In the northeast, on the Sierra crest, are Mt. Maclure and Mt. Lyell, highest point in Yosemite Park. After Lyell passes from view, Rodger Peak, second highest in the Park, appears as the dark triangle beyond the right flank of Peak 12132. Other towering peaks in view this side of the crest don't even have names, but in the company of lesser summits they surely would have. Where our trail extends close to the lip of the Merced River canyon, we can step off the path to an overlook for viewing most of the Clark Range in the southwest, and Clouds Rest in the northwest.

Beyond the top of the ascent, the route winds among large boulders on "gruss"—granite sand—which is the result of the breakup of just such boulders by the fierce erosional forces at work in these alpine climates. After crossing a seasonal stream, the trail ascends to a second broad ridge from which views through the whitebark-pine trees continue to be excellent. About ½ mile beyond this ridge a trail to Foerster Lake veers off to the left. This unsigned trail is indicated by parallel rock borders and occasional flame-shaped blazes on trees. Secluded Foerster Lake has no fish, but swimming and camping there are excellent.

From this spur trail our route makes a long descent, paralleling Foerster Lake's outlet part of the way, to a boulder ford of Foerster Creek. The well-shaded trail then undulates past a number of pocket meadows to another small stream, and yet another not shown on the map. A gentle traverse downward extends almost a mile to a small creek that winds through a flat area densely forested with hemlock and lodgepole pine. From this flat the High Trail begins a climb that doesn't end until it reaches the Yosemite border at Isberg Pass. Very soon the trail fords the outlet of the unnamed lake north of Isberg Peak, and in another 200 yards it reaches a large cairn which marks the junction with a trail down to the Triple Peak Fork. All hikers who arrive here with any surplus energy will greatly enjoy a 4-mile round trip to Isberg Pass before heading down to camp on the Triple Peak Fork.

The trail to the pass first climbs moderately for ¼ mile up a beautiful hillside covered with whitish broken granite in whose cracks a dozen species of alpine wildflowers grow. Looking west and north from this slope, one can see all the peaks of the Clark Range and most of the peaks of the Cathedral Range. Using your *Tuolumne Meadows* map, you can probably make out Tenaya Peak, Tressider Peak, Cathedral Peak, Echo Peaks, Matthes Crest and the Cockscomb. At the top of this little climb a truly marvelous sight comes into view, for here we enter a large, high bowl nearly encircled by great peaks which has in it an enormous meadow and two sparkling lakes. Here and there, clumps of whitebark and lodgepole pines help give scale to the vast amphitheater, and the delicateness of the meadow flowers is a perfect counterpoint to the massiveness of the encircling summits. The setting is absolutely euphoric.

On the far side of the bowl, the trail begins to rise toward the crest and soon comes to a junction where the right fork leads to Post Peak Pass and the left to Isberg Pass, ¾ mile away. The left fork ascends moderately a short way to reach the height of the pass, and then contours over to it. The best views—other than those we have already been enjoying for the last several miles—are to be had from a point on the ridgeline a few hundred yards beyond the sign-marked pass. You can see most of the High Sierra, from the Ritter Range close in the east, to peaks around Mt. Goddard southwest of Bishop.

Back at the cairned junction, our route turns west and starts straight downhill, then veers southwest and switchbacks down into deep hemlock forest, turning north for the last ¾ mile down to the river. There are good campsites around the junction of our trail and the trail to Red Peak Pass, which begins just across the placid Triple Peak Fork (9100′). Fishing is good for brook and rainbow trout to 9″.

5th Hiking Day (**Triple Peak Fork** to **Washburn Lake**, 6.9 miles— 11.1 km): Reverse the 4th and part of the 3rd hiking day, Trip 87, to the good campsites at the head of Washburn Lake.

6th Hiking Day (**Washburn Lake** to **Emeric Lake**, 7.3 miles—11.8 km): The sandy trail along the east side of Washburn Lake leads over slopes dotted with white fir, aspen, juniper, lodgepole pine and Jeffrey pine, and from these slopes on a typical morning, the still water makes a fine mirror for the soaring granite cliffs across the lake. Beyond this lake, our descending trail stays near the singing river in open forest, fording a small stream every quarter mile or so as it descends on a moderate grade. Then the canyon floor begins to widen, and the trail proceeds levelly under a canopy of imposing Jeffrey pines and other tall conifers to a junction with the Lewis Creek Trail beside the Merced Lake Ranger Station. Here we turn right and follow the latter part of the 4th hiking day, Trip 58, to Emeric Lake.

7th Hiking Day (**Emeric Lake** to **Tuolumne Meadows Lodge**, 10.8 miles—17.4 km): Follow the 5th hiking day, Trip 58.

68 Tuolumne Meadows to Agnew Meadows

TRIP   From Tuolumne Meadows Lodge to Agnew
Meadows via Donohue Pass, Island Pass,
Thousand Island Lake, Shadow Lake (shuttle
trip). Topo maps *Tuolumne Meadows, Devils Postpile*. Best mid or late season; 28.2 miles (45.5 km).

Grade	Trail/layover days	Total recom-mended days
Leisurely	5/1	6
Moderate	4/1	5
Strenuous	4/0	4

HILITES   "Sky parlor" meadows, alpine lakes, clear, icy
streams, magnificent peaks—this trip has them
all. Except for the last 4 miles, this route follows
the well-known John Muir Trail as it tours Lyell
Canyon and the view-filled eastern slopes of the
Ritter Range. Because of its fame, this trail sees a
lot of use, but the incomparable scenery enroute
more than compensates for the lack of solitude.

DESCRIPTION (Moderate trip)

1st Hiking Day: Follow Trip 63 to **Lyell Base Camp**, 9 miles
(14.5 km).

2nd Hiking Day (**Lyell Base Camp** to **Rush Creek**, 7 miles—11.3
km): From Lyell Base Camp the trail ascends the steep,
southern terminal wall of Lyell Canyon above the west side of
the Lyell Fork. There is no water here in late season. Just
before the confluence of the Maclure Creek tributary of the
Lyell Fork, our route crosses a bridge to the east side and
switchbacks up to some very used campsites just before
another bridge. The rocky underfooting above here is
pleasantly relieved by superb alpine meadows. Along the first

3 miles of this day's ascent, views of the glaciers on the north faces of Mt. Maclure and Mt. Lyell are superlative.

From this ford our trail climbs steeply up rocky going to Donohue Pass (11,056') at the crest of the Sierra. This pass, lying between Donohue Peak (northeast) and Mt. Lyell (southwest), affords majestic views of the Sierra crest, the Cathedral Range and the Ritter Range—not right at the pass, but just before and just after. From Donohue Pass the trail descends by rocky switchbacks to sparse timber cover at the headwaters of Rush Creek, passing a lateral to Marie Lakes. As the trail levels out somewhat, it meets and then parallels a small, unnamed tributary of Rush Creek descending to join the main stream. In the Rush Creek watershed the forest cover of lodgepole and hemlock becomes denser, and the trail fords two tributaries to the "Improved" campsites on Rush Creek (9600"), where our route meets the Rush Creek Trail. Fishing is good for brook and rainbow (to 10").

3rd Hiking Day (**Rush Creek** to **Shadow Creek**, 8.0 miles—12.9 km): Through a continuing forest cover of lodgepole and mountain hemlock, our route ascends steadily beyond the junction with a trail to Davis Lakes, climbing southeast to the low saddle known as Island Pass (10,200'). Just south of this pass the trail passes two small lakes and then veers eastward across slopes. Along this trail the hiker will discover a verdant growth of wildflowers, including lupine, elephant heads, sulfur flower, Mariposa lily, goldenrod, fleabane, mountain aster, pussy paws, and streptanthus.

The trail emerges from the lodgepole-and-hemlock ground cover to a metamorphic slope above the outlet at the east end of Thousand Island Lake. Views from this rocky slope are sweeping, and the hiker immediately notices the difference between the predominantly darker rock of the Ritter Range and the lighter granite of the Sierra crest's alpine peaks. Geologically, the Ritter Range is made up of somewhat older rocks originally volcanic in nature, and the spectacularly jagged skyline from Banner Peak southward attests to the strength of this rock, which resisted the massive glaciers that gnawed at the range. As the trail switchbacks down to the outlet of Thousand Island Lake, there are classic views across the island-studded waters to the imposing east facades of Banner Peak and Mt. Ritter.

From Thousand Island Lake, proceed to Shadow Creek by reversing the 2nd hiking day of Trip 74.

4th Hiking Day (**Shadow Creek** to **Agnew Meadows**, 4.2 miles— 6.8 km); Reverse the 1st hiking day of Trip 69.

Several fair campsites may be found at the outlet and on the north side of Thousand Island Lake (9834'), the better ones being a mile or two west of the Muir Trail and back from the water. All these sites are somewhat exposed to the wind, but offer unexcelled views. Fishing for brook and rainbow (to 13") is poor-to-fair.

4th and 5th Hiking Days: Reverse the 2nd and 1st hiking days, Trip 74, 9.5 miles (15.3 km).

John Muir Trail, Mt. Lyell

Agnew Meadows to Shadow Creek **69**

TRIP From Agnew Meadows to Shadow Creek (round trip). Topo map *Devils Postpile*. Best mid or late season; 8.4 miles (13.6 km).

Grade	Trail/layover days	Total recommended days
Leisurely	2/0	2
Moderate	....	....
Strenuous	....	....

HILITES Shadow Lake is subject to very heavy use, and in consequence this edition of *Sierra North* no longer recommends camping there but rather, up the inlet stream. If one needs an example to substantiate the necessity of the government's setting aside more wilderness areas, this high-country jewel is a case in point. This is a fine trip for beginning backpackers.

DESCRIPTION

1st Hiking Day (**Agnew Meadows** to **Shadow Creek**, 4.2 miles— 6.8 km): From the trailhead west of the pack station (8335') our route skirts a flowery meadow before crossing a small ridge covered with red fir and lodgepole pine. Just under a mile from the start, and just beyond a long gully, we meet a trail from Agnew Meadows Campground, coming in on the right. In 80 yards the Pacific Crest Trail, which we've started west on, branches left to switchback down to the San Joaquin River while our route ahead descends steadily west toward the river. The first part of this downslope is interesting in that it incorporates many of the ground-cover changes typical of the Mammoth Lakes region. One moment you are in dense pine-and-fir forest, and the next you are walking on an exposed slope of pumice, growing manzanita and abundant wildflowers. In midsummer, watch for varieties of paintbrush, larkspur and streptanthus.

We re-enter forest cover at the canyon bottom and skirt the east side of shallow, lily-padded Olaine Lake. Just beyond it we leave the River Trail and head west to the Middle Fork San

Joaquin River. Crossing this cottonwood-lined stream can be difficult in early season, even if the usual log jam is there. Beyond the ford our trail winds steeply up a sagebrush-and-juniper-dotted slope. This 700-foot climb can be very warm in midsummer, but soon enough we swing over to cascading Shadow Creek and arrive at the outlet of beautiful Shadow Lake. Skirting the north shore, we pass several illegal and abused campsites, and above the head of the lake we find appropriate campsites beyond the junction with the John Muir Trail.

2nd Hiking Day: Retrace your steps, 4.2 miles (6.8 km).

Shadow Lake

Ron Felzer

Agnew Meadows to Ediza Lake **70**

TRIP From Agnew Meadows to Ediza Lake (round trip).
Topo maps *Devils Postpile*. Best mid or late season;
14.0 miles (22.4 km).

Grade	Trail/layover days	Total recommended days
Leisurely	2/1	3
Moderate	2/0	2
Strenuous	....	....

HILITES This is one of the finest routes in the Mammoth
Lakes region for viewing the spectacular Ritter
Range, including Banner Peak, Mt. Ritter and the
Minarets. The alpine beauty of Ediza Lake is
almost legendary. In the shadow of the breathtaking Minarets, one can readily appreciate the
grand processes that formed this very striking
landscape.

DESCRIPTION

1st Hiking Day (**Agnew Meadows** to **Ediza Lake,** 7.0 miles—
11.2 km): First follow trip 69 to **Shadow Creek,** 4.2 miles—6.8
km. From streamside campsites above Shadow Lake we begin
the easy ascent along Shadow Creek to the outlet of Ediza
Lake. Following the John Muir Trail for about ⅔ mile, we wind
in and out of timber, passing some lovely waterfalls and pools
along the creek. After the Muir Trail turns north away from our
route, we cross several meadows, and then we rock hop the
lovely, shaded outlet from Nydiver Lakes. Continuing up
Shadow Creek you will have several choices of trail but you
should have no trouble getting to the outlet of Ediza Lake
(9300′). To get to the legal campsites on the west end of the
lake, you can go around the south side, but the north-side
route is shorter. The delicate environs of this lake are heavily
used, so please be careful. Ediza Lake makes a fine base for
exploring the basin above.
2nd Hiking Day: Retrace your steps, 7.0 miles (11.2 km).

71   Agnew Meadows to Devils Postpile

TRIP   From Agnew Meadows to Devils Postpile Campground (shuttle trip). Topo map *Devils Postpile*.
Best mid or late season; 16.2 miles (1 mile cross
country) (26.0 km).

Grade	Trail/layover days	Total recom- mended days
Leisurely	....	....
Moderate	3/0	3
Strenuous	....	....

HILITES   For those travelers who enjoy spectacular alpine
landscapes this trip is excellent. This route,
however, is difficult, and is recommended for
highly experienced backpackers only. Climbers
use this route to reach the base of the jagged
Minarets.

DESCRIPTION (Moderate trip)

1st Hiking Day: Follow Trip 70 to **Eziza Lake,** 7.0 miles—11.3
km.

2nd Hiking Day (**Ediza Lake** to **Minaret Lake,** 3.0 miles—4.8
km): From the south side of Ediza Lake the trail heads south
up a slope dotted with willows, grassy patches and a few trees.
Occasionally the trail becomes unclear through a willow patch
or a snowbank, but the route is almost straight to the outlet of
Iceberg Lake (9800'). In the meadowed fringes around deep-
blue Iceberg Lake one can find lupine, heather and
paintbrush. Looking up to the south one can see the outlet
from Cecile Lake pouring over the lip of its basin. Heading
around the east side of Iceberg Lake, we want to climb to that
point. The trail becomes faint across a large talus slope above
the lake where there is usually a large snowbank, which may be
icy. At the top of this 500' ascent is windswept Cecile Lake
(10,280'), right at the base of towering Clyde Minaret.

Follow the trail around the east side of Cecile Lake to a grove of stunted whitebark pines on a moraine. Cross over this moraine and descend to a tarn. From here head south and pass between two rock outcrops. The trail descends steeply down a rocky slope to an inlet of Minaret Lake, below. The trail then descends to the north shore of the lake, passes a small lake on the left and rounds the eastern lobe of Minaret Lake (9800') to the outlet. There are many lovely campsites around this lake (campfires illegal), and the trout-filled waters often reflect the Minarets at sunset.

3rd Hiking Day (**Minaret Lake** to **Devils Postpile Campground,** 6.2 miles—10 km): From the outlet of Minaret Lake one gets a last review of the spectacular Minarets over the lake before descending steeply to a forested flat along Minaret Creek. Our trail then crosses a tributary and steepens again to temporarily join the old road from Minaret Mine. We pass through a meadow along the creek before descending an outcrop of red rock down which the creek cascades in a spray of white. After about two miles of gentle and then moderate descent we arrive at a junction with the John Muir Trail in Johnston Meadow. Here we leave the Ansel Adams Wilderness and then cross Minaret Creek on a log. Beyond, we pass a junction with the trail to Beck Lakes and begin a steep, dusty descent to Devils Postpile National Monument. Near the forested canyon floor we leave the John Muir Trail at a junction with the Pacific Crest Trail. Following signs, we cross the Middle Fork San Joaquin River on a bridge and arrive at Devils Postpile. A short walk north brings us to the parking lot at Devils Postpile Campground.

72   Agnew Meadows to Devils Postpile

TRIP   From Agnew Meadows to Devils Postpile Campground (shuttle trip). Topo map *Devils Postpile*.
Best mid or late season; 12.2 miles (19.6 km).

Grade	Trail/layover days	Total recom- mended days
Leisurely	....	....
Moderate	2/0	2
Strenuous	....	....

HILITES   After crossing the Middle Fork San Joaquin, this
interesting route ascends to picturesque Shadow
Lake. Then, doubling back, it traverses the long,
narrow, lake-dotted bench that breaks the slope
from Volcanic Ridge to the river. Dense fir forests,
intimate lakes, and good fishing make this an
excellent beginner's weekend trip.

DESCRIPTION

1st Hiking Day (**Agnew Meadows** to **Rosalie Lake**, 5.4 miles—8.7
km): Follow the 1st hiking day, Trip 69, to Shadow Lake. At
the inlet to beautiful Shadow Lake, this route joins the John
Muir Trail and crosses Shadow Creek on a large log bridge.
The trail rounds the south side of the lake, and begins a series
of 22 switchbacks up a densely forested slope. Breather stops
along this 650-foot climb afford colorful views of the deep blues
and greens of Shadow Lake, and the crest of the ridge is soon
topped at a rocky saddle with a meadowy bottom. This saddle
leads to a good campsite by the outlet of charming Rosalie
Lake (9350'). Fishing is good for rainbow and brook (to 9").
2nd Hiking Day (**Rosalie Lake** to **Devils Postpile Campground**,
6.8 miles—10.9 km): The trail soon climbs over the southeast
ridge that flanks Rosalie Lake. From the outlet of Gladys Lake
(known locally as Vivian Lake) one has views out over the San
Joaquin River canyon. To the west, the black, recrystallized

volcanic rocks of Volcanic ridge are on the skyline, and to the east the rock drops away into the San Joaquin and rises on the far side to red-topped San Joaquin Mountain and the distinctive Two Teats. From here the route drops down into the Trinity Lakes basin. Access to Castle and Emily lakes is via a short, steep foot trail that takes off from the western side of the trail, and fishing at these lakes is fair-to-good for rainbow and brook (to 8″). From the lowest of the Trinity Lakes, the trail descends steeply via dusty trail to Johnston Meadow, where it joins the trail from Minaret Lake. Follow this trail as described in the 3rd hiking day, Trip 71.

Mule ears

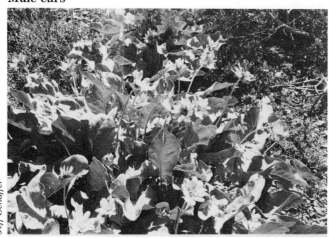

Jeff Schaffer

73 Agnew Meadows to Garnet Lake

TRIP   From Agnew Meadows to Garnet Lake (loop trip).
                 Topo map *Devils Postpile*. Best mid or late season;
                 14.1 miles (22.7 km).

Grade	Trail/layover days	Total recommended days
Leisurely	3/1	4
Moderate	3/0	3
Strenuous	2/0	2

HILITES   Employing about a 4-mile stretch of the well-
                 known John Muir Trail, this trip surveys some of
                 the northern Sierra's most dramatic country. In
                 the region east of the jagged Ritter Range are some
                 of the area's most vivid alpine lakes and spectacu-
                 lar landforms. This route traverses a section of
                 this country in visiting Shadow and Garnet lakes.

DESCRIPTION (Leisurely trip)

1st Hiking Day: Follow Trip 69 to **Shadow Creek**, 4.2 miles (6.8
km).

2nd Hiking Day (**Shadow Creek** to **Garnet Lake**, 4.3 miles—6.9
km): On the John Muir Trail this route ascends west for ⅔
mile through Shadow Creek canyon before turning north. The
trail suffers heavy use, and is likely to be dusty, particularly
in late season. The dust, however, settles as the trail emerges
from pine forest and tops the 1100-foot climb from the Shadow
Creek Trail junction to the rocky ridge above Garnet Lake.
This is an excellent place from which to appreciate the view of
the lake itself, Ritter and Banner, and Mt. Davis to the west.
The traveler will also note the striking change in the country-
side. From the heavily timbered slopes of Shadow Creek canyon, the landscape, except for scattered stands of stunted
hemlock, lodgepole and whitebark is now predominantly gla-
cialy polished rock. From this viewpoint the trail descends 500

feet to the outlet of Garnet Lake (9680′). Fair campsites may be found on the north side of the lake west of the "no camping" zone, and several hundred feet below the outlet. Fishing for brook and rainbow (to 10″) is only fair.

3rd Hiking Day (**Garnet Lake** to **Agnew Meadows via the River Trail,** 5.6 miles—9.0 km): The lateral leading to the River Trail branches from the main trail on the south side of the outlet of Garnet Lake. It is a narrow footpath that descends steeply over a very rocky section, and backpackers should proceed with great caution. Three-fourths mile northeast it strikes the river, crosses on a log, and meets the River Trail, where our route turns right (southeast). The River Trail from this junction is a heavily timbered stretch of trail that passes the Agnew Pass Trail lateral and winds down the canyon. The sound of cascading San Joaquin River is a pleasant part-time accompaniment to this dusty descent when the river is nearby. Fishing on the San Joaquin for rainbow and brook (to 9″) is only fair, and swimming, even in late season, is likely to be somewhat chilly. This route meets the Shadow Lake Trail 2 miles from Agnew Meadows, whence it retraces part of the 1st hiking day.

Mt. Davis from near Rush Creek Trail

74 Agnew Meadows to 1000 Island Lake

TRIP   From Agnew Meadows to Thousand Island Lake via the River Trail (loop trip). Topo map *Devils Postpile*. Best mid or late season; 17.6 miles (28.3 km).

Grade	Trail/layover days	Total recom- mended days
Leisurely	3/1	4
Moderate	3/0	3
Strenuous	2/0	2

HILITES   The climax of this trip is Garnet and Thousand Island lakes. Settings of alpine grandeur make these large lakes favorites of lensmen and naturalists alike. Although this trip can be made in a weekend, the superlative scenery warrants a slower pace. Almost half of this route follows the scenic John Muir Trail.

DESCRIPTION (Leisurely trip)

1st Hiking Day: Follow Trip 69 to **Shadow Creek**, 4.2 miles (6.8 km).

2nd Hiking Day (**Shadow Creek** to **Thousand Island Lake**, 6.3 miles—10.1 km): Follow the 2nd hiking day, Trip 73 to Garnet Lake. Beyond the outlet of Garnet Lake, care should be exercised when crossing the 500-foot talus-covered ridge that separates Garnet and Thousand Island lakes. En route, the trail circles the east shore of dramatic Ruby Lake, and then drops down past colorful Emerald Lake to the outlet of Thousand Island Lake (9834'). The island-dotted lake's wind-swept surface reflects the imposing facade of Banner Peak and the more sharply etched Mt. Ritter. Several exposed campsites (subject to a great deal of wind) may be found on the north side of the lake, the better ones being a mile or more west of the Muir Trail and back from the water. Fishing for rainbow and brook (7-13") is particularly good in early and late season. Camping is also possible at the lakelet about ¼ mile east down the River Trail.

3rd Hiking Day (**Thousand Island Lake** to **Agnew Meadow** via the River Trail, 7.1 miles—11.4 km): This route leaves the John Muir Trail at the meadowy outlet of Thousand Island Lake, and proceeds northeast past several small snow tarns. The alpine setting is soon left behind as the trail re-enters forest cover. Our route then veers southeast to a junction with the High Trail, branches right at this junction, and slants down through dense lodgepole and fir to the Garnet Lake lateral, whence it proceeds as described in 3rd hiking day, Trip 73.

Ritter Range over upper Lost Lake

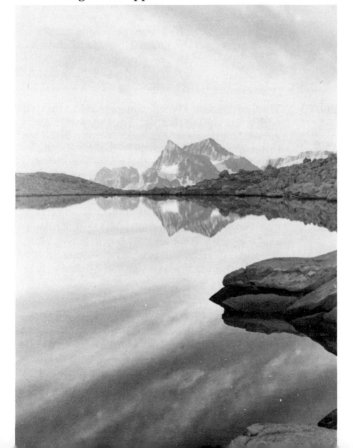

75   Agnew Meadows to 1000 Island Lake

TRIP

From Agnew Meadows to Thousand Island Lake via the High Trail (loop trip). Topo map *Devils Postpile*. Best mid or late season; 17.6 miles (28.3 km).

Grade	Trail/layover days	Total recommended days
Leisurely	3/1	4
Moderate	3/0	3
Strenuous	2/0	2

HILITES

The San Joaquin River drainage provides this trip with a fascinating contrast. The imposing scenery viewed from the west side of the canyon below the Ritter Range has already been described, but few travelers have taken in the altogether different beauty of the slopes of the Sierra Crest. Here on the east side of the canyon the trail traveler passes through an entirely different kind of ground cover and he has unbroken views of the Ritter Range. A first assessment would indicate that this hillside was a scrubby, arid stretch, but it is not. Many streams interrupt the trail, even in late season, and wildflowers line the route.

DESCRIPTION (Leisurely trip)

1st and 2nd Hiking Days: Follow Trip 74 to **Thousand Island Lake**, 10.5 miles (16.9 km).

3rd Hiking Day (**Thousand Island Lake** to **Agnew Meadows,** via the High Trail, 7.1 miles—11.4 km): Follow the 3rd hiking day, Trip 74, to the High Trail junction. From this trail junction, the route ascends past meadowy Badger Lakes and past a secondary lateral to Agnew Pass. On this first slope the trail emerges from the dense forest cover, and then it winds up and down through a ground cover that, except for a few scattered stands of pine, is sagebrush, bitterbrush, willow, and some mountain alder. When the trail descends to one of the many tributaries of the San Joaquin River, the traveler should observe the lush growth of wildflowers, including larkspur, lupine, shooting star, columbine, penstemon, monkey flower, scarlet gilia and tiger lily. For a while views are excellent of the Ritter Range to the west; particularly impressive is the **V**'d view of Shadow Lake directly across the San Joaquin River canyon about 2¾ miles from the trailhead. But views soon disappear, and you make a gradual descent, ending it with a series of well-graded switchbacks to the parking lot north of the pack station.

76   Chiquito Creek to Chain Lakes

TRIP From Chiquito Creek Trailhead to Middle Chain Lake (round trip). Topo map *Merced Peak.* Best mid season; 14.6 miles (23.2 km).

Grade	Trail/layover days	Total recommended days
Leisurely	2/1	3
Moderate	2/0	2
Strenuous	....	....

HILITES Chain Lakes are a traditional and attractive destination for a moderate weekend trip. Though not difficult, this hike is long enough and varied enough to provide the hiker with a feeling of a substantial trip. Fishing is often good at Chain Lakes.

DESCRIPTION (Moderate trip)

1st Hiking Day (**Chiquito Creek Trailhead** to **Middle Chain Lake,** 7.3 miles—11.6 km): From the trailhead parking lot (7320′) the signed Chiquito Lake Trail heads northwest through mixed forest. Although it is designated a hiker trail only, horses use this trail, and even motor vehicles travel the first ¼ mile. After the first ¼ mile, the dusty trail steepens and climbs a hot, sunny hillside; then it levels off to pass the old trail coming in on the left. Soon we cross a small creek and climb another hot hillside before swinging into shade to come within earshot of Chiquito Creek.

The trail continues on a moderate ascent until it fords the creek just below Chiquito Lake. From the lake's south shore we head briefly west and then pass a junction with a trail to the Sky Ranch Road. Then we traverse north to the Yosemite Park boundary. Leaving the cows behind, we go through a barbed-wire fence to another junction. Turning right here, we stroll to a sharp-crested moraine, cross it, and descend gently for ½ mile to ford the seasonally wide outlet of Spotted Lakes. From the ford our trail ascends moderately through red fir up a large moraine to a small meadow. This meadow marks the top of the moraine, and the remainder of this 500-foot climb takes us past a few bedrock outcrops. Past the top of the ridge, we descend gently through mixed forest to ford Chain Lakes creek. On the other side of the creek is a junction; here we turn right (east) and then ascend steeply to lower Chain Lake, singed CHAIN LAKES. From here the trail swings around the north side of the lake, turns south, crosses a seasonal stream and makes a rocky, 150-foot ascent to the middle lake, also signed CHAIN LAKES. Camping is best on the south side of this lake.

Those wishing to visit the upper lake can reach it from the abused campsite near the middle lake's outlet. From here the trail to the upper lake climbs steeply above the north shore of the middle lake onto a rocky ridge. The trail then passes a tarn, turns left around a small lake and crosses the creek. From here a short ascent leads to the timbered west side of beautiful Upper Chain Lake. All three lakes contain rainbow or brook trout, or both.

2nd Hiking Day: Reverse your steps, 7.3 miles (11.6 km).

Middle Chain Lake

77 Chiquito Creek to Rutherford Lake

TRIP
From Chiquito Creek Trailhead to Fernandez Trailhead via Rutherford Lake (shuttle trip). Topo map *Merced Peak.* Best mid or late season; 25.4 miles (40.9 km).

Grade	Trail/layover days	Total recommended days
Leisurely	4/1	5
Moderate	3/1	4
Strenuous	3/0	3

HILITES
This hike can be done in three days, during which the hiker will encounter a great variety of terrain and scenery, going from dense red-fir forests to alpine lakes and back again. Fishing on both sides of Fernandez Pass is good-to-excellent.

DESCRIPTION (Moderate trip)
1st Hiking Day: Follow Trip 76 to **Middle Chain Lake,** 7.3 miles (11.6 km).

2nd Hiking Day (**Middle Chain Lake** to **Rutherford Lake,** 9.4 miles—15.1 km): This hiking day takes one through a wide variety of landscape features: forests, meadows, streams, lakes and passes. After we retrace our steps to the junction by the outlet of Chain Lakes, we turn right and continue the steep descent beside the creek. The grade soon eases where there is a newly formed clearing along the creek. Here are downed trees and a jumble of boulders—the remains of a debris flow. A debris flow is something like a combination flood and landslide—a thick, slow-moving, water-saturated mixture of rock, soil, trees and anything else lying around.

Turning north away from the creek, we soon pass a signed junction with a trail to Buck Camp. Continuing north, our trail winds among glacial erratics and over bedrock outcrops under a partial forest cover, climbs steeply over a low ridge, and passes a glacial tarn. The trail then descends along a small watercourse to a lodgepole-pine-covered flat where a zealous CCC and Park Service crew has dug trenches in order to lower the water table. The excavated soil has been used to build a causeway nearby. From here a very short ascent brings us past a packer campsite on the left, and then to the Merced River in Moraine Meadows. Beyond the ford (wet in early season) the trail passes more campsites and arrives at a signed junction with another trail to Buck Camp. Here we turn right and then ascend gently under lodgepole pine over a very maintained trail. After an easy mile the trail turns south and fords the flower-lined Merced River (wet in early season). The grade soon steepens as we begin a two-stage climb to Fernandez Pass. For 400 vertical feet the shaded trail winds up to a shallow, meadow-fringed lake, crossing a seasonal stream enroute. Here the grade eases, and in another ¾ mile we reach a signed junction with the trail south to Breeze Lake. This trail leads past a small lake, then becomes faint, and the last stretch is a ducked route over slabs to the hemlock-lined north shore of large, scenic Breeze Lake.

From the junction we begin the second stage of the climb to the pass, and immediately the trail becomes very steep and rocky. The trail ascends through lodgepole and silver pine over weathered granite for 600 feet to signed Fernandez Pass (10,175′). Here we leave the Park and then ascend a bit more before descending past another tree-dotted saddle. The trail now winds down ledges into the headwaters of Fernandez Creek, and we get good views of the Ritter Range to the east. The grade eases temporarily where we cross a small meadow, and steepens again before we arrive at a signed junction with a trail to Rutherford Lake (9800′). This eroded trail begins in a small forested flat and climbs very steeply for ¼ mile to the small dam at the south end of this well-used alpine lake. Campsites can be found on the lake's east side.

3rd Hiking Day (**Rutherford Lake** to **Fernandez Trailhead,** 8.7 miles—14 km): From the small dam at the south end of Rutherford Lake we descend the steep trail ¼ mile back to the Fernandez trail and turn left onto it. This rocky trail switchbacks down the sunny canyon wall to a gentler descent under tall red fir. About 1½ miles from Rutherford Lake we ford Fernandez Creek (wet in early season) and arrive at a junction with the Post Peak Pass Trail. We continue right, on the Fernandez trail, and traverse past a low exfoliation dome.

Soon we pass over a low ridge, descend a wooded gully, and arrive at the signed trail to Rainbow Lake. From here it is an easy 1½ miles down gentle slabs through open lodgepole and juniper to the northern junction with the Lillian Lake Loop. From this junction our trail heads east and begins a long descent to Madera Creek. Initially, the trail descends gently, enters a forested gully, and crosses a small creek. Continuing southeast under red fir, lodgepole pine and occasional Jeffrey pine and juniper, our trail gains the crest of a moraine where we get views east through the trees. The trail then becomes steep, completes two sets of switchbacks and passes a junction with the Timber Creek Trail. After some more dusty switchbacks we arrive at a shaded flat along peaceful Madera Creek. Proceeding across this flat, we pass a signed junction with the Walton Trail, left, and some good campsites, and then ford wide Madera Creek (wet in early season). The trail climbs steeply up the south bank and then continues on a moderate ascent through lodgepole pine and red fir. Along this ascent you notice a mixture of light and dark rocks on the ground. Many times during the Pleistocene Epoch glaciers originating near Madera Peak flowed over this area, and the darker, metamorphic rocks came from the vicinity of Madera Peak while the lighter, granitic rocks came from farther east, perhaps around Staniford Lakes.

Forest cover thins and views improve until we reach the southern end of the Lillian Lake Loop. Here, atop a broad ridge, we leave the Ansel Adams Wilderness and begin the 2-mile descent southeast to the Fernandez trailhead. This section of trail, which passes two laterals to the Norris Creek trailhead, is described (in reverse) in the first day of Trip 79.

Chiquito Creek to Bridalveil Creek 78

TRIP   Chiquito Creek Trailhead to Bridalveil Campground (shuttle trip). Topo maps *Merced Peak*,
Yosemite. Best mid or late season; 29.4 miles (48.6
km).

Grade	Trail/layover days	Total recommended days
Leisurely	4/1	5
Moderate	4/0	4
Strenuous	3/0	3

HILITES   This is a shuttle trip that crosses some of the more
scenic southern Yosemite National Park bound-
ary country. Some of the finest fishing in the Park
is found along this route at Chain and Royal Arch
lakes, and bonus angling spots can be explored on
layover days at Breeze, Spotted, Johnson and
Crescent lakes. The gigantic, sweeping effects of
glacial action are seen throughout this trip. The
resulting cirques, **U**-shaped valleys, jagged
ranges, and polished granite are a constant source
of awe and delight to the traveler.

DESCRIPTION (Leisurely trip)

1st Hiking Day: Follow Trip 76 to **Middle Chain Lake** (7.3
miles (11.9) km).
2nd Hiking Day (**Upper Chain Lake** to **Royal Arch Lake**, 9 miles—
14.5 km): First, retrace your steps to yesterday's junction, and
then continue downstream. In ⅓ mile the trail veers north to a
junction, where we turn left (west) and parallel the outlet
creek from Chain Lakes as it falls to rendezvous with the
South Fork Merced. Just before the South Fork a signed lateral trail leads south ¼ mile to good camping at Soda Springs.

Our route fords the South Fork and swings southwest over a lodgepole-covered slope. The depth of the U-shaped, glacially formed slopes gives a good account of the forces that were at work when the ice flow originating in the Clark Range to the north was in its heyday.

After fording Givens Creek the trail passes a southbound trail to Chiquito Pass. Just 60 yards farther we choose a well-used left fork over a little-used right fork and then continue ½ mile to meet the Buck Camp/Merced Pass Trail on a ridgetop. Turning southwest, we descend through red-fir forest and then climb northwest to the meadowy precincts of Buck Camp. At Buck Camp Yosemite National Park has a summer ranger station, and emergency services may be obtained. From Buck Camp the trail ascends a tough 750 feet via switchbacks, then drops 350 feet to a junction with the Royal Arch Lake Trail. From this point it is but ¾ mile to Royal Arch Lake (8700'). Large, black, rainbow-arched striations across the eastern wall of polished granite gave this picturesque lake its name. These distinctive markings are the result of water discoloration due to centuries of seepage. They make a magnificent backdrop to the excellent fishing for brook and rainbow (8-14") and anglers may well regard this relatively small lake as the high point of the trip. Numerous good campsites are on the west shore, and this lake makes an excellent base camp for scenic and angling excursions to nearby Buena Vista, Johnson and Crescent lakes. Swimming is good in late season.

3rd and 4th Hiking Days: Reverse the steps of the 2nd and 1st hiking days, Trip 82, 13 miles (20.9 km).

Royal Arch Lake   *National Park Service*

Granite Creek Road to Rutherford Lake 79

TRIP   From **Fernandez Trailhead** to **Rutherford Lake**.
(semiloop trip). Topo map *Merced Peak.* Best
mid or late season; 20.7 miles (33.3 km).

Grade	Trail/layover days	Total recom- mended days
Leisurely	3/1	4
Moderate	3/0	3
Strenuous	2/0	2

HILITES   The lake-filled area east of Gale and Sing peaks
provides a choice trip for the angler. Except for a
midsummer slack period, these lakes are good
producers of brook, rainbow, and even golden
trout. Add to this benefit the dramatic peaks that
lie to the west, and the 35-mile views to the south,
and every hiker will find cause for visiting this
country. This trip is the answer for the hiker with
a short time for travel who wishes to get into the
spectacular south boundary country.

DESCRIPTION (Moderate trip)

1st Hiking Day (**Fernandez Trailhead** to **Vandeburg Lake** 4.5
miles —7.3 km): From the west side of the turnaround loop at
the end of the road, the signed Fernandez Trail begins a gentle
ascent through a forest of white fir, Jeffrey pine and lodgepole
pine. In ⅓ mile our route arrives at a signed junction with a
lateral to the Norris Creek trailhead. Here we turn right and
soon begin a moderate ascent to another signed junction with
a trail to the Norris Creek trailhead. From here we gain an open
ridgetop, where we meet a signed junction with the Lillian
Lake loop. With grand views over our shoulder, we turn west
onto the loop and enter the Ansel Adams Wilderness. In a
mixed forest of red fir, mountain hemlock, and lodgepole and
silver pine, we pass two cow-infested meadows on the left, and

then swing north and climb steeply up a rocky ridge. From the ridgetop we descend for a short distance through hemlock forest to ford the outlet of Vandeburg Lake. A little uphill to the west are the well-used campsites on the north side of this attractive lake.

2nd Hiking Day (**Vandeburg Lake** to **Rutherford Lake,** 7.5 miles—12.1 km): From the northwest side of Vandeburg Lake our trail ascends west up slabs to a signed junction with a trail to Lady Lake, at the edge of a lodgepole-pine-covered flat. A moderate ¾-mile ascent up this trail would bring one to the shady campsites on the northeast side of Lady Lake.

From the Lady Lake junction the main route continues up more slabs dotted with lodgepole pines. Where the trail tops a low ridge, we can pause to take in the expansive views of the Ritter Range to the northeast. After a short descent to the north we arrive at the first of the trout-filled Staniford Lakes. Our scenic trail passes above the largest Staniford Lake and boulder-hops Shirley Creek. Continuing north across slabs our trail crosses several seasonal creeks before swinging west to ford the shaded outlet of Lillian Lake. Instead of proceeding to the well-used campsites on the northeast side of this large lake, our route turns east and descends moderately under lodgepole pine and hemlock for about a mile. Then the grade levels off and we ford the creek from Rainbow and Flat lakes, and after an easy ¼ mile arrive at a junction with the Fernandez Trail. We turn left on it and ascend gently over juniper-and-lodgepole-pine-covered slabs for over a mile to a junction with a trail to Rainbow Lake. (If you want to visit this lovely lake, this trail would take you there in 1½ miles. Follow the trail across the creek and ascend southwest through timber and slabs for ¾ mile. The ducked trail then turns northwest and descends to cross the same creek above Flat Lake. A short ascent leads to the wooded east side of fishless Rainbow Lake, where overnight camping is prohibited.)

From the Rainbow Lake trail junction, the Fernandez Trail heads north and climbs up a shaded ravine onto a flat ridge. For another mile the route is a gentle stroll through open lodgepole-pine forest to a junction with the Post Peak Pass Trail. Here turn left and ford Fernandez Creek. The Fernandez Trail then swings west and ascends moderately under tall red firs for about ½ mile. Then the trail begins a series of switchbacks up the rocky, sun-drenched north canyon wall. This ascent passes through sections of red metavolcanic rock, and views to the south and east are good reasons to pause and rest in the shade of a juniper or a silver pine. Our trail re-enters timber at a small flat where we arrive at a junction with the short trail to Rutherford Lake. This very steep and badly eroded trail ascends ¼ mile to the small dam on the south side of well-used Rutherford Lake (9800'). The shores of this scenic lake have been abused, so camp well away from the water. This deep lake contains a number of large golden and brook trout.

3rd Hiking Day: Follow the 3rd hiking day, Trip 77, 8.7 miles (14 km).

80 Granite Creek Road to Isberg Lakes

TRIP   From Fernandez Trailhead to Granite Creek
                Campground (shuttle trip). Topo map *Merced
                Peak.* Best mid or late season; 28.7 miles (46.2
                km).

Grade	Trail/layover days	Total recommended days
Leisurely	5/1	6
Moderate	4/1	5
Strenuous	3/1	4

HILITES   This is a challenging hike, with an altitude gain of
                over 3000 feet. Scenery varies from the cloisters of
                dense forests and the intimacy of small meadows
                to the overwhelming panoramas from two high
                passes. Fishing is best in early or late season, and
                ranges from fair to excellent.

DESCRIPTION (Leisurely trip)

1st Hiking Day: Follow Trip 79 to **Vandeburg Lake**, 4 miles (6.4
km).

2nd Hiking Day (**Vandeburg Lake** to **Post Peak Pass Trail**, 5.7
miles—9.2 km): Follow the 2nd hiking day, Trip 79, to the
junction of the Fernandez Trail and the Rainbow Lake Trail,
by a small marsh. From the junction turn right on the
Fernandez Trail and climb a short, shaded ravine up to a low
ridge. On the ridge the trail makes a northwest traverse
through open lodgepole-pine forest, passing a broken dome on
the west. After a nearly level mile and then a short, gentle
descent we arrive at a junction with the Post Peak Pass Trail
going right. There is a good campsite just north of the junction, by Fernandez Creek, and more are to be found several

hundred yards down the Post Peak Pass Trail to the east, near the confluence of Fernandez Creek and the creek from Slab Lakes. Both of these small creeks contain brook trout.

3rd Hiking Day (**Post Peak Pass Trail** to **Lower Isberg Lake,** 7.8 miles—12.6 km): This hiking day takes one over two steep passes that have excellent views. Heading east from the Fernandez Trail, the Post Peak Pass Trail soon crosses Fernandez Creek on logs. A short distance beyond we ford the creek from Slab Lakes and pass a junction with a trail to the lakes. We continue northeast over a low, wooded ridge past two glacial tarns where one may sometimes see families of mallards. Beyond the second tarn the trail descends to ford seasonal Post Creek (9040') and begins a steep, three-stage ascent to Post Peak Pass. The first stage takes us up a densely forested hillside to marshy Isberg Meadow. Beyond this meadow our route leaves timber and ascends on a washed-out trail along a flower-lined creek. Then the grade eases and the trail enters the extraordinary "beachball" landscape around Porphyry Lake (10,100'). The dark blotches in this bedrock are inclusions of quartz diorite in a lighter-colored granite.

The last stage of the climb to Post Peak Pass is a steep ascent over a rocky, washed-out trail under the western ramparts of Post Peak. The last several hundred feet of this climb may be snowbound into summer, but a sign marks obvious Post Peak Pass (10,750'). From the wind-swept pass, the trail actually climbs a little more as it skirts a low peak ¼ mile northwest of the pass, where one can have excellent views. Our trail stays near the ridge as we pass high above Ward Lakes before descending west into Yosemite Park. A ⅓-mile descent brings us to a junction with the Isberg Trail, which we turn onto and then ascend back up to the Park boundary. This rocky ascent brings us to a point above Isberg Pass, which is a short descent away over ledges to the north. At the pass (10,520') we again enter the Ansel Adams Wilderness, and then descend towards Upper Isberg Lake. The trail makes a very long traverse to the northeast, and if there is a lot of snow when you're there, it may be more efficient to descend directly east to the north side of the lake. From this lake the trail crosses the outlet and swings near a viewpoint above McClure Lake, then veers north and descends to the meadowed north side of Lower Isberg Lake. Scenic campsites can be found in the trees on the low moraine on the southeast side of the lake.

4th Hiking Day (**Lower Isberg Lake** to **Middle Cora Lake,** 5.7 miles—9.2 km): After rejoining the Isberg Trail we head east into forest cover, cross a small creek and swing south. Soon our lodgepole-pine-shaded trail becomes steep as it winds down to the meadowed fringes of trout-filled Sadler Lake (9345'). Camping is legal only on the south and west sides of this popular lake. Rounding the east side of the lake brings us to the outlet, and then to a junction with the trail to McClure Lake. From here our trail descends moderately under lodgepole pines, then through a stretch of avalanche-downed trees, before fording East Fork Granite Creek. Descending more gently now, the trail follows the orange bedrock channel for ½ mile before veering away from the creek and passing a junction with the Timber Creek Trail. Our trail continues to descend, crossing several small creeks before it levels off in the cow-infested environs of the East Fork. Then the trail crosses to the east side of the creek (wet in early season), skirts a number of meadows, and swings away from the creek to cross a low bedrock ridge. Over a mile from the ford we pass a junction with a lateral to the Stevenson Trail. From this junction it is an easy ½ mile over a low moraine down to the shaded east shore of middle Cora Lake. Camping is legal only on the southwest side of the lake.

5th Hiking Day (**Middle Cora Lake** to **Granite Creek Campground,** 4.6 miles—7.4 km): From the outlet on the southeast side of middle Cora Lake, our trail heads south through lodgepole forest, and in 1¼ miles we ford East Fork Granite Creek for the last time (wet in early season). The trail descends the west bank for ½ mile and then swings west and passes a wilderness boundary sign. Soon we turn south again and the descent steepens as the trail winds down a ravine under red fir, lodgepole pine and Jeffrey pine. The grade eases before the last, dusty descent brings us to a trailhead parking lot on the east side of West Fork Granite Creek. A bridge downstream takes us to the east end of Granite Creek Campground (7040').

Yosemite Valley to Merced Lake

TRIP   From Yosemite Valley to Merced Lake (round trip). Topo maps *Yosemite, Merced Peak*. Best early season; 27.8 miles (44.8 km)

Grade	Trail/layover days	Total recom- mended days
Leisurely	4/0	4
Moderate	3/0	3
Streuous	2/0	2

HILITES   An early-season trip (low altitude, early snow-melt), this route offers all the scenic grandeur of the Valley attractions, plus the intimate knowledge of the back country that only the backpacker can have. Fishing is good during early season on the Merced River and at Merced Lake. Swimming is poor during the early season, owing to the chilly waters, but photographers and naturalists will find an exciting area of geologic spectacle and history.

DESCRIPTION (Leisurely trip)

1st Hiking Day (**Yosemite Valley** to **Little Yosemite Valley,** 4.7 miles—7.6 km): Though this trip is graded leisurely, the first hiking day is rigorous, with over 2000 feet of climbing, but the route is so spectacular that the hiker can easily forget his aches and pains. This trip starts at the beginning of the John Muir Trail, across the Merced River from the Happy Isles Trail Center. Ascending steeply south, we leave the wide, level Valley floor behind and begin to climb the steep, narrow canyon of the Merced River. This section of canyon is steep partly because neither the Merced River nor the glaciers that were here was able to erode two masses of very resistant bedrock very much. Over the edges of these two masses flow the two waterfalls, Vernal and Nevada.

The John Muir Trail—which is more like a road here—climbs steeply under canyon live oak and California bay. Where the trail rounds Sierra Point we can look back at Yosemite Falls, while below us are the river and the intake and reservoir for the Valley's water supply. Soon we arrive at the Vernal Fall bridge, and several hundred feet beyond we meet the Mist Trail. Ascending from here to the top of Nevada Fall, most people use the less steep John Muir Trail, but if you have not been up the Mist Trail, it is recommended. Returning via the John Muir Trail is both easier and safer. Both routes will be described here.

If you ascend the Mist Trail you will usually get wet. Climbing toward Vernal Fall, the trail soon becomes extremely steep as it ascends large, rocky steps where the mist can be a driving rainstorm in spring. As we rise above the base of the 320-foot fall, we pass through a hole, and then reach the base of a large, dripping overhang. Then we turn left on a ledge that exits onto slabs above Vernal Fall. From the railing by the fall proceed up past Emerald Pool to a junction with a lateral leading to the right to the Muir Trail. Here we turn left, then cross the river and ascend to a level area below Nevada Fall. The last section of the Mist Trail switchbacks up a steep, rocky gully several hundred yards north of Nevada Fall.

If you take the John Muir Trail to the top of Nevada Fall, you start by ascending a long series of switchbacks. After passing a junction with a lateral to the Mist Trail we climb more switchbacks and get very good views of Half Dome, Mt. Broderick and Liberty Cap. These last two, though rounded like Half Dome, were overridden by glaciers while Half Dome was not. Our trail then passes a junction with the Panorama Trail and arrives at the top of Nevada Fall. While admiring the view of Glacier Point you may notice patches of shiny, smooth bedrock at your feet—glacial polish—indicating that a glacier has been here recently. There is very little glacial polish below this point, which marks the farthest extent of a glacier that was here about 13,000 years ago.

The John Muir Trail meets the Mist Trail several hundred yards northwest of Nevada Fall. From the top of the Mist Trail it is a short ascent and then a gentle descent into Little Yosemite Valley. Our trail passes a lateral to the Half Dome Trail, and ½ mile farther we leave the John Muir Trail at a junction near the well-used camping area by the summer ranger station.

*2nd Hiking Day (***Little Yosemite Valley** to **Merced Lake,** 9.2 miles—14.8 km: From the well-used, misused and abused camping area, our shaded route heads toward the east end of Little Yosemite Valley. The trail—40 feet wide in places— swings away from the complacent river and stretches along the flat valley floor under Jeffrey pines and white firs. The double phone lines we see will parallel our route all the way to Merced Lake. As an indication of how thick glaciers were here, look up at Moraine Dome to the east: ice filled the valley almost to its summit 750,000 years ago. Since then glaciers have repeatedly entered this valley, but none that thick.

At the east end of Little Yosemite Valley the trail swings close to the river again. Here the lofty canyon walls converge and the grade steepens as we pass another camping area. The next section of our route is through a short, narrow gorge leading to Lost Valley. In this section of canyon, glaciers did very little to modify the pre-existing **V**-shaped, stream-cut canyon.

Soon we arrive in wide, level Lost Valley, where the vertical walls reflect the vertical jointing in the bedrock. At the east end of Lost Valley we enter yet another short, narrow section of canyon, which leads to yet a smaller valley, on the north side of exfoliating Bunnell Point. Before the canyon narrows again, the trail crosses one branch of the river via an island, and a second branch on a new wood bridge. The lumber for this bridge was hewn in 1984 from a 175-year-old sugar pine that stood just below the trail.

From the bridge our rocky trail stays near the river until we begin the steep stretch up to Echo Valley. The trail avoids the gorge bottom by climbing 400 feet south and traversing over open slabs where glacial erratics have been rearranged to mark the trail. Our route then descends to cross the river on a bridge at the west end of Echo Valley. Following the river, then turning north, the trail arrives at a junction and a multibridged crossing of Echo Creek. We continue east through a very dense young forest of lodgepole pines.

Soon our route winds up slabs, and where the river is confined in yet another gorge we walk right above the fast-moving water. The grade eases once again as we arrive at yet another wide, flat valley, this one containing Merced Lake. Following the north shore, the trail passes a drift fence and arrives at the camping area at the lake's east end. Bears are plentiful. The lake contains a population of brook and rainbow trout.

3rd and 4th Hiking Days: Retrace steps, 13.9 miles (22.8 km).

82 Bridalveil Creek to Royal Arch Lake

TRIP   From Bridalveil Campground to Royal Arch Lake (round trip). Topo map *Yosemite*. Best early-to-mid season; 26 miles (41.8 km).

| | Trail/layover days | Total recom- |
Grade	days	mended days
Leisurely	4/0	4
Moderate	3/0	3
Strenuous	2/0	2

HILITES   In early season this trip route is lush with wildflowers of every variety, and color film is a must for the photographer. Anglers will find few lakes within the Park to rival the fishing at Royal Arch Lake. The easy grade of the topography makes this an excellent early-season choice.

DESCRIPTION (Leisurely trip)

1st Hiking Day (**Bridalveil Campground** to **Turner Meadows**, 6.3 miles—10.1 km): From the trailhead at the southeast end of the campground, the trail begins winding southeastward along meandering Bridalveil Creek. The grade is gentle as the trail winds through the dense lodgepole forest. Periodically, the thick undergrowth gives way to intimate, mountain-bluebell-filled meadows. Beyond a left-leading trail to the Glacier Point Road, near Lost Bear Meadow, the trail veers south beside one of the larger tributaries of Bridalveil Creek. It crosses this tributary, passes a lateral to the Ostrander Lake trail, and in ½ mile crosses the tributary again, and each fording is heralded by banks covered with lavendar shooting stars. The second crossing marks the beginning of an easy 400-foot climb over the ridge that separates the Bridalveil Creek and Alder Creek watersheds. In early and mid season this ridge is colorfully decked out in lush pink and white fields of pussy paws, brodiaea, mat lupine and Douglas phlox. From the top of this ridge, the trail drops to the

Deer Camp Trail junction, climbs over Turner Ridge and then offers a short walk to Turner Meadows and the four campsites at the southern end. The cabin site at the head of the meadows (indicated by the rock fireplace) is all that remains of Bill Turner's pioneer abode. He occupied these grasslands while running cattle around the turn of the century. There is stream water except in late season.

2nd Hiking Day (**Turner Meadows** to **Royal Arch Lake**, 6.7 miles—10.8 km): Before leaving Turner Meadows, one should take the opportunity to study the wildlife that frequents the meadows, particularly in the early morning. On the trail you will pass many little rills supporting colorful wildflower gardens before you reach, in ½ mile, the Wawona Trail, which branches south, and ¾ mile farther, the Chilnaulna Lakes Trail, branching east. These trails were used by U.S. Cavalry patrols at the turn of the century. Their purpose was to facilitate administration of the Park, which at that time meant keeping the poachers, cattlemen and sheepmen out.

Just after the last junction you ford swirling Chilnaulna Creek (difficult in early season), and then climb on switchbacks over an eastward-rising ridge to a junction with a second lateral trail to Wawona, leading left. South of the ridgecrest, where views to the south open up, we turn east up the valley of Grouse Lake's little outlet stream and ascend gently for 2 miles. You can leave the trail where it veers a bit northward away from the creek and follow that stream to Grouse Lake, should that be your goal, or you can stay on the trail for another ¼ mile to find a spur trail leading to the right to the lake.

From the spur-trail junction your trail provides an easy, shaded walk over a small rise and thence down to cross the inlet of shallow Crescent Lake, just out of sight in the south. Another mile of level walking into increasing mosquito-infested forest brings us to Johnson Lake, with its good fishing for brook and rainbow (9-13″). Johnson Lake and its perimeter were one of the last acquisitions of private property within the Park's boundaries, and two crumbling cabins remain to remind us of our home-steading era.

The next ¾ mile, to a junction with the Royal Arch Lake Trail, is a 250-foot ascent up a lodgepole-covered slope. Here our route leaves the Buck Camp Trail and turns north for a small climb through dense forest that gives way to open hillside as we approach dramatic Royal Arch Lake (8700′). This lake is small but it is deep, and it supports an excellent, self-sustaining fishery of brook and rainbow (8-14″). Its regal name derives from the blackened granite streaks that rainbow across the steep eastern face of the lake basin. There are numerous good campsites not far from a seasonal lakelet beside the west shore, which is perfect for bathing when it has warmed up by mid-season.

3rd and 4th Hiking Days: Retrace your steps, 13 miles (20.9 km).

83 Bridalveil Creek to Glacier Point

TRIP   From Bridalveil Campground to Glacier Point (shuttle trip). Topo map *Yosemite.* Best early-to-mid-season; 29.1 miles 46.9 km).

	Trail/layover	Total recom-
Grade	days	mended days
Leisurely	5/1	6
Moderate	4/1	5
Strenuous	3/0	3

HILITES   This long circle trip covers some of the more scenic portions of the southern part of the Park, and has the advantage of a very short shuttle between the beginning and ending points. Anglers have a wide choice of lake and stream fishing which is among the best in Yosemite. Despite the attractions, the route is not heavily traveled, and those seeking some solitude will find it on this trip.

DESCRIPTION (Moderate trip)

1st and 2nd Hiking Days: Follow Trip 82 to **Royal Arch Lake**, 13 miles (20.9 km).

3rd Hiking Day (**Royal Arch Lake** to **Buena Vista Creek Tributary,** 11.0 miles—17.7 km): The mileage this day is long, in order to get beyond a large burn that begins after 5½ miles, shortly beyond the outlet stream from Hart Lakes. Our 2-mile ascent from Royal Arch Lake to the Buena Vista summit is an easy one across granite slabs dotted with stands of lodgepole and through open meadows that retain a springlike freshness well into the summer. Beyond the crest, at Buena Vista Lake, anglers can unlimber their rods for good fishing for brook and rainbow (9-13″). About ⅓ mile beyond the lake, at the Chilnualna Lakes Trail junction, photographers may wish to capture the sweeping views.

Cathedral Peak, the Cockscomb, Matthes Crest, Mt. Clark, Gray Peak, Red Peak, Merced Peak, Triple Divide Peak, Gale Peak, Sing Peak and Madera Peak, It is only another 0.7 mile, but a 480-foot descent, to Upper Chilnualna Lake (8500'). Fishing on this small (7-acre) lake is excellent for brook (8-14"). From Buena Vista summit our trail drops down to cross and recross Buena Vista Creek and then climb abruptly back onto the shoulder of Horse Ridge, crossing the seasonal outlet of Hart Lakes as it does so. Dropping north, we reach the unmarked junction with a ducked footpath to Edson Lake (8160'). Fair campsites may be found on the north shore. Fishing at the lake is only fair for rainbow.

4th Hiking Day (**Edson Lake** to **Illilouette Creek**, 6.7 miles—10.8 km): Back on the Buena Vista Trail, the first part of this day's walk is a long, steady descent of 1000 feet on dusty, rocky underfooting. From Buena Vista Creek the 700-foot descent to Illilouette Creek is sandy. The dense red-fir forest is often interrupted by clumps of dead lodgepole pines, and the contrast is much like stepping from a cathedral into the adjoining graveyard. Periodically, the fir cover opens to give peephole views of the granite domes to the north and northeast, of which Mt. Starr King stands out above all the rest. Our trail dips close to the confluence of Buena Vista and Illilouette creeks, and then veers away from the latter as we follow its canyon downstream, jumping across several small tributaries. As we approach Illilouette Creek again, we meet the trail from Mono Meadow, and near this junction find campsites on both sides of the creek. Fishing on the creek is fair for rainbow (to 8").

5th Hiking Day (**Illilouette Creek** to **Glacier Point**, 3.5 miles—5.6 km): The trail descends gently beside Illilouette Creek for about 1½ miles before beginning to climb. As it ascends past the junction with a trail down to Illilouette Fall, each foot of altitude gain improves the view, giving the trail here its meaningful name, the Panorama Trail. From this trail, on a clear day (and it is clearer in the morning), one can look across the vast chasm of the Merced River, and with the aid of binoculars see hikers on the summit of Half Dome. Nearer at hand, we can see the work of avalanches that have thundered down from the heights, carrying rocks, trees and soil across the trail. The fine views from just below Washburn Point include Nevada Fall, Vernal Fall, Half Dome, Mt. Starr King, and many high peaks of eastern Yosemite, marching off to the southeast horizon. The last half mile to Glacier Point (7214') is accomplished by switchbacks that rise through a fine stand of red fir to the parking circle near this famous overlook.

84 Bridalveil Creek to Yosemite Valley

TRIP   From Bridalveil Campground to Yosemite Valley
                (Happy Isles), (shuttle trip). Topo maps (15′) *Yose-
                mite, Merced Peak*. Best early-to-mid season; 32.7
                miles (52.6 km).

Grade	Trail/layover days	Total recommended days
Leisurely	5/1	6
Moderate	4/1	5
Strenuous	3/0	3

HILITES   This route traverses some of the finer forest stands
                in Yosemite, crosses the Buena Vista Crest, and
                concludes via the famous Panorama and Nevada
                Fall trails into the Valley. A feeling of remoteness
                from the start, combined with excellent fishing on
                several lakes, makes this a fine early-to-mid
                season trip.

DESCRIPTION (Leisurely trip)

1st and 2nd Hiking Days: Follow Trip 82 to **Royal Arch Lake**, 13
miles (20.9 km).

3rd and 4th Hiking Days: Follow the 3rd and 4th hiking days
of Trip 83 to **Illilouette Creek**, 12.3 miles (19.8 km).

5th Hiking Day (**Illilouette Creek** to **Yosemite Valley**, 7.4
miles—11.9 km—via the John Muir Trail, or 6.7 miles—10.8
km—via the Mist Trail): A short way up the east bank of
Illilouette Creek from the campsites is a junction, where our
route turns north across a sandy meadow. After jumping a

small, unnamed stream, we climb moderately to meet a trail coming in on the right. Continuing northward, our trail crosses a low, forested saddle and descends to the blacktopped Panorama Trail, where we turn right (east). This route skirts the edge of the sheer Panorama Cliff and then switchbacks down 500 feet to the lip of Nevada Fall, joining the John Muir Trail shortly before reaching the top of the fall. One of the finest falls in Yosemite, Nevada Fall drops 594 feet in one vertical plunge. Other falls in the Valley drop greater distances, but none has the volume of water that the Merced River has. The result is a thunderous roar that can be heard for miles. As the viewer stands facing out over the fall, the granite dome on his right is Liberty Cap; directly ahead and slightly above him is Glacier Point. Unfortunately, a shelf of the slope on the left hides the 370-foot Illilouette Fall. Should the traveler determine to conclude this day's hike via the John Muir Trail he will have to retrace his steps to the last junction and then retrace part of the 1st hiking day, Trip 81.

The more spectacular route, however, is the Mist Trail. As this route is spectacular, it is also quite difficult, owing to its steepness. The Mist Trail begins 0.2 mile northeast of the top of Nevada Fall. Progress down the Mist Trail is easily measured in relation to Nevada Fall, since the trail at one point comes down to the very base of the fall. At this point the immense power of the fall makes itself known. This route imposes an unforgettable humility on all those who tread it, for no sooner is Nevada Fall left behind than one is at the man-made railing on the brink of Vernal Fall. This site is a point of contrasts. Emerald Pool, just above the fall, is a placid flow of water that elicits a feeling of calm. Ten seconds away, the same water is catapulted with a roar into the misty chasm below. It is into this same chasm that the trail winds. On this trail section the trail's name gains meaning, and one emerges from the cloud of mist 800' lower with clothing damp and ears ringing with the sound of crashing water. At the Vernal Fall bridge the Mist Trail rejoins the John Muir Trail, which descends rather steeply to Happy Isles.

85 Bridalveil Creek to Royal Arch Lake

TRIP   From Bridalveil Campground to Royal Arch Lake
              (semiloop trip). Topo map *Yosemite*. Best early-to-
              mid season; 27.2 miles (43.7 km).

	Trail/layover	*Total recom-*
Grade	*days*	*mended days*
Leisurely	5/1	6
Moderate	4/1	5
Strenuous	3/0	3

HILITES For the first-timer, exploring Yosemite's south
             boundary country is a memorable experience, and
             this loop trip provides an exciting route. Angling
             on the many lakes around Buena Vista Peak is
             excellent, particularly in early season, and the
             easy access and return recommend this trip as an
             early-season "warm up."

DESCRIPTION (Leisurely trip)

1st Hiking Day: Follow Trip 82 to **Turner Meadows**, 6.3 miles
(10.1 km).

2nd Hiking Day (**Turner Meadows** to **Upper Chilnualna Lake**, 4.9
miles—7.9 km): From Turner Meadows the trail continues
southeast. One half mile from the campsites at the south end of
the meadow our route passes the Wawona Trail, and ¾ mile
later it turns east along Chilnualna Creek. This junction
marks the beginning of a long, easy ascent that is pleasantly
accompanied by the creek. Fishing along this cascading
stream is fair (small brook and rainbow); most anglers will
keep their lines dry until they reach Chilnualna Lakes
(8480'). Here, all except the lowest lake provide excellent
fishing for brook and rainbow (7-12"). Small (7-acre) upper
Chilnualna Lake, alongside the trail, has several good
campsites on its north side, but the best and most secluded
Chilnualna Lake is the southernmost one.

3rd Hiking Day (**Upper Chilnualna Lake** to **Royal Arch Lake**, 3.0 miles—4.8 km): From the north side of the lake, the trail climbs steeply up the 480-foot, densely forested slope to a junction with the Buena Vista Trail. Our route turns right (southeast) and climbs the ridge to beautiful Buena Vista Lake (9080′). On this high lake fishing is good for rainbow and brook (9-13″) and anglers may wish to tarry. After a switchbacking 300-foot climb, the remaining 2 miles to Royal Arch Lake is a gentle descent across granite that exhibits a sprinkling of lodgepole pine and hemlock. Royal Arch Lake (8700′) is a fine fishing lake (excellent angling for brook and rainbow to 14″), and there are numerous good-to-excellent campsites on the west shore. The lake's name is well-suited, deriving from the blackened granite streaks that rainbow across the sheer eastern facade of the lake basin.

4th and 5th Hiking Days: Reverse the steps of the 2nd and 1st hiking days, Trip 82, 13 miles (20.9 km).

Lyell Fork of the Tuolumne River

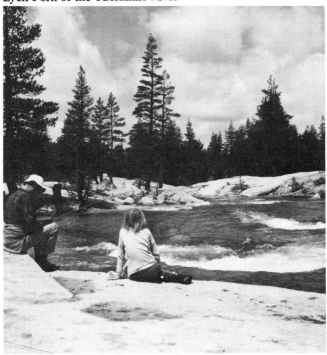

86   Glacier Point to Merced Lake

TRIP   From Glacier Point to Merced Lake (round trip). Topo maps *Yosemite, Merced Peak*. Best early season; 31.8 miles (51.2 km).

Grade	Trail/layover days	Total recommended days
Leisurely	4/1	5
Moderate	4/0	4
Strenuous	3/0	3

HILITES   This early-season excursion has all the scenic advantages of the Yosemite-Valley-to-Merced-Lake trip (Trip 81) without the 2000-foot climb from Happy Isles to Nevada Fall. Beginning high above the Merced River canyon, one gets an airy view that provides a better feeling for the glacial history of the area. Mild elevation change and solid mileage make this route a fine choice for the hiker who wants to shake winter's kinks out of early-season muscles.

DESCRIPTION (Leisurely trip)

1st Hiking Day (**Glacier Point** to **Little Yosemite Valley,** 6.7 miles—10.8 km): This trip begins near the snack bar east of the parking-lot restrooms. If you haven't seen the views from the actual point, you should walk 200 yards north to the fenced-in-overlook. Views are very impressive of the east end of Yosemite Valley, Half Dome, Vernal and Nevada falls, and domelike Mt. Starr King in the southeast. From the picnic area by the snack bar our route climbs a short distance south to a signed junction with the Pohono Trail, where we turn left and enter forest. Like the trails in Little Yosemite Valley, this one is big and wide, receiving a lot of day use. The trail begins a moderate-to-steep descent, and makes one switchback before angling south toward Illilouette Creek. Views of Half Dome and the sound of the falls filter through a forest cover that includes white fir, sugar pine, Jeffrey pine and black oak. Under them, manzanita, huckleberry oak and deer brush form most of the ground cover.

After 1⅔ miles we find a junction with the Buena Vista Trail, leading up-canyon. We turn left here and switchback down to seasonally raging Illilouette Creek. Just before the bridge a short spur trail leads down to an airy overlook of Illilouette Fall. Beyond the large steel, rock and concrete bridge, the now-less-used trail begins a 800-foot ascent to the top of Panorama Cliff. On this ascent, at about 6500 feet, we see some Douglas-firs. This is an unusually high elevation for this species. Warm air flowing up the Merced River canyon rises up Panorama Cliff, creating an unusually warm and favorable microclimate here.

Our route traverses along the top of aptly named Panorama Cliff to a junction with the Mono Meadow Trail, (leading right), and then our now-paved trail begins the 800-foot descent to Nevada Fall. Via a long series of switchbacks the trail descends through a dense forest of tall, water-loving Douglas-firs and incense-cedars. Near the bottom we pass some sections of abandoned trail, a drainage diversion wall and the phone lines that run to Merced Lake Ranger Station, 9 miles up-canyon. Then our route joins the John Muir Trail and soon arrives at the slabs above Nevada Fall. On these slabs you may notice large patches of smooth, shiny rock—glacial polish. All these slabs were polished by glaciers of the Tioga glaciation—the last time glaciers were here—at the end of the Pleistocene epoch, about 12,000 years ago. There is much, much less glacial polish below this point, indicating that no glaciers may have entered Yosemite Valley from the Merced River canyon during the late Pleistocene. In fact, the last time glaciers flowed through the Valley was probably 750,000 years ago.

Beyond Nevada Fall the trail ascends past a junction with the Mist Trail and switchbacks over a low bedrock ridge under Liberty Cap. After ½ mile we pass a cutoff to the John Muir Trail north of this valley and soon reach a junction where the John Muir Trail turns left (north). Here is the main, heavily used camping area, where there are outhouses, a ranger station and anti-bear boxes. If this area doesn't suite you, you could continue for about 2 level miles to the less crowded sites at the east end of Little Yosemite Valley.

2nd Hiking Day: Follow the 2nd hiking day, Trip 81, to **Merced Lake,** 9.2 miles (14.8 km).

3rd and 4th Hiking Days: Retrace your steps, 15.4 miles (24.8 km).

87 Glacier Point to Rutherford Lake

TRIP   From Glacier Point to Rutherford Lake (loop trip).
Topo maps *Yosemite, Merced Peak*. Best mid or late
season, 69.5 miles (111.9 km).

Grade	Trail/layover days	Total recommended days
Leisurely	12/2	14
Moderate	11/2	13
Strenuous	7/2	9

HILITES   Designed for the experienced backpacker, this trip
offers a combination of excellent fishing and
superlative vistas. Almost a dozen angling lakes,
most of them in high-country settings, also
provide swimming to alleviate the trail dust.
Three major passes challenge the most ambitious
hiker, and the wide variations in plants and
wildlife will satisfy the most discriminating
naturalist.

DESCRIPTION (Moderate trip)

1st Hiking Day: Follow Trip 86 to **Little Yosemite Valley**, 6.7
miles (10.8 km).

2nd Hiking Day: Follow the 2nd hiking day, Trip 81, to **Merced
Lake,** 9.2 miles (14.8 km).

3rd Hiking Day (**Merced Lake** to **Lyell Fork, Merced River,** 5.8 miles—9.3 km): From Merced Lake High Sierra Camp the trail ascends slabs to a drift fence and enters an area much used by livestock. A shaded ¾-mile stroll brings us to an engineered ford of multibranched Lewis Creek, a junction with the Lewis Creek Trail, and the Merced Lake Ranger Station. From the station we continue our level stroll to a riverside drift fence. Staying closer to the river now, our trail soon begins a moderate ascent along the east canyon wall, crossing several small creeks before traversing above the outlet of Washburn Lake (7600'). The outlets of Merced and Washburn lakes are similar, as both lakes are dammed by similar bedrock ribs. Skirting the east shore of the lake, we cross a small creek and pass the shaded campsites at the head of the lake, near a fine sandy beach for swimming. Beyond the lake our trail ascends a dry slope and then swings over to riverside by a lovely waterfall. The gentle ascent continues as the trail passes through very large stands of bracken fern under a beautiful, tall forest of huge white firs and Jeffrey pines, with smaller lodgepole pines and aspens. An emerald-green, placid Merced River flows near the trail in places along this idyllic setting. Where the Lyell Fork comes down on the left we meet the main river, and good campsites can be found in the vicinity of the bridge. Fishing in the river is fair-to-good for rainbow trout (to 9").

4th Hiking Day (**Lyell Fork, Merced River**, to **Triple Peak Fork Meadow**, 4.2 miles—6.8 km): Beyond the sturdy wood bridge spanning the Merced River, our trail soon begins to climb south into the great granite **V** carved by the lower stretches of the Merced Peak Fork of the river. This ascent steepens as it enters the zone of red fir and juniper, and then the path levels momentarily where it crosses the Merced Peak Fork on another wooden bridge, which spans a short section of quiet water between roaring cascades above and below. Our trail leaves the riverside and climbs by long switchbacks up the north side of the bowl, leading to excellent viewpoints for visual enjoyment of the huge granite slabs, the aspen grove and the pockets of conifers below. Another overlook at a switchback turn is close beneath a cascade and a waterfall on the Triple Peak Fork, whose upper reaches our trail is searching out. It was in these upper reaches of the river that the Merced glacier began, and the polished granite on every hand is a constant reminder of its presence. Above the switchbacks our trail ascends gently to a verdant flat where the green Triple Peak Fork slowly winds among the tall trees. After one more steep—but short— climb, the trail ascends gradually near the river under a moderate forest cover of lodgepoles for 2 miles to the foot of long Triple Peak Fork Meadow. The river curves in lovely fashion through this mile-long grassland, past many campsites made illegal by the prohibition against camping within 100 feet of streams. Side pools out of the main current warm up enough to provide pleasant swimming in midsummer. The best campsites are at the south end of the meadow, near the junction with the Red Peak Pass Trail (9100'). Fishing is good for brook and rainbow trout (to 9").

5th Hiking Day (**Triple Peak Fork Meadow** to **Post Creek**, 7.2 miles—11.6 km): This hiking day begins with a gradually increasing climb for a long mile southward away from the Triple Peak Fork, out of lodgepole forest into dense hemlock. Then the duff trail turns northeast and climbs almost a mile on a traverse interrupted by two short switchbacks, to arrive at the rock monument at the junction with the high trail that goes along the top of the east wall of the Merced River canyon. Here our route turns right (south) and quickly ascends a beautiful hillside with broken, light-colored granite close on the left and the soaring Clark Range across the canyon on the right. The trail then levels off in a spectacular high bowl, encircled by Triple Divide Peak, Isberg Peak and some unnamed peaks between. The feeling of spaciousness here is worth the four days' hike to get to this Shangri-la, and in midseason the green grass and many-hued flowers add enough stimulation to surfeit the senses. After fording the unmapped, unnamed outlet of the unnamed but mapped lakes in this bowl, our trail dips into a bowl-within-the-bowl and there crosses another clear stream.

Finally we ascend out of the huge meadow and cross another stream before arriving at a hillside junction with the Isberg Pass Trail, where we turn right (south). Our Post Peak Pass Trail climbs to the ridgeline north of Post Peak, then follows this ridge south to the actual pass (10,700'). This ascent is not without compensation, for the views from the trail are among the most outstanding in the South Boundary Country. From this divide between the Merced and the San Joaquin River, the traveler has views of the Clark Range to the west, the Cathedral Range to the north and the tops of Banner Peak, Mt. Ritter and the Minarets to the east.

At this point our route leaves Yosemite, later to recross the boundary at Fernandez Pass—6 miles away. The trail descends 600 feet to little Porphyry Lake (10,100'), where fishing is fair for brook and rainbow. Below the lake, the trail improves slightly in the stretch to Isberg Meadow, then becomes fairly good. Conies and marmots may appear on the rocky portions of this trail, and deer, grouse and quail in the meadowy parts. After going almost level for ½ mile through several meadows, we enter lodgepole forest and descend moderately to the good campsites at Post Creek (9040'). Fishing along the creek is good for brook trout (to 8").

6th Hiking Day (**Post Creek** to **Rutherford Lake**, 3.9 miles—6.3 km): From Post Creek the trail crosses a small rise, passes two small, unnamed lakelets (no fish), and fords the West Fork Granite Creek. Shortly beyond, the trail fords Fernandez Creek and strikes the Fernandez Pass Trail. Here our route turns right (west) along a gently ascending, densely timbered stretch that offers fine views across Fernandez Creek. After a long ½ mile the trail switchbacks moderately up a morainal slope, trending northwest, to a junction with the Rutherford Lake lateral. Here our route turns right (north) and climbs steeply to the cirque nestling 28-acre Rutherford Lake (9800'). There are fair-to-good campsites on the west side of the lake south of the outlet. Views from these sites are excellent, and fishing is fair for brook and golden (to 16").

7th Hiking Day: Reverse the steps of the 2nd hiking day, Trip 77, to **Middle Chain Lake**, 7.7 miles (12.4 km).

8th Hiking Day: Follow the 2nd hiking day, Trip 78, to **Royal Arch Lake**, 9 miles (14.5 km).

9th, 10th and 11th Hiking Days: Follow the 3rd, 4th and 5th hiking days, Trip 83, 15.8 miles (25.4 km).

Clark Range from near Post Peak Pass

88   Glacier Point to Granite Creek

TRIP   From Glacier Point to Granite Creek Campground
                 (shuttle trip). Topo maps *Yosemite*, *Merced Peak*.
                 Best mid or late season, 41.5 miles (66.8 km).

Grade	Trail/layover days	Total recommended days
Leisurely	7/2	9
Moderate	6/1	7
Strenuous	4/1	5

HILITES   This route traverses the very heart of Yosemite's
                 South Boundary Country, and crosses the divide of
                 the Merced and San Joaquin River watersheds at
                 Isberg Pass. Fishing on the lakes and streams is
                 fair-to-excellent, and the life zones range from
                 Canadian to Arctic-Alpine. Remoteness and
                 panoramic vistas beckon the traveler to choose
                 this trip.

DESCRIPTION (Leisurely trip)

1st Hiking Day: Follow Trip 86 to **Little Yosemite Valley**, 6.7
miles (10.8 km).

2nd Hiking Day: Follow the 2nd hiking day, Trip 81, to **Merced
Lake,** 9.2 miles (14.8 km).

3rd and 4th Hiking Days: Follow the 3rd and 4th hiking days,
Trip 87, to **Triple Peak Fork Meadow**, 10 miles (16.1 km).

5th Hiking Day (**Triple Peak Fork Meadow** to **Isberg Lakes**, 4.9
miles—7.9 km): First, follow the 5th hiking day, Trip 87, to the
junction of the Post Peak Pass and Isberg Pass trails. From
this junction at timberline, our route turns left (northeast) and

climbs steadily among large blocks of talus. The views north and west, which already have been excellent, become even better as our route switchbacks farther up the ridge, as high as the pass we are approaching. Then the tread goes more or less level to signed Isberg Pass (10,500') and beyond it continues to weave sinuously along the crest. Finally it passes through a tiny defile between two stunted whitebark pines which frame a very dramatic view of the Ritter Range a few miles east. In the distance to the right of this dark range, most of the High Sierra is visible, and hikers who have rambled among its summits will spy some of their favorite monuments. From this pass between the Merced River and the San Joaquin River watersheds, the trail descends by switchbacks to rocky upper Isberg Lake, and then more gradually to lower Isberg Lake (9800'). Fishing in these lakes is fair-to-good for brook and some rainbow (to 8"). There are a few fair campsites at lower Isberg.

6th and 7th Hiking Days: Follow the steps of the 4th and 5th hiking days, Trip 80, 10.7 miles (17.2 km).

Unnamed lake, Triple Divide Peak

National Park Service

Fish Creek/Mono Creek

Surmounting Duck Pass from the north, one looks south across Cascade Valley to the Silver Divide. In the light of midday, the bleached granite of the divide imparts a glowing crown to the whole range and the impression is one of a royal diadem. Views such as this make the region a special place—a favorite to which one must return time and again lest a nuance of memory be lost. Since most of the region is now part of the John Muir Wilderness, its Sierran tranquility is assured.

The Silver Divide country, composed of the Fish and Mono Creek watersheds, lies southeast of Devils Postpile. It is bounded on the north by the Mammoth Crest, on the east by the Sierra crest, and on the south by the Mono Divide. Both Fish Creek and Mono Creek flow west from the Sierra crest, and their flow is augmented by feeder streams emanating from pocket lakes and cirque lakes of the Mono Divide, the Silver Divide and the Mammoth Crest. These feeder streams plunge and splash down from their alpine settings to densely forested canyon floors. The forest carpet in the canyons contrasts sharply with the barrenness of surrounding peaks, like Red Slate Mountain, Mt. Morgan, Mt. Mills, Mt. Gabb and Mt. Hilgard, all over 13,000 feet.

Glacially wrought, the Fish and Mono Creek canyons exhibit typical "hanging valleys," broad expanses of polished granite, amphitheater cirques, and arc-shaped moraines. An outstanding example of a terminal moraine may be seen when one looks back toward Long Valley from the eastern ascent to McGee Pass. The glacier that once filled this canyon was one of the Sierra's most ancient, and it is fitting that it was eroding the oldest rocks in the Sierra. Recent fossil identification has dated these rocks at four hundred million years. Nowhere in the Sierra is the birthplace of a glacier more vividly portrayed than in the Little Lakes Valley on the east side of Mono Pass. Backed by Mts. Mills, Abbot and Dade and Bear Creek Spire, this charming valley has the typical **U**-shaped profile. Lateral moraines pushed to the sides of the valley by the ebb and flow of ice are now topped by tiny lakelets.

The Indians were the first to appreciate the charm of high-country retreats like the Little Lakes Valley. On the east side, it was the Mono Indians who sought the high country in summertime. This country provided a plentiful natural larder, but the Indians, like us, also fled to the heights to escape the midsummer valley heat.

Prospectors, following the lure of "that one big strike," soon penetrated into the high country, but most of their efforts were confined to the area around Mono Lake. The first recorded visit to Mono Pass and the San Joaquin River was by the Brewer party in 1864. Led by an army cavalryman who claimed he had once pursued Indians over the pass, this tiny survey team topped the Sierra crest and followed the descent of the present Mono Creek Trail to Vermilion Valley (now covered by man-made Lake Thomas A. Edison). Using the valley as a base camp, they made an unsuccessful attempt to ascend Mt. Goddard before returning to Yosemite.

The Brewer party journals do not indicate the quality of fishing available in the area at the time. However, it is difficult to imagine much better angling than is offered there today. The appropriately named Fish Creek boasts a varied fish population of brook, rainbow and some golden trout—as does Mono Creek. On the Fish Creek side of the Silver Divide some of the better fishing spots are Cascade Valley, Tully Hole, Helen Lake and Warrior Lake. The Mono Creek watershed offers equally fine angling at Grinnell Lakes, Graveyard Lakes and Laurel Lake, and on the upper reaches of Mono Creek. State fishing licenses are required.

The Trailheads

Vermilion Campground. Go east from Clovis (near Fresno) 81 miles on State Highway 168 to the Florence Lake/Lake Edison junction, then 8 miles north on a mostly paved road to Vermilion Campground.

Coldwater Campground. Go west from U.S. 395 4 miles to Mammoth Lakes and take the Lake Mary Road. Follow it 3.5 miles to the northeast shore of Lake Mary, turn left on a road signed for Coldwater Campground, go ½ mile, and turn left into the campground. Go 1 mile to the trailhead at campground's end.

Mosquito Flat. Go 25 miles north from Bishop or 15 miles south from the Mammoth Lakes turnoff on U.S. 395 and then 11 miles on paved road to road's end in Mosquito Flat beside Rock Creek.

McGee Creek Roadend. Go 32 miles north of Bishop or 8 miles south of the Mammoth Lakes turnoff to a dirt road that leads west 4.0 miles to a roadend parking area.

89   Lake Edison to Graveyard Meadows

TRIP   From Vermilion Campground (Lake Thomas A.
               Edison) to Graveyard Meadows (round trip). Topo
               maps *Kaiser Peak, Mt. Abbot.* Best mid season;
               10.4 miles (16.8 km).

Grade	Trail/layover days	Total recommended days
Leisurely	2/0	2
Moderate	....	....
Strenuous	....	....

HILITES   The grail at the end of this quest is a pretty,
               meadowed campsite within the boundaries of the
               John Muir Wilderness Area. This route travels
               densely forested country abounding in wildlife,
               and tops a crest offering superlative views.

DESCRIPTION

1st Hiking Day (**Vermilion Campground** to **Graveyard Meadows**,
5.2 miles—8.4 km): To reach the trailhead, proceed beyond the
turnoff to the campground and follow the dirt road 0.15 mile to
a parking area, turn right, up the hill, and go past the turnoff
to the packstation (on the left) to a parking area at a Forest
Service sign. Park here under the tall Jeffrey pines. After a
stroll of 0.3 mile we reach a signed junction with the trail to
Quail Meadows, and we veer right onto it and down, to the
collapsed bridge across Cold Creek. Beyond the bridge, our
route reaches a junction, where we take the Goodale Pass
Trail, the left fork, and proceed under Jeffrey pines, white firs
and junipers. We soon begin a long, dusty ascent under a dense
cover of mostly Jeffrey pines. Our route passes a meadow on
the lower part of this climb, but the ascent is fairly monoto-
nous until very near the top, where we are rewarded with good
views of Lake Edison and the peaks of the Mono Divide. From
the crown of the climb it is but a short distance to Cold Creek,
which we ford in order to join a jeep road for a short distance
before we arrive at the signed boundary of the John Muir

Wilderness. Graveyard Meadows (8850') are on the right, and secluded camping can be found at the head of the meadows. Or if one prefers, one can stay at the more well-used sites near the ford. Fishing in Cold Creek is poor-to-fair for brook (to 8"). *2nd Hiking Day*: Retrace your steps, 5.2 miles (8.4 km).

Cold Creek bridge before it collapsed

90   Lake Edison to Graveyard Lakes

TRIP

From Vermilion Campground (Lake Thomas A. Edison) to Lower Graveyard Lake (round trip). Topo maps *Kaiser Peak, Mt. Abbot.* Best mid or late season; 16.8 miles (27.2 km).

Grade	Trail/layover days	Total recom- mended days
Leisurely	4/1	5
Moderate	3/1	4
Strenuous	2/1	3

HILITES

The California Department of Fish and Game has never been called overly creative, but it named the lakes in the Graveyard Lakes chain well. Beneath tombstone-granited Graveyard Peak lie lakes with DF&G names like Vengeance, Murder, Phantom, Headstone, Spook and Ghost. This country is worth investigating if for no other reason than to satisfy one's curiosity about these names. The truth is that this particular lake basin is one of the loveliest and most regal in the Silver Divide country.

DESCRIPTION (Leisurely trip)

1st Hiking Day: Follow Trip 89 to **Graveyard Meadows**, 5.2 miles (8.4 km).

2nd Hiking Day (**Graveyard Meadows** to **Lower Graveyard Lake**, 3.2 miles—5.2 km): From the south end of Graveyard Meadows, the trail enters the John Muir Wilderness and skirts the north edge of the meadows under a dense cover of lodgepoles and red firs. Birdlovers should keep an eye out for the Brewer blackbird, whitecrowned sparrow, Cassin finch, robin and sparrow hawk that inhabit this mountain field. At the north end of the meadow, the trail begins climbing moderately, and soon we cross Cold Creek on rocks (difficult in early season). This forested, duff trail ascends the narrowing Cold Creek valley, fording the creek in two places at the south end of Upper Graveyard Meadow. The trail continues its gentle-to-moderate ascent under lodgepoles to a junction with the trail to Graveyard Lakes. We turn left onto it and ford Cold Creek in Upper Graveyard Meadow. Beyond the ford, the trail enters a cover of lodgepole and hemlock and begins a steep, rocky climb to the basin above. The lodgepole pine and mountain hemlock at the top of this 600-foot ascent give way to lush meadows at the eastern fringes of beautiful lower Graveyard Lake (9950'). Good though heavily used campsites may be found in the lodgepole stands where the trail first meets the lake, or along the east side of the lake between this point and the inlet stream.

From any of these places, the camper has marvelous views of Graveyard Peak and the tumbled granite cirque wall that surrounds the entire Graveyard Lakes basin. It is easy to derive the logic behind the name, "Graveyard Peak." Tombstone-makers have for years shown a preference for this particular kind of salt-and-pepper granite. These campsites along the east side of lower Graveyard Lake make an excellent base camp from which to fish and explore the remaining five lakes in the basin. The three small lakes directly above offer pretty and cleaner camping, and they can be reached by following the trail around to the head of the lake and climbing the hill. Fishing is good on lower Graveyard Lake for brook trout (to 13") and fair-to-good on the upper lakes, due to poor spawning waters.

3rd and 4th Hiking Days: Retrace your steps, 8.4 miles (13.6 km).

Looking south over Lake Edison

91 Rock Creek to Gem Lakes

TRIP   From Mosquito Flat (on Rock Creek) to Gem
Lakes (round trip). Topo maps *Mt. Tom, Mt.
Abbot.* Best mid or late season; 8 miles (12.8 km).

Grade	Trail/layover days	Total recom- mended days
Leisurely	2/0	2
Moderate	....	....
Strenuous	....	....

HILITES   Majestic scenery dominates this short, popular
trip. Because of its moderate terrain and high
country "feel" this route through the Little Lakes
Valley has been a long-time favorite of the beginning hiker, and the varied and good fishing for
brook and rainbow makes it also an excellent
angling choice.

DESCRIPTION

1st Hiking Day (**Mosquito Flat** to **Gem Lakes**, 4 miles—6.4
km): The magnificent Sierra crest confronts the traveler at the
very outset of this trip. From the trailhead at Mosquito Flat
(10,200′), the wide, rocky-sandy trail starts southwest toward
the imposing skyline dominated by soaring Bear Creek Spire.
In a few minutes we enter John Muir Wilderness and then
reach a junction at which the Mono Pass Trail is the right fork
and our trail, the Morgan Pass Trail, is the left fork. Soon our
route tops a low, rocky ridge just west of Mack Lake, and from
this ridge one has good views of green-clad Little Lakes Valley.
Gazing out, one cannot help but feel a sense of satisfaction
that this beautiful valley enjoys protection as part of John
Muir Wilderness. Aside from some early, abortive mining ventures, this subalpine valley remains relatively unspoiled.

   From the ridgetop viewpoint our trail descends to skirt a
marsh that was the west arm of Marsh Lake before it filled in.
Anglers may wish to try their luck for the good fishing for
brown and brook trout in Marsh Lake and the nearby lagoon
areas of Rock Creek. While fishing on the numerous lakes and
streams of Little Lakes Valley, one has views south into the

long glacial trough to the south—a long-time favorite of lens-men. Flanked by Mt. Starr on the right and Mt. Morgan on the left, the valley terminates in the soaring heights of Mts. Mills, Abbot, Dade and Julius Caesar, and Bear Creek Spire, all over 13,000 feet. Still-active glaciers on the slopes of these great peaks are reminders of the enormous forces that shaped this valley eons ago, and the visitor cannot help but feel contrasting reactions of exhilaration and humility.

From the meadowed fringes of Marsh and Heart lakes, the trail ascends gently past the west side of Box Lake to the east side of aptly named Long Lake. For the angler with a yearning to try different waters, the unnamed lakes on the bench just to the east offer good fishing for brook and rainbow. Beyond Long Lake the trail ascends through a moderately dense forest cover of whitebark pines past a spur trail branching left to Chickenfoot Lake. Then we dip to cross a seasonal stream, climb slightly, and dip again, to the outlet stream of the Gem Lakes. Ahead on the left we see the last switchback on the trail up to Morgan Pass, through which the abandoned road that has been our trail once reached the tungsten mines in the Pine Creek drainage.

Just after a rockhop ford of the Gem Lakes outlet, we take the trail that leads 150 yards up beside this stream to the lowest of the three main Gem Lakes. Many campsites in clumps of whitebark pines are scattered around these emerald-green lakes, under the sheer north wall of peak 11645. Fishing is fair-to-good for brook and rainbow trout to 10″. The Treasure Lakes, located in barren cirques above here, are traditional basecamp locations for climbers bound for the high peaks to the west.

2nd Hiking Day: Retrace your steps, 4 miles (6.4 km).

92 Rock Creek to Ruby Lake

TRIP   From Mosquito Flat to Ruby Lake (round trip).
Topo maps *Mt. Tom, Mt. Abbot*. Best mid or late
season; 5 miles (8 km).

Grade	Trail/layover days	Total recommended days
Leisurely	2/0	2
Moderate	....	....
Strenuous	....	....

HILITES   From the Little Lakes Valley upward to the
heights of the Ruby Lake cirque, the traveler
gains an appreciation of glacially formed country.
One can almost see the main trunk of the glacier
flowing northeast through the valley and being
joined by the feeder glacier from the cirque that
now holds Ruby Lake. The terminus of this trip,
Ruby Lake, lies amidst the barren peaks of the
awe-inspiring Sierra Nevada crest.

DESCRIPTION

1st Hiking Day (**Mosquito Flat** to **Ruby Lake,** 2.5 miles—4 km):
First, follow Trip 91 to the junction of the Morgan Pass and
Mono Pass trails. Here our route branches right (west) and
ascends steeply over rocky switchbacks. In the course of this
switchbacking ascent, the traveler will see the moderate-to-
dense forest cover of whitebark and lodgepole diminish in
density as we near timberline. Views during the climb include
the glacier-fronted peaks named above, and, midway up the
ascent, Mt. Morgan. Immediately below to the east, the deep
blue of Heart and Box lakes and some of the Hidden Lakes
reflects the sky above, and the viewer looking at the panorama
of the valley can readily trace the glacial history that left these
"puddles" behind.

Near the meadowed edge of the outlet stream from Ruby
Lake is a junction, where we turn left. It becomes apparent
that a cirque basin is opening up, although one cannot see

Ruby Lake, which completely fills the cirque bottom, until one is actually at water's edge (11,000'). This first breathtaking view of the lake and its towering cirque walls makes the climb worth the effort. Sheer granite makes up the upper walls of the cirque, and the crown is topped by a series of spectacular pinnacles, particularly to the west. To the north, also on the crest, a notch indicates Mono Pass, and close scrutiny will reveal the switchbacking trail that ascends the south ridge of Mt. Starr. The lower walls of the cirque are mostly made up of talus and scree that curve outward to the lake's edge, and it is over this jumbled rock that ambitious anglers must scramble to sample the fair fishing for brook, rainbow and brown (to 12"). Good campsites can be found below the outlet of the lake. Lakeside campsites are exposed and usually windy.

2nd Hiking Day: Retrace your steps, 2.5 miles (4 km).

Outlet of Ruby Lake

93   Mcgee Creek to Steelhead Lake

TRIP   From McGee Creek Roadend to Steelhead Lake
(round trip). Topo maps *Mt. Morrison, Mt. Abbot.*
Best mid or late season; 9 miles (14.4 km).

Grade	Trail/layover days	Total recom- mended days
Leisurely	2/1	3
Moderate	2/0	2
Strenuous	....	....

HILITES   Travelers new to east-escarpment entry to the
Sierra will find the ascent to Steelhead Lake fascinating because of the swirling patterns in the
highly fractured red metamorphic rocks of the
canyon wall. Though Steelhead Lake is relatively
easy to reach, the hiker may find seclusion there.

DESCRIPTION

1st Hiking Day (**McGee Creek Roadend** to **Steelhead Lake**, 4.5
miles—7.2 km): From the parking area (8100′) the trail
ascends a short distance to a Forest Service sign proclaiming
the eastern boundary of the John Muir Wilderness. The route,
an old jeep road leading to the defunct Scheelore Mine,
traverses the north and then the west side of McGee Creek
canyon. The canyon is mostly sage- and rabbitbrush-covered
except for an anomalous grove of aspen in an apparently dry
area. Near the creek are more aspen, cottonwood, birch and
willow. Soon our trail fords the streams emanating from the
springs above Horsetail Falls, and the canyon narrows. As the
trail passes close to the creek, the grade eases, and our route
enters a lush area with a lovely floral display.

The gentle ascent continues to a ford of tree-lined McGee
Creek, where there is sometimes a log (difficult in early season). Then the unshaded trail climbs more steeply until it
passes a beaver dam. Above the dam, the creek wanders

through a meadow, above which the trail fords the creek via logs and boards to the west bank. As the trail loops west it becomes steeper and enters a moderately dense lodgepole forest. Then our route leaves the jeep road at a signed junction and continues its winding ascent to a junction with the Steelhead Lake lateral. (This junction is farther than indicated on the map; it is where the trail finally returns to creekside. Fording McGee Creek, this lateral climbs steeply by switchbacks along the north side of the outlet stream from Grass Lake. Fishing from the meadowed fringes of little Grass Lake is poor-to-fair for rainbow and brook. From Grass Lake the trail once more switchbacks up an abrupt, timbered slope, and ends at the good camping sites at the north end of fairly large (about 25 acres) Steelhead Lake (10,350'). Views from these campsites take in the granite grandeur of Mt. Stanford and Mt. Crocker to the south and west, and rust-and-buff-colored Mt. Baldwin to the north. Fishermen will find the angling for rainbow and brook excellent (best in early and late season). They will also find the name "Steelhead" Lake a misnomer, though an understandable error. Over the years, catches of rainbow trout from this lake have exhibited pale, faded-out markings, giving an appearance much like their silver cousins of coastal waters.

2nd Hiking Day: Retrace your steps, 4.5 miles (7.2 km).

94   McGee Creek to McGee Lake

TRIP From McGee Creek Roadend to Big McGee Lake (round trip). Topo maps *Mt. Morrison, Mt. Abbot.* Best mid or late season; 13 miles (21 km).

Grade	Trail/layover days	Total recommended days
Leisurely	2/1	3
Moderate	2/0	2
Strenuous	....	....

HILITES In an alpine setting close under the Sierra crest, Big McGee Lake shares a large granite basin with three other fishable lakes. This beautiful spot nestles under the sheer, colorful walls of Red and White Peak, and close to impressive Mt. Crocker.

DESCRIPTION

1st Hiking Day (**McGee Creek Roadend** to **Big McGee Lake,** 6.5 miles—10.5 km): First, follow Trip 93 to the trail intersection with the Steelhead Lake lateral, where the trail continues, south over a forested, rocky slope. The ascent eases as the trail passes a drift fence, and then we pass a tarn, climb above a meadow where there is a campsite, and emerge from timber into another meadow. The trail then undulates under a sparse cover of whitebark pine to join the creek briefly and skirt a smaller meadow from where an older section of trail heads back down-canyon. Soon the trail reaches the rocky, open slopes just north of Big McGee Lake (10480'). Fair-to-good campsites may be found along the north shore. Fishermen will enjoy the fair-to-good fishing for rainbow and brook (to 13") on Big McGee Lake, and, if time and inclination allow, will want to explore the equally good fishing at nearby Little McGee Lake, Crocker Lake, or picture-book Golden Lake.

2nd Hiking Day: Retrace your steps, 6.5 miles (10.5 km).

McGee Creek to Lake Edison

95

TRIP From McGee Creek Roadend to Vermilion Campground (Lake Thomas A. Edison) (shuttle trip). Topo maps *Mt. Morrison, Mt. Abbot, Kaiser Peak.* Best mid or late season; 33.6 miles (54.3 km).

Grade	Trail/layover days	Total recommended days
Leisurely	7/2	9
Moderate	5/2	7
Strenuous	4/2	6

HILITES This trans-Sierra route is one of the finest in the northern Sierra. Two scenic passes, both over 11,000 feet, cross the Sierra crest and the Silver Divide. Between them the route visits alpine lakes and streams offering excellent fishing for rainbow, brook and golden trout. Pristine meadows, spectacular peaks, and dense forest mark this trip as a must for any serious wilderness traveler.

DESCRIPTION (Leisurely trip)

1st Hiking Day: Follow Trip 94 to **Big McGee Lake,** 6.5 miles (10.5 km).

2nd Hiking Day (**Big McGee Lake** to **Tully Lake,** 5.5 miles—8.9 km): With the colorful and majestic heights of Red and White Mountain to the left (southwest) the route ascends steeply to Little McGee Lake, passing a signed junction with the route to Hopkins Pass. Fishing at this rockbound lake is fair for rainbow and brook. From Little McGee Lake our route swings northward and ascends a narrow, rocky canyon toward McGee

Pass. The red rock walls of the canyon look very desolate, and the trail briefly disappears under snow until late season. The last few hundred feet of ascent are accomplished via rocky switchbacks up the west wall of a barren cirque. From McGee Pass (11,900′) views to the west are good of the peaks above Fish Creek.

An interesting turn-of-the-century legend has it that two Indian sheepherders running sheep around the headwaters of McGee Creek were returning from the high country. En route, a pack on one of their mules shifted, and they jury-rigged a large rock to balance the shifting action. Upon reaching their destination, they unloaded the jury-rigged balance and discovered that the rock felt abnormally heavy. As in all good gold legends, the rock assayed rich, and, ostensibly, neither the two Indians nor subsequent treasure-seekers have found the lode from which the rock was taken.

From the pass much of the descent to timberline is on new trail that has too many switchbacks for most people's taste. We reach timberline above a large meadow, and from here our trail follows a route north of that shown on the topo map. The trail descends through sparse timber and meets the creek at the foot of a meadow. Just below, the creek and the trail drop steeply and turn right. Ford the creek here and head south up a grassy swale to the good campsite in the trees above Tully Lake. Good campsites may also be found on the meadowed fringes along the northeast side of the lake. Tully Lake (10,400′) is a small (about 10 acres) high-country lake that sustains fair-to-good fishing for golden and brook (to 13″). Anglers will want to try the nearby waters of Red and White Lake, about 1 mile over the ridge to the east. Fishing here is also fair-to-good for rainbow that often run to 16″. Those wishing stream fishing can find smaller rainbow, brook and some golden along meandering Fish Creek.

3rd Hiking Day (**Tully Lake** to **Tully Hole**, 3 miles—4.8 km): This short trail day allows the traveler who admires wild back-country scenery to absorb the primitive beauty of this area. Anglers, particularly fly fisherman, will find the leisurely pace along Fish Creek satisfying. From Tully Lake retrace the route to the main Fish Creek Trail, where it turns left (west). The trail now follows the south bank of Fish Creek as it descends below treeline ¼ mile to a ford of Fish Creek, where it meets the trail that follows the outlet from Tully Lake. Our trail soon fords the creek again and enters timber. Here we pass a signed junction with the trail to Cecil and Lee Lakes. Then the descent steepens and the trail switchbacks down to lush Horse Heaven. Through the meadow, the trail is muddy into late season, and the ford at the west end of the meadow is difficult in early season. Beyond this ford the trail passes a drift fence and descends through lodgepole and hemlock on the south side of the creek to Tully Hole (9500'). Like the meadows at Horse Heaven, the grasslands of Tully Hole (9500') are also rife with wildflower color. The stream is sometimes bowered with willows, but the long, swirling, curved line of Fish Creek is for the most part an open, pleasant stretch of water with grassy, overhung banks and several deep holes. Good campsites at the northwest edge of the meadow near the John Muir Trail junction take advantage of the fine views up the meadow.

4th Hiking Day (**Tully Hole** to **Lake of the Lone Indian**, 5 miles— 8.1 km): The route at this point joins the John Muir Trail, and leaves Tully Hole by a gentle descent. From the trail, the traveler has splendid views and access to the numerous small falls and holes that characterize nearby Fish Creek. The trail then passes the junction with the Cascade Valley Trail and climbs steeply over a densely forested slope east of the outlet stream from Squaw Lake. Midway up this stretch the trail levels off, fords the stream twice in quick succession, and passes several campsites situated in picturesque meadows. Then it begins the final, long, steep climb to Squaw Lake. This section of trail is rocky, eroded and exposed.

Meadow-fringed Squaw Lake is a good place to stop and ponder the effects of glacial erosion—the clean granite cliffs the large erratics here and there, and the lake basin itself. Anglers will wish to fish Squaw Lake—and Warrior Lake above it—which offer good-to-excellent fishing for brook (to 9").

From Squaw Lake our route winds up the rocky slope to the southwest, and in ½ mile meets the Goodale Pass Trail at a small pool. Our route leaves the John Muir Trail here, turns right, tops a ridge, and descends through rocky meadows to the foot of turquoise Papoose Lake. This small lake (under 5 acres) affords good fishing for brook, as does Chief Lake, up the granite slope to the east. At the outlet of Papoose Lake our route branches north, and then descends over a long dusty traverse to the good campsites in the grassy pockets at the southwest end of Lake of the Lone Indian (10,200'). Angling is good for brook and rainbow (8-14").

5th Hiking Day (**Lake of the Lone Indian** to **Lower Graveyard Lake**, 5.2 miles—8.4 km): First retrace the steps of the previous day to the Goodale Pass Trail at the foot of Papoose Lake.

Our route then turns right (southwest), and 100 yards beyond
the ford of Papoose Lake's outlet is a signed junction with the
trail to Minnow Creek. Here our trail begins a steep, rocky
ascent to a long, grass-bottomed swale below Goodale Pass.
Where the trail levels off momentarily an unsigned trail goes
right, down the hill to Lake of the Lone Indian. The exfoliating, rocky slopes of the Silver Divide show the usual signs of
glaciation—polish, rounding and striation. The whistling of
marmots that inhabit the jumbled slopes accompanies the
traveler as he climbs the last leg to Goodale Pass (11,000′).
From the pass views extend as far north as the Ritter Range
and Yosemite, and south over the San Joaquin River watershed to the peaks beyond the Mono Divide. The first part of the
descent down the south side of Goodale Pass is rocky and steep.
As the switchbacking trail progresses, it offers fine views of
the nearby cirque that feeds Cold Creek.

Soon the trail levels out somewhat and stepladders down
through a series of charming green pocket meadows. As the
trail descends in and out of lodgepole-pine stands, it crosses
many small streams which pour out of the canyon's north wall.
Unfortunately, some of these may be fouled by the summer
cattle population. Soon after the ford of Cold Creek (difficult in
early season) the trail arrives at the junction with the
Graveyard Lakes Trail. Here our route branches right (west)
onto it and follows the last part of the 2nd hiking day, Trip 90.
6th Hiking day: Reverse the steps of the 2nd hiking day, Trip
90, 3.2 miles (5.2 km).
7th Hiking Day: Reverse the steps of the 1st hiking day, Trip
89, 5.2 miles (8.4 km).

Rock Creek to Lake Edison

96

TRIP   From Mosquito Flat (on Rock Creek) to Vermilion Campground (Lake Thomas A. Edison) via Mono Creek (shuttle trip). Topo maps *Mt. Tom, Mt. Abbot, Kaiser Peak*. Best late season; 21.4 miles (34.5 km).

Grade	Trail/layover days	Total recom- mended days
Leisurely	4/1	5
Moderate	3/1	4
Strenuous	2/1	3

HILITES   Taking this trans-Sierra crossing in late season gives the traveler three distinct plusses: First, the luxuriant aspen groves along Mono Creek take on their golden hue about this time. Second, the mid-season fishing slump usually ends as the weather cools off. Last, this popular route sees heavy foot and animal traffic during early and mid season, but this activity tapers off when the leaves begin to turn.

DESCRIPTION (Leisurely trip)
1st Hiking Day: Follow Trip 92 to **Ruby Lake**, 2.5 miles (4 km).
2nd Hiking Day (**Ruby Lake** to **Fish Camp**, 7.8 miles—12.6 km); First, retrace your steps back to the Mono Pass Trail. From the junction, the trail ascends steeply over the rocky switchbacks on the south slope of Mt. Starr to Mono Pass (12,000′), a notch in the cirque wall just west of Mt. Starr. Views from the pass are excellent, but those wishing a panoramic outlook on the

spectacular Sierra crest should ascend the granite shoulder of Mt. Starr, an easy climb to the east. From this vantage point one has a complete perspective of Pioneer Basin and Mts. Stanford, Huntington, Crocker and Hopkins, and Red and White Mountain to the north. To the south one has an "end-on" view of Mts. Abbot and Dade, Bear Creek Spire, and Mt. Humphreys.

From Mono Pass the trail descends over granite slopes past barren Summit Lake, and then drops more severely as it veers west above Trail Lakes (poor-to-fair fishing for brook). Our route then turns northward and fords Golden Creek. Following the north side of the stream in a moderately dense forest cover, the trail passes the lateral to Pioneer Basin (north) and the lateral to Fourth Recess Lake (south). Anglers may elect to try their luck at the good fishing for brook (8-14") at Fourth Recess Lake, ½ mile south over a gentle climb.

Our route continues to descend, fording the outlet streams from Pioneer Basin and paralleling the westward course of Mono Creek. As the Mono Creek valley opens up beyond Mono Rock, the trail passes the steep lateral to Third Recess Lake (south), and, about a mile farther, descends past the turnoff to Lower Hopkins Lake and the Hopkins Lake basin. Anglers will find the many fine holes that interrupt dashing Mono Creek good fishing for the brook, rainbow and occasional golden (to 12"). In late season the groves of quaking aspen that line the stream's banks are an incomparably colorful backdrop to an otherwise steady conifer green. Owing to heavy traffic, this segment of trail becomes somewhat dusty where it passes the Grinnell Lake lateral and descends to Fish Camp (8500'). This traditional camping place marks the junction of the Mono Creek Trail with the Second Recess lateral. Due to heavy use here, the Forest Service encourages you to camp downstream.

3rd Hiking Day (**Fish Camp** to **Quail Meadows**, 5 miles—8.1 km): As this day's route descends along the north side of Mono Creek, the rich yellows of the aspen groves accompany the stream. Occasionally the traveler has views of the stern northern face of Volcanic Knob to the south, and from several spots along the trail one looks up the long, chutelike valley of the First Recess to the granite-topped heights of Recess Peak. Fishing for the brook, rainbow and occasional golden is much like that of the previous day, but the stream is somewhat less accessible from the trail. About 2½ miles below Fish Camp the trail turns right, away from the narrowing canyon, and climbs by rocky switchbacks to the crown of a ridge, where it joins the John Muir Trail. Thence it descends a short distance on the east side of the North Fork of Mono Creek, and fords the North Fork (difficult in early season) just above its confluence with Mono Creek. From the ford to the edge of Quail Meadows is a gentle downhill walk through dense forest cover. Fair-to-good campsites can be found on the forested fringe of Quail Meadows (7760'), downstream from the point where the John Muir Trail branches left (south) and crosses Mono Creek.

4th Hiking Day (**Quail Meadows** to **Vermilion Campground**, 6.1 miles—9.8 km): Our route from Quail Meadows proceeds west on a level stretch. Mono Creek now casades over a series of granite-bedrocked holes (fine swimming in late season) before flowing into the northeast tip of Lake Edison. This man-made, granite-edged lake dominates the views to the south for the remainder of this trip. A boat-taxi service operates the length of the lake, based at a resort adjoining Vermilion Campground, but advance inquiry should be made about length of operating season and ferry schedule. (Write to Vermilion Valley Resort/Mono Hot Springs/California 93642.) The ferry lands at the northeast tip of the lake, and the marked footpath giving access to this point can be seen from the trail.

The trail along the upper reaches of the north side of Lake Edison undulates severely over alternately rocky and dusty stretches. At some points the trail crosses granite ridges 600 feet above the lake surface, and from these ridges the traveler has fine views of heavily timbered Bear Ridge across the lake. The forest cover reflects the lower altitude, as Jeffrey pine and red fir mix with ever-present lodgepole. This forest becomes quite dense as our route passes the trail going right (north) to Graveyard Meadows and Goodale Pass. A faint trail to the left (south)leads to another landing point, on a nearby bay. Our route continues west, crosses the bridge over Cold Creek, and passes the trail to Devils Bathtub. Beyond this junction the hiker leaves the worst of the dust behind as the trail winds through Jeffrey pine to a Forest Service road. This sandy road descends gently to the east edge of Vermilion Campground (7650').

97   McGee Creek to Rock Creek

TRIP   From McGee Creek Roadend to Mosquito Flat (on Rock Creek) via McGee Pass, Red and White Lake, Grinnell Lakes and Fish Camp (shuttle trip). Topo maps *Mt. Morrison, Mt. Abbot, Mt. Tom.* Best late season; 29.3 miles (47.1 km).

Grade	Trail/layover days	Total recommended days
Leisurely	6/2	8
Moderate	4/2	6
Strenuous	3/1	4

HILITES   For *experienced knapsackers only*, this rugged route (some cross-country) offers excitement and challenge sufficient to satisfy the most jaded appetite. High-country lakes surrounded by rampartlike peaks characterize this colorful route, and the fishing is good-to-excellent.

DESCRIPTION (Leisurely trip)

1st and 2nd Hiking Days: Follow Trip 95 to **Tully Lake**, 11 miles (17.7 km).

3rd Hiking Day (**Tully Lake** to **Grinnell Lake**, 3.5 miles—5.6 km—cross country): From the east shore of Tully Lake our route ascends the grassy swale that lies due east of the lake. At the outlet stream from Red and White Lake our route turns right (south-east) and follows this stream to the lake itself. Fishermen will wish to try these icy, clear, blue waters for large rainbow (to 18″), although there's no good camping, Red and White Lake offers an excellent vantage point from which to take in the spectacular and aptly named heights of Red and White Mountain. The saddle (11,600′) that this day's route traverses is clearly discernible on the lowest point of the right shoulder of Red and White Mountain, and the easiest route to the saddle takes the traveler around the rocky east shore of the lake. The steepest part of the ascent is over treacherous shale—or snow in early and mid season—and the climber is well-advised to take it slow and easy. Rope should be carried and used, especially if ascending the west side of the pass.

From the top one obtains a well-deserved and exciting view of the surrounding terrain. To the north the immediate, dazzling blue of Red and White Lake sets off the buff browns and ochre reds of the surrounding rock. Beyond this basin the meadowy cirque forming the headwaters of Fish Creek is a large greensward that contrasts sharply with the austere, red-stained eminence of Red Slate Mountain, and the distant skyline offers sawtooth profiles of the Ritter Range, with its readily identifiable Minarets, and the Mammoth Crest. To the south, the barren, rocky shores of the Grinnell chain of lakes occupy the foreground, and, just beyond, the green-sheathed slopes of the Mono Creek watershed drop away, rising in the distance to the Mono Divide. Like the ascent of this saddle, the descent should be taken with some care. The sudden, shaley drop terminates in a large "rock garden," a jumble of large boulders, just above Little Grinnell Lake. Our rock-hopping route takes us along the east shore of this tiny lake to the long, grassy descent leading to the west side of Grinnell Lake (10,800'). Midway along this side, where the most prominent peninsula infringes on the long lake, our route strikes the marked fisherman's trail that veers southwest down a long swale to tiny Laurel Lake. There are several fair campsites at this junction which offer excellent views due to their situation on a plateau above the lake. Fishermen will find Grinnell Lake fair-to-good fishing for brook and rainbow (8-14"). Alternative good campsites can be found along the meadowy fringes of Laurel Lake (10,300'), about 1 mile southwest. Fishing on this lake is excellent for brook (to 10").

4th Hiking Day (**Grinnell Lake** to **Fish Camp**, 4.5 miles—7.2 km): The fisherman's trail from Grinnell Lake to Laurel Lake descends via a long, scooplike swale to the grassy meadows forming the headwaters of Laurel Creek. The trail, though very faint from Grinnell to Laurel Lake, becomes clearer as it descends gently along Laurel Creek. At this point the creek is still a "jump-across" stream, but a careful approach along the banks will reveal an abundance of brook trout (to 9"), and fly fishermen who favor stream angling will find this tiny watercourse a delight.

The gradual descent along the creek becomes somewhat

steeper just above the larger meadows. The pleasant, timber-fringed grassland is divided by the serpentine curves of Laurel Creek. The trail across the meadow is difficult to follow, and the traveler who loses it should cross to the west side of Laurel Creek and look for the trail in the vicinity of the campsites at the south end of the meadow. The dense lodgepole cover at the end of the meadow soon gives way to manzanita thickets and occasional clumps of quaking aspen as the trail reaches the steep, switchbacking descent above Mono Creek. These switchbacks are unmaintained, and are subject to heavy erosion. However, the difficult going is more than compensated for by the excellent views across the Mono Creek watershed into the Second Recess. Particularly impressive are the heights of Mt. Gabb and Mt. Hilgard, which guard the upper end of this side canyon. When our route strikes the Mono Creek Trail, it turns right (west) for a gently descending ½ mile to the campsites at Fish Camp (8500'). Due to heavy use here, the Forest Service encourages you to camp downstream. Fishing is good for brook and rainbow (to 12") on Mono Creek.

5th Hiking Day: Reverse the steps of the 2nd hiking day, Trip 95, 7.8 miles (12.6 km).

6th Hiking Day: Reverse the steps of the 1st hiking day, Trip 92, 2.5 miles (4 km).

Mammoth Lakes to Purple Lake **98**

TRIP From Coldwater Campground (Mammoth Lakes) to Purple Lake (round trip). Topo map *Mt. Morrison*. Best late season; 16 miles (25.8 km).

Grade	Trail/layover days	Total recommended days
Leisurely	3/1	4
Moderate	2/1	3
Strenuous	2/0	2

HILITES The rewards for crossing a mountain pass amount to more than the views that are presented. Most experienced knapsackers know that passes have a way of separating the day hikers from over-nighters. So it is with this trip across the Mammoth Crest. Those seeking the satisfaction of seeing what lies beyond the top of the hill, will find this hike a worthwhile choice.

DESCRIPTION (Moderate trip)

1st Hiking Day (**Coldwater Campground** to **Purple Lake**, 8 miles—12.9 km): From Coldwater Campground (8960') the Duck Pass Trail ascends on an alternately sandy and rocky section along a moderately forested slope, soon entering John Muir Wilderness. The first four miles of this trail, from the trailhead to Barney Lake, receives a good deal of day hiker and fisherman use, so by midseason the trail is fairly dusty. As the going levels off, after the first rise, Arrowhead Lake is visible off to the left (east). Then the trail ascends again to Skelton Lake. The lake was named for the brothers Skelton, who, during this mining area's heyday, established and maintained a stamp mill at the lower end of the lake. Owing to heavy fishing pressure on these lakes, the angling is only fair. As our route crosses the rolling terrain south of Skelton Lake, the barren canyon walls along the Mammoth Crest show the scouring action of the ancient glaciers that once covered the land. From the rocky shores of emerald-green Barney Lake the steep ascent to Duck Pass is easily seen. The switchbacks ascending this steep slope leave hemlock and lodgepole pine behind and except for an occasional whitebark pine this climb is barren and exposed.

Just before Duck Pass (10,790′) there are views of the Mammoth Creek watershed and the Mammoth Crest to the northwest. Beyond, the skyline is dominated by the distinctive spires of the Ritter Range. Just beyond the pass we see Pika and Duck lakes, which occupy the basin immediately below; and these blue, still waters are flanked by somber, dark metamorphic peaks. Across Cascade Valley the Silver Divide's granite peaks occupy the horizon. The descent to the outlet of large Duck Lake begins by passing a trail to Pika Lake. This lake offers perhaps the best camping in the basin. The main trail, which stays high at first, eventually drops to the outlet of Duck Lake. Except for a few gnarled whitebark pines, the jumbled slopes and rocky crags surrounding the lake are barren and austere.

From Duck Lake our route crosses the outlet and descends to join the scenic John Muir Trail. It then turns left (south), rounds a rocky, granite shoulder, and veers east to the several good campsites near the outlet at the south end of Purple Lake (9860′). Fishing is fair-to-good for rainbow and some golden and brook (8-13″). Purple Lake's partly timbered, rocky shoreline gives way to meadow at the northeast end of the lake. The rocks above the meadow give this lake its name; they have a rosy tint during the day, but around sunset they turn purple and violet.

2nd Hiking Day: Retrace your steps, 8 miles (12.9 km).

Mammoth Lakes to Lake Edison   **99**

TRIP   From Coldwater Campground (Mammoth Lakes) to Vermilion Campground (Lake Thomas A. Edison) via Cascade Valley and Goodale Pass (shuttle trip). Topo maps *Mt. Morrison, Mt. Abbot, Kaiser Peak*. Best late season; 29.9 miles (48.1 km).

Grade	Trail/layover days	Total recommended days
Leisurely	6/1	7
Moderate	5/1	6
Strenuous	4/1	5

HILITES   This trans-Sierra route explores two watersheds, ascends two passes, and offers a world of fine fishing along the way. About one fourth of the route follows the famous John Muir Trail, and high, alpine scenery alternates with intimate, friendly meadows, fast-running streams, and lonely, placid lakes. Long mileage and stiff climbs make this a trip for the hiker who has prepared himself with a couple of early- or mid-season warm-ups, but the rewards, in views and fishing, repay him for the required effort.

DESCRIPTION (Moderate trip)

1st Hiking Day: Follow Trip 98 to **Purple Lake**, 8 miles (12.9 km).

2nd Hiking Day (**Purple Lake** to **Cascade Valley/Fish Creek ford**, 3.5 miles—5.6 km): From the outlet of Purple Lake our route

branches right (southwest) from the John Muir Trail and
descends gently at first, parallel to Purple Creek. The forest
cover along this switchbacking descent is primarily lodgepole
pine, giving way to Jeffrey pine and juniper near the valley
floor. Manzanita is the main shrub on the steeper part of the
descent. The hiker has fine views of the Silver Divide across
the valley. The long switchbacks of this steep descent
terminate in a large meadow on the floor of Cascade Valley.
Here our route strikes the Cascade Valley Trail and turns left
(east) along Fish Creek. The fairly level going along the valley
floor gives the angler ample opportunity to test the good
fishing for brook and rainbow (to 9″). California's DF&G
Anglers' Guide says about Cascade Valley: "One of the finest
trout streams left in the High Sierra; meandering and scenic
with splendid campsites and forest cover." As the hiker works
his way up the valley, Fish Creek rushes and then meanders
on his right, and open meadow fringes beckon. Where this trail
crosses Fish Creek via a wading ford, this hiking day ends at
one of the many campsites (8560′). Fishing is good, as noted
above.

3rd Hiking Day (**Cascade Valley/Fish Creek ford** to **Lake of the
Lone Indian**, 4.8 miles—7.7 km): Beyond the ford of Fish Creek
the trail ascends somewhat more steeply over rocky stretches.
Fish Creek, now on the left, changes as the canyon narrows.
The water flows faster and the creek becomes a riotous tumble
of waterfalls and tiny holes. Just below the point where our
route rejoins the John Muir Trail, the canyon wall on the north
side of the valley becomes a sheer, dramatically polished
granite surface. Our trail crosses the outlet stream from Helen
Lake and meets the John Muir Trail, onto which we turn right
(south). From this junction to Helen Lake the ascent is steep.
The first part of the climb is densely forested as it works its
way up the east side of the outlet stream from Helen Lake, and
midway up, the trail passes several alternative meadowed
campsites on the right. Beyond these campsites the trail
becomes rocky, exposed and eroded as it makes the last steep
climb to Helen Lake. One has excellent views back down the
U-shaped valley with which to fill the breather stops, and as
the trail crests at the granite lip of the Helen Lake cirque, one
can see whence the glacier emanated that carved the valley
below. Anglers will want to fish Helen Lake—and Bobs Lake
about ½ mile southeast. Both offer good-to-excellent angling
for brook (to 9″).

The trail then rock-hops the outlet of Helen Lake, passes
two small alpine tarns, and branches right, leaving the John

Muir Trail, which continues south to Silver Pass. Our route passes below rocky Papoose Lake, which offers good fishing for brook trout, as does Warrior Lake, a short distance over the granite to the east. At the outlet stream of Papoose Lake our route branches north, away from the Goodale Pass Trail, and descends over a dusty traverse to the good, grassy-pocketed campsites at the southwest end of Lake of the Lone Indian (10,200′). Fishing is good for brook and rainbow (8-14″).

4th Hiking Day: Follow the 5th hiking day, Trip 95, 5.2 miles (8.4 km).

5th Hiking Day: Follow the 2nd hiking day, Trip 90, and the 1st hiking day, Trip 89, 8.4 miles (13.5 km).

Polemonium

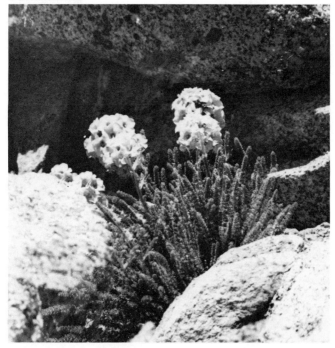

00   Mammoth Lakes to Lake Edison

TRIP   From Coldwater Campground (Mammoth Lakes)
to Vermilion Campground (Lake Thomas A. Edison), via Cascade Valley, Tully Lake and Grinnell
Lakes (shuttle trip). Topo maps *Mt. Morrison, Mt.
Abbot, Kaiser Peak*. Best late season; 35.9 miles
(57.8 km).

Grade	Trail/layover days	Total recommended days
Leisurely	8/2	10
Moderate	5/2	7
Strenuous	4/2	6

HILITES   This is a trip for *experienced backpackers only*.
Employing a short but strenuous cross-country
route over the Silver Divide, this unusual and
remote trip should appeal to fisherman, hiker and
naturalist—or any combination thereof. Travelers
looking for a trip of lonely alpine grandeur will
find it in the Silver Divide country.

DESCRIPTION (Leisurely trip)

1st and 2nd Hiking Days: Follow Trip 99 to **Cascade Valley/Fish
Creek ford**, 11.5 miles (18.5 km).

3rd Hiking Day (**Cascade Valley/Fish Creek ford** to **Tully Hole**, 2.8
miles—4.5 km): From the Fish Creek ford the trail ascends the
sometimes-rocky valley floor on the south side of Fish Creek.
This section offers splendid access to nice deep holes and
gurgling riffles, but as the canyon narrows, the trail becomes
steeper and the creek becomes faster, small waterfalls
alternating with noisy cascades. Looking up at the sheer

canyon walls, the hiker cannot help but be impressed with the glacial forces that polished their granite faces. Just below the junction with the John Muir Trail, the trail fords the outlet stream from Helen Lake. Here our route turns left (north) onto the John Muir Trail and crosses to the north side of plunging Fish Creek via a steel bridge. The trail then climbs steeply by switchbacks, offering fine views back to the falls above the bridge. The climb is short, and the trail levels out somewhat as it rejoins Fish Creek. The reunion with the creek is startling, for its waters are now almost placid as they flow through deep green holes. The roar and thunder of the falls are but an echo, and beside the now-mellow Fish Creek the trail ascends to the lovely, open meadows of Tully Hole (9500'). Fish Creek is a pleasant, meandering background to the good campsites at the northwest edge of the meadow. Here the angler should break out his rod for the good-to-excellent fishing for brook, rainbow, and some golden (to 12").

4th Hiking Day: Reverse the steps of the 3rd hiking day, Trip 95, 2.5 miles (4 km).

5th and 6th Hiking Days: Follow the steps of the 3rd and 4th hiking days, Trip 97, 8 miles (12.9 km).

7th and 8th Hiking Days: Follow the steps of the 3rd and 4th hiking days, Trip 96, 11.1 miles (17.9 km).

Mts. Dana and Gibbs, Dana Fork of the Tuolumne River

Trip Cross-reference Table

Trip Number	No. Hiking Days	Season			Pace			Trip Type			
		Early	Mid	Late	Leisurely	Moderate	Strenuous	Round	Shuttle	Loop	Semiloop
1	2		x		x			x			
2	4		x		x			x			
3	6		x		x			x			
4	2		x		x			x			
5	4		x			x		x			
6	5		x			x			x		
7	2		x		x			x			
8	2		x		x				x		
9	3		x		x				x		
10	2		x			x					x
11	2		x	x		x			x		
12	3		x				x		x		
13	4		x		x						x
14	2		x	x	x						x
15	4		x		x				x		
16	6		x	x	x				x		
17	2		x		x			x			
18	2		x		x				x		
19	2	x	x		x			x			
20	4		x	x	x			x			
21	4		x	x	x			x			
22	5		x	x	x						x
23	7		x	x	x					x	
24	7		x	x	x				x		
25	2		x	x	x			x			
26	4		x	x	x			x			
27	2	x	x		x			x			
28	6		x	x	x			x			
29	5		x	x	x				x		
30	5		x	x	x				x		
31	7		x	x	x				x		
32	2		x	x	x			x			

Trip Number	No. Hiking Days	Season			Pace			Trip Type			
		Early	Mid	Late	Leisurely	Moderate	Strenuous	Round	Shuttle	Loop	Semiloop
33	3		x	x	x			x			
34	4		x	x		x					x
35	5		x	x		x					x
36	5	x	x			x			x		
37	2		x	x		x		x			
38	2		x	x		x		x			
39	4		x	x		x		x			
40	3		x	x		x			x		
41	3		x	x		x					x
42	6		x	x			x		x		
43	6		x	x		x		x			
44	8		x	x		x					x
45	2	x	x	x	x			x			
46	4		x	x		x			x		
47	2		x	x	x				x		
48	2	x			x			x			
49	4	x			x			x			
50	2		x	x		x		x			
51	3		x	x		x			x		
52	5		x	x		x			x		
53	2		x	x		x					x
54	2		x	x	x			x			
55	2		x	x	x			x			
56	2		x	x	x			x			
57	4		x	x	x			x			
58	5		x	x	x				x		
59	4		x	x	x				x		
60	5		x	x	x				x		
61	3		x	x	x				x		
62	2		x	x		x		x			
63	2		x	x	x			x			
64	2		x	x	x			x			
65	4		x	x	x						x
66	6		x	x		x					x

Trip Number	No. Hiking Days	Season			Pace			Trip Type			
		Early	Mid	Late	Leisurely	Moderate	Strenuous	Round	Shuttle	Loop	Semiloop
67	7		x	x		x					x
68	5		x	x		x			x		
69	2		x	x	x			x			
70	2		x	x	x			x			
71	3		x	x		x			x		
72	2		x	x		x			x		
73	3		x	x	x					x	
74	3		x	x	x					x	
75	3		x	x	x					x	
76	2		x	x	x			x			
77	3		x	x		x			x		
78	4		x	x	x				x		
79	3		x	x	x						x
80	5		x	x	x				x		
81	4	x			x			x			
82	4	x	x		x			x			
83	5	x	x		x				x		
84	5	x	x		x				x		
85	5	x	x		x						x
86	4	x			x			x			
87	11		x	x		x				x	
88	7		x	x	x				x		
89	2		x		x			x			
90	4		x	x	x			x			
91	2		x	x	x			x			
92	2		x	x	x			x			
93	2		x	x	x			x			
94	2		x	x	x			x			
95	7		x	x	x				x		
96	4			x	x				x		
97	3			x		x			x		
98	2			x		x		x			
99	5			x		x			x		
100	8			x	x				x		

Recommended Reading

Bateman, Paul C. and Clyde Wahrhaftig. "Geology of the Sierra Nevada," in *California Division of Mines and Geology, Bulletin 190,* 1966, pp. 107–72.

Brewer, William H. *Up and Down California.* Berkeley, University of California Press, 1966.

Browning, Peter. *Place Names of the Sierra Nevada.* Berkeley, Wilderness Press, 1986.

Bunnelle, Hasse. *Food for Knapsackers.* San Francisco: Sierra Club, 1971.

Farquhar, Francis. *History of the Sierra Nevada.* Berkeley: University of California Press, 1965.

Darvill, Fred. *Mountaineering Medicine.* Berkeley: Wilderness Press, 1985.

Hill, Mary. *Geology of the Sierra Nevada.* Berkeley: University of California Press, 1975.

Ingles, Lloyd G. *Mammals of the Pacific States.* Stanford, CA: Stanford University Press, 1965.

King, Clarence. *Mountaineering in the Sierra Nevada.* New York: Lippincott, 1963.

Matthess, Francois. *The Incomparable Valley.* Berkeley: University of California Press, 1964.

McDermand, Charles. *Yosemite and Kings Canyon Trout.* (Out of print.)

Muir, John. *My First Summer in the Sierra.* Boston: Houghton Mifflin, 1979.

⎯⎯⎯⎯ , (ed. Fred Gunsky). *South of Yosemite.* Berkeley, Wilderness Press, 1987.

Murie, Olaus J. *A Field Guide to Animal Tracks.* Boston: Houghton Mifflin, 1975.

Niehaus, Theodore. *Sierra Wildflowers.* Berkeley: University of California Press, 1974.

Peattie, Roderick (ed.). *The Sierra Nevada: The Range of Light.* New York: Vanguard Press, 1947. (Out of print.)

Peters, Ed (ed.). *Mountaineering: The Freedom of the Hills.* Seattle: The Mountaineers, 1982.

Peterson, P. Victor and P. Victor Peterson, Jr. *Native Trees of the Sierra Nevada.* Berkeley, University of California Press, 1975.

Peterson, Roger Tory. *A Field Guide to Western Birds.* Boston: Houghton Mifflin, 1961.

Roper, Steve. *Climber's Guide to the High Sierra.* San Francisco: Sierra Club, 1976.

_____ . *Sierra High Route.* San Francisco: Sierra Club, 1982.

Roth, Hal. *Pathway in the Sky: The Story of the John Muir Trail.* Berkeley: Howell-North Books, 1965. (Out of print.)

Russell, Carl P. *100 Years in Yosemite.* Yosemite: Yosemite Association, 1968.

Schaffer, Jeffrey P. *Yosemite National Park.* Berkeley: Wildernesss Press, 1983.

_____ . *Carson-Iceberg Wilderness.* Berkeley: Wilderness Press, 1987.

Storer, Tracy I. and Robert L. Usinger. *Sierra Nevada Natural History.* Berkeley: University of California Press, 1964.

Watts, Tom. *Pacific Coast Tree Finder.* Berkeley: Nature Study Guild, 1973.

Weeden, Norman. *A Sierra Nevada Flora.* Berkeley: Wilderness Press, 1986.

Whitney, Stephen. *A Sierra Club Naturalist's Guide to the Sierra Nevada.* San Francisco: Sierra Club, 1979.

Index